Erikson:
Identity and Religion

ERIKSON:
Identity and Religion

J. EUGENE WRIGHT, JR.

THE SEABURY PRESS · NEW YORK

1982
The Seabury Press
815 Second Avenue
New York, N.Y. 10017

Library of Congress Cataloging in Publication Data

Wright, J. Eugene, 1931–
   Erikson, identity and religion.

   Includes bibliographical references and index.
   1. Erikson, Erik Homburger, 1902–
2. Identity (Psychology)   3. Developmental
psychology.   4. Moral development.   5. Psychoanalysis.   I. Title.
BF713.E74W74   150.19'5'0924   81-14502
ISBN 0-8164-2362-8   AACR2

Grateful acknowledgment is made to the following publisher for permission to quote from copyrighted material:

From *Pastoral Care: A Thematic Approach,* by Donald Capps. Copyright © 1979 The Westminster Press. Used by permission.

To My Wife
Jeannette Oestreich Wright
And To Our Children
Jay
Nancy
John

*"Babies control and bring up their families
as much as they are controlled by them;
in fact, we may say that the family brings up
a baby by being brought up by him."*

Erik H. Erikson, *Childhood and Society*

Contents

Introduction

Erik H. Erikson wrote his book on Martin Luther because he found him to be such an interesting person that he just had to do it. That expresses precisely my own position regarding Erikson; that, together with the fact that he has not received the degree of attention deserved from contemporary psychological, social, religious, and other appropriate fields of study.

If one walks through a large university bookstore, one often sees stacks of Erikson books on display. But interpretations of his life and theory as they relate to other areas are still lacking. I am not alone in feeling this concern. A group of scholars who convened a conference in Chicago to discuss Erikson's theory as it relates to religion said they took that action in part because of their embarrassment at the neglect of Erikson in contemporary studies.

I am firmly convinced that Erik H. Erikson, as an original thinker, as an observer of human nature from both a scientific (psychoanalytic) and artistic viewpoint, sees within that very nature many of those characteristics and needs that religion also sees. In that sense, I consider him to be a prophet for our period of history who needs to be read and understood. I hope that what I have done in the pages to follow will encourage readers to study Erikson's original writings as well as those interpreters who have found him to be stimulating.

Why is Erikson so important for our particular historical era? First, he, himself, experienced the "identity crisis" of which he writes. This caused him to reflect upon it, describing what had happened and what needs to happen if, when moving through this crisis of life, one is to find resolution. Secondly, in analyzing our historical period, he has found that the uprootedness, mobility, and rapid change in our century are productive of identity confusion. As Erikson worked to solve his own crisis, he helped to clarify just what it is that youth today encounters in identity confusion, thereby lifting his own patienthood to a universal level and helping to solve for others "what he could not solve for himself alone." Thus he describes Luther, who also lived in an era of great ideological upheaval, and I, in turn, apply the description to Erikson.

This book is divided into two parts. The first concentrates upon Erikson as a person, his method, and the development of the eight stages of the life cycle. Part Two relates his theory to ethical and religious areas.

I have cast Erikson's own identity crisis of not quite belonging in stepchild imagery, a concept he uses for a description of himself in his autobiographical reflections. In this book, the stepchild motif will be used for more than just the family orientation. Identity confusion results for Erikson, and for all of us, because we feel that we do not quite belong, in families, ideologies, religious perspectives, and in other ways to be described.

There is an existential dimension to my own inquiry. This book is dedicated to my wife and children. During the days after the book was completed I listened (unavoidably at first, then intentionally) to words that were being played and sung by my youngest son, John, with his electric guitar and accompanied by a Pink Floyd record on the stereo. The words remind us of questions youth are asking the adult world. Questions that are similar to, but more serious than, those asked in Erikson's own youth: Is the blue sky gone? Will our future be one of bombs and fear? Where shall we turn for shelter? What does life have to promise—blue sky—or must we say goodbye to that reality? Is there anybody out there, or only a wall?

For Luther's age, and for Erikson's own years of the identity crisis, there was great social change. However, today the upheaval and threat is more ominous, both from within and without. Bombs from the sky, diseases from within, escapes through drugs. These are the realities youth encounter. Is there any answer? Is there anyone out there?

Erikson does have some very interesting answers, and his questions and observations also have a transcendent dimension beyond the physical and natural. He assumes a predetermined order in the development of the human organism in society. This growth process may be identified according to physical, social, and personal changes which he has designated as stages of development. He concludes that these are eight in number. His pioneering work has contributed to the thinking of many who have expanded and refined the eight to even more explicit and manageable periods of development. His interest in childhood is that for which he was first noticed.[1] Later, he realized that youth was the period being overlooked as an insignificant transition from childhood to adulthood.[2] In more recent years he has suggested that perhaps it is time to focus our attention upon adulthood,[3] for it is the adult who cares for the children and youth and holds up a vision of what life may become. This latter theme will be developed in those chapters of this book following Chapter V.

Erikson is significant for study because he realistically observes that the development of the human organism in society is faced with difficulties from within and without. The reality of negative forces in the physical world has a somewhat comparable formulation in religion, in which the reality of evil is always over against the power of good. Indeed, Erikson sometimes speaks of the negative forces he observes by using such words as sin and evil.

Further, what makes Erikson so significant is his interdisciplinary approach. From whatever perspective we come to this study we are very likely to have tunnel vision. Erikson reminds us that the individual organism, from birth, has a history that is always interacting with the present moment; that we have an ever-enlarging social world which begins with the one who first holds us and then grows to include the family, the community, our school experience, vocational setting, and ultimately the universe. The complexity of our interaction with society, with ourselves intrapsychically and historically, is staggering. It is also threatening, for it demands interdisciplinary interpretation, and we all tend to be stepchildren when we are out of our given area of interpretation. Such an enlargement of our perspectives as Erikson demands is threatening to our securities. He forces us to expand our horizons.

As a product, himself, of our technological age, Erikson appreciates the modern scientific frame of mind. He is deeply concerned for that which is true, for the objective, verifiable, and demonstrably real. However, truth is more than just the facts. There is that which is actual in lived experience. Our brain is more than the left hemisphere which produces the rational, logical propositions of the right hand. The brain has its right hemisphere, a place for aesthetic truth, intuition, subjective sensing of what is actual; a place for feelings; and knowledge of the left hand.

Erikson has a vision for a better society in an age needing a new utopian goal. His society would care for its children and youth, guided by a larger concern than just its own unique race, nation, sex, or lifestyle. His vision is of a responsible, wider identity which will realistically accept its individual specieshood, but not lock itself into an exclusive pseudospecies kind of mentality that excludes those who are different.

I find in Erikson an ethical orientation that makes sense of former systems while offering integration and innovation. From childhood's need for rules (law and order), through youth's search for a meaningful world-image (ideology), to which it may pledge its loyalty (fidelity), Erikson moves to the adult stage of caring, of being responsible for the next generation and the world. His ethics integrates the right and the good into the larger concept of the responsible. Responsibility assimilates its earlier contributions, it does not ignore or dispose of them.

As a psychoanalyst, Erikson acknowledges his Freudian orientation. But he documents the reality that while we may be driven by instinctual forces we do something with our drives. In that point of view we have an acknowledgment of much that Freud was saying about the unconscious forces at work in all of our protests and pronouncements. We also have an enlarged vision of what it means to be "man (or woman) come of age." We take responsibility for who we are and what we will become. Erikson has encouraged that kind of thinking in his move beyond the id and libidinal forces to a concentration upon the ego, the I who steers her own ship and chooses her stars.

In Erikson's way of thinking, to perceive the importance of religion is not alien to technological persons. Rather, as I have interpreted him, it is essential for wholeness.

While these introductory comments may sound as though I am uncritical of Erikson, such is not the case. From my own point of view he does not go far enough in his ambivalence toward religion. He offers us a very challenging way of interpreting human nature, however, that far exceeds the usual psychoanalytical approach. In this he is a prophet for our age, worthy of our thoughtful study. Other areas of criticism will appear later.

In often citing Erikson's own works, it has been my intention to allow us to sense his style, complexity, interdisciplinary approach, and as much as possible attempt to live with the ambiguity he sometimes presents. Only as we read his original books will that be completely possible, but it is my hope that this interpretation will encourage new readers to discover him.

Erikson opens up the issue of the sexual revolution through which we are presently living. He uses the masculine nouns and pronouns generically, as I have usually done, and I know that this will not please some readers. I hope, however, that the theory to which he points, that male and female are gifted equally in their own orientation will be of greater importance. Some in the feminist movement have not appreciated Erikson's emphasis upon anatomy's differences, which then relate to social differences. One has to read him carefully, however, to realize that he is highly critical of our male-dominated heritage. His vision includes a new day in which both sexes will be appreciated for their equally important contributions to society.

In conclusion, let me acknowledge the larger context out of which I have approached the subject and express my indebtedness to those who have enabled me to produce this book. It was in my first postgraduate educational experience that I was challenged to think more deeply and with greater integration by Culbert G. Rutenber.[4] It was in his Philosophy of Religion course that "hints of transcendence" were pointed out as being in evidence in the realm of everyday experience. I consider that to be a vital foundation to my later studies of Erikson.

My introduction to Erikson came through a sabbatical study experience under the guidance of Ross Snyder.[5] With the philosophical base of phenomenology and existentialism, he was Eriksonian in his orientation. I well recall the class session in which he had a student bring her infant child into the classroom to demonstrate basic trust, an effective technique that supplemented the usual rational study of a great thinker, and a method for which Snyder is well known in Christian educational circles.

In the Social Ethics program at the University of Southern California, it was the director, John B. Orr, who first suggested to me that Erikson would be an interesting study for a doctoral dissertation. John P. Crossley, Jr., then became my mentor in a project centering upon Erikson's ethics. Time and again John Crossley pushed me with the probing question, "Was Erikson really any different from others in his field who merely wish for a harmony of conflicting forces both within the person and society? Was it not just adjustment that was the goal of psychoanalysis and therefore of Erikson's theory?" The pages to follow will develop my own answer to that question, but, as I have already indicated, Erikson wants more than adjustment. He has a vision of a new age that must come if we are to escape the destructive course upon which we are now moving.

In the years since my studies at the University of Southern California I have often taught students in religion classes about Erikson's theory, and, as most teachers will agree, it was the student questions and challenges that continued to cause me to rethink my own position. I am grateful to those who interacted with me in those classes.

It has been within the immediate context of a sabbatical study leave from Eastern Baptist Theological Seminary that I have had the time to think and write, and I express my appreciation to that institution for the sabbatical. Marian Oehrig has often supplied me with bibliographical information that I might otherwise have missed. Duron Rutenber has typed the manuscript with a thoughtfulness and alertness superseding that of most typists. A product of college and postgraduate work herself, she has often brought pages back to me, asking, "Is this what you really mean?" And usually her question was helpful and productive of greater clarity.

Finally, but certainly not least in importance, Jerry Gill, whose writings will be acknowledged in the pages to follow, was a most significant contributor to this work. At a time when the book might have foundered hopelessly he read what I had done and encouraged and prodded me to continue. He offered to read each chapter, interacting in an extremely helpful way. He suggested changes in chapter titles, ways of organizing, as well as helping me clarify my writing, as acknowledged in Chapter II. He is a professor, philosopher, and artist, and as such provided me with a perspective much needed in continuing my work.

No one enters into the project of writing a book without a great deal of tolerance, support, and encouragement from his or her family. Therefore, I express my deep gratitude to my wife, Jeannette, as well as to John and Nancy, who have lived with books and papers and a sometimes preoccupied and absent-minded husband and father. (While our oldest son, Jay, lives on the opposite coast, I would include him in this expression of gratitude to my family.)

Erik Erikson, himself, was helpful, not only through his writings, but in a brief telephone conversation and exchange of letters. One has to have a certain audacity to attempt to interpret the ideas of a great man. However, as will be noted later, there is a playfulness in Erikson's own writing and spirit. He encourages that approach on the part of others. Therefore, what follows is a kind of playing with ideas, the core concept of identity, religion, and the way in which these subjects have relevance for this modern, or perhaps postmodern age.

NOTES

1. Erik H. Erikson, *Childhood and Society,* 2d. ed., revised and enlarged (New York: W. W. Norton, 1963).
2. Erik H. Erikson, *Identity: Youth and Crisis* (New York: W. W. Norton, 1968).
3. Erik H. Erikson, *Dimensions of a New Identity: The 1973 Jefferson Lectures in the Humanities* (New York: W. W. Norton, 1974). See his "Conclusion: A Century of the Adult?" pp. 121–25. See also his edited book, *Adulthood* (New York: W. W. Norton, 1978).

4. Culbert G. Rutenber, Professor Emeritus, Philosophy of Religion, Eastern Baptist Theological Seminary, Philadelphia, Pa.
5. Ross Snyder was the former Senior Professor of Christian Education, Chicago Theological Seminary, Chicago, Ill. He is presently teaching part time in San Anselmo, Calif.

PART ONE

Erik H. Erikson:
His Identity,
Method, and Theory

CHAPTER I

An American Stepchild

In reflecting upon Martin Luther's identity struggle, Erikson observes that from time to time one person becomes representative of an age. The struggle of an individual crisis is the call of destiny, for as that person solves his own problem, he addresses a universal need.[1] This ingenuous insight reflects Erikson's conviction that Luther had contributed significantly to his own historic period and to those who have been enslaved by any system. Erikson's conclusion is also applicable to himself, however.

The stepchild imagery in this chapter's title is appropriate for Erikson, whose fatherland was another country yet who made the United States his home. It is all the more appropriate as it is applied to one who has endeavored to help technology's confused children find their identity in an impersonal economic and social system.

As one who felt he did not belong, for more reasons than just national origin, Erikson lifted his patienthood to the universal level. He has thereby contributed to society new terms and new concepts relating to personal and social identity.

In reflecting on Erikson's life, one is reminded of Paul Tillich's claim to have lived "On the Boundary"[2]—between continents, philosophy and theology, and theory and practice. Erikson, like Tillich, has been an occupier of many boundaries; however, he refers to himself in typical clinical terms, as a stepchild, a motif not unlike the boundary one.[3]

Erikson's Danish father abandoned his mother prior to the date of

Erik's birth in Frankfurt, Germany, June 15, 1902. For three years mother and infant son lived alone in Germany. During those impressionable years and later, Erik's mother was friendly with a number of artists, which Erikson himself feels was an early influence and helps to account for the fact that during adolescence, and throughout his life, art has been an interest and has contributed to his style of observation and the tracing of impressions.

When Erikson was three years old, he became ill and in need of a pediatrician. As Coles puts it graphically, he was taken to "Dr. Homburger, who cured the patient and fell in love with the patient's mother. When they were married, the boy Erik was given his stepfather's name."[4] For many years he was not told that Dr. Homburger was his stepfather.

A new home was made for Erik Homburger and his mother in Karlsruhe, Germany, where the Danish boy was reared in a Jewish home. He recalls feeling "different" although not because of mistreatment by his stepfather. It was rather because of his Danish characteristics— blond, blue-eyed, and tall—which made him distinct in his Jewish family. To his schoolmates he was a "Jew"; to his stepfather's friends he was a "goy" (gentile). These biographical elements are felt by Erikson to have had an early effect upon his own "identity," a concept which will be described in a later chapter when youth and the identity crisis are discussed.

Erikson remembers his mother as being pervasively sad during his early youth, but also as being "deeply involved in reading what I later found to have been such authors as Brandes, Kierkegaard, and Emerson and I could never doubt that her ambitions for me transcended the conventions which she, nevertheless, faithfully served."[5] He also credits both mother and stepfather as being courageous in allowing him to experiment with life-styles in his quest to find himself, a characteristic which Erikson contends is an essential ingredient of responsible parenthood.

Erikson describes his family as bourgeois, and it appears that his doctor stepfather was able to provide a comfortable living for the family in a location near universities, commerce, and natural beauty. It was in Karlsruhe that Erikson attended grammar school and gymnasium. He was never fond of the regimentation of school life and is today one of those rare exceptions to the normal course by which one becomes an academician, having simply refused to conform to the routine of college or graduate school.

Following gymnasium, Erikson attended art school, but preferred the role of the wandering artist to that of a settled student. Sensing and choosing alienation from his family and society, he adopted a life-style that he refers to as narcissistic—sketching, making wood carvings, and ignoring the world's social and political problems. The life of the wandering artist was in Erikson's view similar to today's antiestablishment youth culture. He views the sketching, however, as "a fundamental exercise in tracing impressions,"[6] the beginning of a methodology that would later be adopted as a way of making his unique contribution to the social-psychoanalytic field, a style referred to in the next chapter as "left-handed."

Beyond these years of moratorium—a concept more fully described below in the development of the identity stage of the life cycle—Erikson implies that there was a move toward identity in the call that came to him from his childhood friend from Karlsruhe, Peter Blos, to become a teacher of art in the newly founded progressive school in Vienna in which Blos was working. It was at this time, Erikson recalls, that "I learned to work regular hours, and I met the circle around Anna Freud—and Freud."[7]

Again, applying his own theory to himself, Erikson sees in Freud "a mythical figure and above all a great doctor who had rebelled against the medical profession."[8] In the practice of psychoanalysis the Freudian circle allowed him the healing role, not unlike that of his stepfather, the pediatrician, without the rigor of a medical school.

It is interesting to note that in Erikson's revision of his earlier autobiographical reflections, he changes the wording in such a way as to identify more positively with his stepfather. In the earlier account he describes his identification with Freud as being "an ambivalent identification with my stepfather."[9] In his later revision he changes the word ambivalent to read that in Freud he found a "strong identification with my stepfather, the pediatrician, mixed with a search for my own mythical father."[10]

This slight changing of words is significant because it is one of Erikson's contentions that the crises of the life cycle are never settled once and for all. There is a reliving of those cycles, a reworking, which can help develop the virtues of each crisis positively. It would seem that in Erikson's own case, as he reflected on his identification with Freud, it was not so much an "ambivalent" identification with his stepfather as it was a "positive" identification. Erikson may have seen the identification as one of ambivalence in his earlier writing but, upon reviewing, reliving, and revising that period, he no longer sensed the ambivalence as much as the positive relationship with his stepfather.

Of the Freudian circle, Erikson observes that here also was the social milieu, the circle of friends and co-workers, which accepted him into its ranks. In this, he visualizes the group's adoption of a stepson.[11]

During these early years in Vienna, Erikson thought of himself as an artist, and while he was interested in the psychoanalytic movement, he had no intention of making it a vocation. He was fascinated by the intense loyalty of the Vienna group of Freudian followers. Many of the learning experiences came in evening gatherings in which papers were read and discussed in a free university style that would be envied by many today. There was a devotion to the cause that often typifies a new movement, and this loyalty to a freeing concept and methodology was attractive to Erikson.

In those days one was chosen for psychoanalytic training and that honor came when Anna, Sigmund Freud's youngest daughter, accepted Erikson as a fellowship candidate. On the basis of his teaching of children both as a private tutor and in the Vienna school with Blos, he had been selected for training analysis. "Anna Freud had founded the Vienna version of the subspecialty of child analysis, and I, too, was to be primarily trained as a psychoanalyst of children, although such training included the supervised treatment of adolescent and of adult patients."[12]

Coles states that in addition to his daily analytic hour with Anna Freud, Erikson was being trained as a clinician in the Vienna school by August Aichhorn and others in the group. "He also studied with a Montessori group in Vienna, and was one of two men to graduate from the Montessori teachers' association, the Lehrerinnenverein."[13]

It was at this time in Vienna that Erikson met and fell in love with a talented American, Joan Serson. She was a teacher of modern dance and a student in Europe doing research for a possible doctorate in education from Columbia. She was also a part of the Vienna school experience in psychoanalysis. They married, and, by the time Erikson graduated from the Vienna Psychoanalytic Society in 1933, they were the parents of two sons, Kai and Jon. Later, in America, a third child, a girl, would be born to the Eriksons.

Mention of the 1930s is reminder enough that Hitler was coming to power in Germany. It was becoming increasingly difficult for the Freudian group to work freely. The Eriksons at first planned a return to Erik's native Denmark, but citizenship procedures proved too difficult. Through a chance meeting with Hanns Sachs, a native of Vienna, but living in Boston and a part of its psychoanalytic community, Erikson was urged to move to the United States and was assured that Boston would welcome his talent as a child psychoanalyst.

The remainder of Erikson's biography is inevitably related to his developing theory, a matter to be considered when attention is given to his methodology and life cycle concepts. Thus, a less detailed outline here will suffice to complete this sketch of his life.

In Boston, Erikson was one of the few nonmedical psychoanalysts. In fact, even without degrees he was given positions at Harvard Medical School and the Massachusetts General Hospital. He also began his own private practice, working primarily with children. It was at this time that Erikson made his last futile attempt to conform to the rigors of formal education, enrolling "at Harvard as a candidate for a Ph.D. in psychology, though in a matter of months it became clear that his mind still could not accommodate itself to formal, academic study. He had become a clinician, and he wanted to spend his time with people."[14] It is to Erikson's credit that without formal degrees he would attain the stature that is his today.

In Boston, as in other regions where Erikson was to move in the following years, he divided his time between clinical work and research. He also sought to investigate the nature of psychological health as well as the symptoms of pathology, and this must be understood as a lifelong interest that is significant for his theory.

In 1936 Erikson was invited to Yale University to accept a position in the Institute of Human Relations. He was appointed to a full-time research position by the Yale Medical School. He was first an instructor and soon an assistant professor. He also found that the Yale Institute of Human Relations, led by John Dollard, provided the kind of interdisciplinary stimulation that has challenged him throughout his lifetime. Here were sociologists, anthropologists, and psychiatrists working together on common problems.

In 1938 Erikson made one of his trips into another culture to observe and theorize concerning the relationship of individual development and cultural patterns. He had already broadened his base of interest to include anthropology and history, and was now invited by Scudder Mekeel to accompany Mekeel on an expedition to the Pine Ridge Sioux Indian Reservation in South Dakota.

The forties—both the century's and Erikson's, for his age roughly corresponds to the decades of this century, and he views his own life in that perspective—he spent in California. He conducted a private practice in San Francisco and was associated with the Institute of Child Welfare at the University of California, Berkeley, as well as serving as consultant to a number of other clinics. He again broadened his base of study with another field trip to an Indian reservation, the home of the Yurok tribe of Northern California. In this study, as in his work at Berkeley as a professor, Erikson was formulating his own theory that would culminate in his first major work, *Childhood and Society* (1950). The significance of this volume, which was a culmination of his concern for normal growth and development, will be discussed later.

At Berkeley the McCarthy era had produced a climate in which the loyalty oath was required of professors. Erikson refused to sign the oath, though a loyal American citizen, and he was dismissed and then reinstated. He then resigned, however, in protest against the firing of others from their teaching positions.[15]

Following the University of California "loyalty oath debacle," as Erikson refers to it, he received many invitations from other institutions to teach and do research. He accepted the one that came to him from the Austin Riggs Center in Stockbridge, Massachusetts. There the opportunity presented itself to study more directly the troubled adolescent, whose period was at that time, unbelievable as it may be to the present day proliferation of adolescent studies, often overlooked as a fleeting, almost unimportant, transitory time between determinative childhood and mature adulthood.

During the decade of the fifties Erikson also commuted regularly to the University of Pittsburgh's Western Psychiatric Institute. In contrast to the well-to-do youth of Riggs,

> in Pittsburgh he saw the children of workers and of would-be workers who were jobless. He joined the staff of the Arsenal Health Center, worked with Dr. Benjamin Spock, and watched how relatively poor mothers—many recent immigrants—handled their children. . . . He was interested in the relationship between "the environment" and the mind, and he did not intend to forget that by and large psychiatrists see patients who come from a particular (middle class) kind of environment.[16]

Erikson's studies of this period increasingly turned to the whole "identity" question and culminated in 1958 with the publication of *Young Man Luther: A Study in Psychoanalysis and History.* Coles points out that it was also during these years that Erikson was concerned with a study of Freud. He wrote three separate articles about Freud, coming to appreciate more than ever the dimensions of Freud's theory so often neglected—the historical and cultural. His study of Luther reflects much of this growing concern for the application of psychoanalytic theory to the lives of great men.

In 1960 Erikson was appointed a professor at Harvard. His reputation was now firmly established, not only as a psychoanalyst, but also as a scholar of interdisciplinary dimensions. Increasingly he was asked to be a guest lecturer at scholarly convocations all over the world. When he spoke in the Cambridge, Massachusetts, area, his meetings were often a standing-room-only event.

Erikson's speeches and journal articles became the foundation for two more books, *Insight and Responsibility* (1964), and *Identity: Youth and Crisis* (1968). These titles describe the progression of his thought, the growing interest in the historical and social dimensions to be added to the psychoanalytic and anthropological.

Erikson reports that Freud had initially desired to become a statesman, that he wanted his new discipline to be kept from the hands of the medical profession as their exclusive possession, and that he saw philosophy, not specialized medicine, as his ultimate goal. Erikson himself has fulfilled Freud's ambitions in a way in which perhaps no other psychoanalyst has done. When reading Erikson one is aware of reading philosophy. He has been successful in lifting psychiatry from its often narrowly defined medical limits and relating psychoanalytic theory to society, history, and religion. For this he is sometimes blamed more than praised by his professional colleagues. The evidence of his contribution to society is being appreciated more and more, however, as the popularity of his books and theory, as well as the demands upon his time, bear witness.[17]

Erikson's speeches and articles turned from questions of childhood and adolescent identity to those of ethics. *Insight and Responsibility* is one evidence of this interest, its last chapter dealing specifically with the Golden Rule as applied to ethical issues. The most decisive ethical treatment, however, is his book *Gandhi's Truth: On the Origins of Militant Nonviolence* (1969). Here is an emphasis reflective of a desire to round out his life cycle theory with the same attention devoted to wholeness in life and history, to maturity, wisdom and integrity as was originally given to the early stages of childhood in his first writings.

Since his book on Gandhi, Erikson has published four other books and also participated in taped conversations which were then put into book form. As Professor Emeritus of Human Development and Lecturer in Psychiatry at Harvard University, he agreed to enter into dialogue with Huey P. Newton of the Black Panther Party. Transcripts of these discussions were made and from them *In Search of Common Ground: Conversations with Erik H. Erikson and Huey P. Newton* was published.[18]

In 1973 the National Endowment for the Humanities invited Erikson to deliver two lectures on Thomas Jefferson. Here again he dealt with the identity question peculiar to America. He also addressed himself to the challenge facing generative man in providing an ethically wholesome world for those entrusted to its care. These lectures became the basis of the book *Dimensions of a New Identity*.

As mentioned earlier in this chapter, in 1975 Erikson combined a number of his previous journal articles and speeches into the volume entitled *Life History and the Historical Moment.* He revised the articles and added some new material. The theme is how life histories relate to historical moments both for leaders and those who follow. In the Preface, however, Erikson adds a sentence supporting the claim that ethics are a primary interest. Reflecting on the book's contents, he states that "it concerns the awakening of those groups of contemporaries (young people, modern women) to a need for *inner* as well as political liberation; and it concerns, throughout, the life histories of us, the observers, defined as we are by our own past, by the history of our field, and by the tasks of the times."[19]

In 1977 Erikson produced *Toys and Reasons: Stages in the Ritualization of Experience.* Based upon the Godkin Lectures that were given in 1972 at Harvard, this book develops the "relationship of childhood play to political imagination."[20] His most recent publication is a revised and enlarged edition of an earlier issue of the journal *Daedalus.* It is simply entitled *Adulthood,* having one chapter by Erikson, its editor.[21]

Now living in semiretirement in Tiburon, California, Erikson remains active. Since 1972 he has served as a senior consultant for the Mount Zion Hospital, San Francisco. In correspondence with this writer on questions relating his theory to religion and how others have interpreted those issues, he has agreed to give time and thought and to write his response when ready. In typical Eriksonian style, he states that "here, context is everything."[22]

Context *is* everything for Erikson. His life as it intersects with history is the ultimate context for his thought, and it is hoped that in these biographical pages his spirit, like that of Gandhi, whose presence he sought to find in his book, may be sensed. If that happens at all, then readers will turn to the writings of Erikson for more intimate investigation and encounter with his profound insights.

Before concluding with a summarizing comment on the stepchild theme, two other biographical observations are in order. One, Erikson has a delightful sense of humor that is often subtle but obvious to those who read his works extensively.[23] Most of the pictures used on the book jackets show him in a very somber mood. It is therefore refreshing to note that one of his latest publications, *Toys and Reasons,* reveals a smiling profile, perhaps reflective of that playfulness which comes when one can look back on one's one-and-only life cycle with integrity.

Secondly, it would appear that Erikson is in many ways a very private person. When referring to the pathological side of his own identity crisis, he simply indicates that it need not be described except to say that with the aid of psychoanalysis he was helped to formulate his later developmental theory.[24] Yet it is perhaps this honesty concerning the negative polarities of life crises that has enabled him to maintain a balanced position between the extremes of naive optimism and despairing pessimism. His quietness in dealing with his own position is also revealed in his treatment of religion, the concern of the last chapter of this book.

Erikson has dealt at great length with what he calls "homo religiosus." Ultimately we must ask to what extent he himself is a religious man. Our answer may not be as satisfying as we might wish, whether we come to study Erikson from the Freudian or the religious perspective. However, "context is everything," and when the background not only of his life, but of his method and theory have been examined, we will raise the questions that relate his life cycle and historical period to the ultimate concern of faith and trust.

Finally, in returning to the stepchild theme, it is obvious that Erikson fits that typology in many ways. He also recognizes the danger of making "not belonging" into a life-style. He points out that the negative identity of a stepson is that of a bastard. To exploit the role of stepchild might lead one "to avoid belonging anywhere quite irreversibly; working between the established fields can mean avoiding the disciplines necessary for any one field; and, being enamored with the aesthetic order of things, one may well come to avoid their ethical and political as well as their methodological implications."[25]

Admitting that one might find some of these weaknesses in his work, Erikson goes on to point out that he has consciously attempted to counteract them. Appealing to his fellow countryman Kierkegaard, who clearly distinguished between the aesthetic and ethical man, Erikson notes that he has moved consistently in his writing to consider questions of a social and political nature, and "to religious actualists such as Luther and Gandhi."[26]

Erikson has indeed lifted his own stepchild identity to a universal level in exploring the borderlines in a world in which many today feel that they simply do not belong. In his own quest he illustrates a life, a method, and provides a conceptual model for us to understand the nature of belonging.

It is possible that for any person or group belonging may be interpreted too narrowly, thereby excluding others. This exclusive provincialism is what Erikson calls "pseudospecies." One of his strong ethical concerns is that the vision of a wider identity may emerge within our world in which too often we exclude those of other races, nations, or religions. If, in lifting his stepchild patienthood to a universal level of a wider identity, Erikson has helped to build bridges leading to a sense of belonging that is authentic for the entire species of humanity, then his words about Luther with which this chapter opened surely apply to Erikson as well.

NOTES

1. Erik H. Erikson, *Young Man Luther* (New York: W. W. Norton, 1958, 1962), p. 67.
2. Paul Tillich, *On the Boundary: An Autobiographical Sketch* (New York: Charles Scribner's Sons, 1966). Erikson used this Tillichian concept to describe his own life when he revised his original "Autobiographic Notes on the Identity Crisis," *Daedalus*, 99 (Fall 1970), for inclusion in his book, *Life History and the Historical Moment* (New York: W. W. Norton, 1975).
3. See Erik H. Erikson, *Life History and the Historical Moment*, pp. 29–30.
4. Robert Coles, *Erik H. Erikson: The Growth of His Work* (Boston: Little, Brown, 1970) p. 13. How Erik Homburger later came to adopt the name, Erikson has several interpretations in contemporary mythology. Roazen suggests "an identification with the Norwegian discoverer of America." Later he calls it a family decision to avoid confusion with hamburger; and a conscious choice by Erikson, the fatherless one, to indicate that in a sense he is his own father, Erik's son. Roazen is also critical of Erikson at this point, feeling that the dropping of Homburger was a kind of "repudiation of his German-Jewish stepfather." See Paul Roazen, *Erik H. Erikson: The Power and Limits of a Vision* (New York: Free Press, 1976), pp. 93, 98–99. Gail Sheehy reflects a similar mood as she follows Marshall

Berman, who, in a book review for *The New York Times* (March 30, 1975), accused Erikson of evading or denying his Jewishness and of repudiating his stepfather when he dropped Homburger as his last name. See Gail Sheehy, *Passages* (New York: Bantam Books, 1977) pp. 18–19, and note 5, p. 516.

5. Erikson, *Life History*, p. 31.
6. Ibid., p. 28.
7. Ibid., p. 29.
8. Ibid.
9. "Autobiographic Notes on the Identity Crisis," p. 744.
10. *Life History*, p. 29.
11. Ibid.
12. Ibid., p. 24.
13. Coles, p. 23.
14. Ibid., p. 33.
15. Erikson, *Life History*, p. 42.
16. Coles, p. 171.
17. See two articles in which Freud's desire to have his discipline apply more widely is discussed: Erik H. Erikson, "On the Nature of Psycho-Historical Evidence: In Search of Gandhi," *Daedalus*, 97 (Summer 1968), p. 710. This article has also been reprinted and revised in Erikson's book *Life History and the Historical Moment*, pp. 113–168. Erikson, "Freud's 'The Origins of Psycho-analysis,' " *International Journal of Psycho-analysis*, 36 (Jan-Feb 1955), p. 4.
18. Kai T. Erikson, ed., *In Search of Common Ground: Conversations with Erik H. Erikson and Huey P. Newton* (New York: Dell Publishing Co., Laurel Edition, 1973).
19. Erikson, *Life History*, p. 10. Italics mine.
20. Erik H. Erikson, *Toys and Reasons* (New York: W. W. Norton, 1977), p. 11.
21. Erik H. Erikson, ed., *Adulthood* (New York: W. W. Norton, 1978).
22. Personal letter, November 17, 1979. When reflecting on his own earlier writing about women, he writes ". . . in these matters context is all . . ." See "Once More the Inner Space," Erikson, *Life History*, p. 225.
23. For a few random examples of his humor, see *Life History*, pp. 46, 250; and *Toys and Reasons*, pp. 53–54, 132, 153.
24. Erikson, *Life History*, p. 26.
25. Ibid., p. 31.
26. Ibid.

CHAPTER II

Left-Handed Knowing

Understanding the eight stages of development in Erikson's system is far less difficult than explaining how he gets there. In fact, it is probably Erikson's method that has been the most perplexing aspect to those who seek to comprehend his theory but who sense the significance of his wisdom. The stepchild imagery remains an appropriate one for Erikson's method as well as his life. He warns his readers that being at home in the hyphen between psychology and history, and between psychology and sociology, will not be comfortable. There are other hyphens in his interdisciplinary approach and it is the purpose of this chapter to explore that unfamiliar terrain.

Left-handedness

Perhaps a reminder of Erikson's early artistic experiences, his lifelong interest, and his artistic perspective is the place to begin. Art is occasionally referred to as being an activity of the left hand. Culturally, left-handedness has often symbolized that which does not fit neatly with the rational schemes of right-handed categories.

Jerome Bruner[1] and others list such activities as dreams, art, sentiment, intuition, subjectivism, feelings, and, in general, all nonrational categories as being left-handed. To the right hand belong order, logic, science, reason, and action.[2]

Erikson, the artist-turned-clinician, presents an unusual combination. He is neither totally committed to art, nor is he a cold rationalist. He is a stepchild seeking relation, an explorer discovering new frontiers of knowledge best described in Bruner's symbolism of left-handed knowing. Before seeing how Erikson fulfills this model, let us note a significant conclusion of Bruner.

In an extremely perceptive observation, Bruner helps anyone who may have a problem understanding someone like Erikson. It is not uncommon to find readers of Erikson expressing resistance and frustration in seeking to comprehend the interdisciplinary complexity of his method. Here is Bruner's insight:

> . . . There is, perhaps, one universal truth about all forms of human cognition; the ability to deal with knowledge is hugely exceeded by the potential knowledge contained in man's environment. To cope with this diversity, man's perception, his memory, and his thought processes early become governed by strategies for protecting his limited capacities from the confusion of overloading. We tend to perceive things schematically, for example, rather than in detail, or we represent a class of diverse things by some sort of averaged "typical instance."[3]

Our conventional schemes and types are challenged by Erikson. His left-handed knowing forces us to abandon the prejudices of either objective rationalism or subjective intuition. Yet, the positive aspects of each must be reclaimed, enlarged, and related to new perspectives.

Bruner cites Whitehead's suggestion that "both for the exploration of the metaphysical and the poetic, the language of the poet may be the only appropriate medium."[4] Later in this chapter we will have occasion to hear Erikson express a somewhat similar point of view as he notes the subjective basis of Einstein's scientifically verifiable theory. For now, it is sufficient to note that in his left-handed knowing, Erikson challenges our simplistic dichotomies and offers to lead us into a new appreciation for an integrative approach to understanding.

Disciplined Subjectivity[5]

At the conclusion of an interview, Erikson made the following comment which reveals not only the main thrust of his approach, but his humor as well: "You have heard of the rabbi who felt inhibited when he was asked to make a speech in heaven. 'I am good only at refutation,' he said. My difficulty is different. I find it hard to put up a good argument, because I am more at home in observation and illustration."[6]

It is at this point that Erikson is often criticized by his more rationalistic colleagues. In concluding a lengthy treatment of Erikson's theory, the author of a textbook on personality theory has this to say: "A criticism with more merit . . . focuses on the quality of the empirical foundations upon which the theory is based." He goes on to praise Erikson for his observational data, his experience in clinical practice, and many other virtues in his approach. But he follows his praise with this criticism: "Despite these qualities, however, description based upon personal observation, although constituting the raw data of any scientific undertaking, is not sufficient. It is well recognized—indeed Erikson recognizes it himself—that observation can be very subjective."[7]

Impression, observation, word-sketches and illustrations are a part of Erikson's method. In describing his search for Gandhi, "On the Nature of Psycho-Historical Evidence," he writes, "I had to offer some observations of a 'markedly personal nature,' and this not only from predilection but because the only methodological certainty that I could claim for my specialty, the psychotherapeutic encounter, was 'disciplined subjectivity.' "[8]

"Disciplined subjectivity" means that in the psychotherapeutic relationship there is an element of intuition and inference not to be measured in any objective way. Yet in the depths of this encounter with emotions and the irrational, the therapist must be intellectually disciplined enough to relate the subjective element to theory and concepts. He must ever be aware of his own reactions and way of relating to his client.[9]

In light of this aspect of Erikson's method, it would appear that Robert Coles is more accurate than Henry W. Maier in stating the relationship between theory and method in Erikson's writings. The latter claims that Erikson begins with theory, substantiating it with his observations.[10] Coles would appear to be more true to the Eriksonian approach in his conclusion that (at least with regard to his interdisciplinary approach) Erikson begins inductively, developing his theory in the process.[11]

In Erikson's Preface to *Insight and Responsibility*, he comments on his use of insight. "This is a form of discernment hard to define and harder to defend, for it includes those preconscious assumptions which both precede and follow proven knowledge and formulated theory, and it includes enlightened common sense and informed partisanship."[12] He concludes that in this respect he has expressed his insights more fully than he has built a theory.

In Erikson's differentiation between reality and actuality, a distinction we will have occasion to note repeatedly, he is concerned with the limits of verifiability in the so-called "outer world." Science and rationalism are no guarantee of success in psychoanalysis. He states that "maybe our habitual reference to man's environment as an 'outer world' attests, more that any other single item, to the fact that the world of that intuitive and active participation which constitutes most of our waking life is still foreign territory to our theory."[13]

Rationalism can be what Erikson calls a "Cartesian straitjacket (which) we have imposed on our model of man ..." To remove the straitjacket we must differentiate between reality and actuality, the latter being "the world verified in immediate immersion and interaction."[14] Here the emphasis is upon experience, the unconscious and preconscious, inspiration and mutual activation, a different dimension from the objective verifiability of reality.

However, lest one conclude that Erikson, the subjective artist, is all there is to know, let us turn to the "discipline" side of his disciplined subjectivity. His protest against Cartesian straitjacketing in no way limits him to the categories of intuition, subjectivism, or insight alone. Erikson is a theoretician and it is to his Freudian foundation that we must now turn our attention.

Foundation in Freud and Psychoanalysis's Second Stage

Erikson proudly identifies himself with Sigmund Freud.[15] One way of describing Erikson's Freudian orientation would be to note his revisions of Freudian theory. Actually, Erikson considers himself to be more true to Freud than to psychoanalytic practice as it has developed. He often claims that Freud never intended the kind of restriction in practice that has resulted in psychiatry's present general confinement to the medical field.

Along with most of Freud's concepts (e.g., id, ego, and superego), Erikson accepted the five basic principles of psychoanalysis: inner resistance, repression, the reality of the unconscious, the power and significance of the sexual nature from infancy and throughout life, and the need to give attention to infantile experience. Erikson believes that Freud's discoveries of transference and countertransference should be added as principles of equal importance to the first five.[16]

Erikson also credits as foundational to his discipline what Freud called his "points of view."[17] We shall simply list these here, commenting only upon that which Erikson feels must be added to Freud's scheme. The four points of view Freud taught his students to identify are: topographic, dynamic, economic, and genetic.[18]

Erikson attributes a fifth point of view to David Rapaport, the adaptive.[19] In his own moving beyond mere adjustment to new levels of adaptation, Erikson becomes extremely creative. It is in the facing and solving of a psychosocial identity crisis such as Luther's that the adaptive power of the human ego is revealed to be of greater significance than libidinal drives. More must be said about this as we see Erikson move beyond Freud.

Acknowledging, then, Erikson's Freudian base, it must be reiterated that he revises Freud. Erikson also expands upon the work of Freud's interpreters, moving into what he alludes to as a possible "second stage" for psychoanalysis.

From Pathology to Normative Health

Erikson's shift of emphasis from pathology to health will be discussed in later chapters as the schedule of virtues is explored. However, this is an important methodological change from Freudianism that has been developed by Erikson, and it is essential to note it at this point.

Erikson admits to a pathological orientation in the introduction to his *Childhood and Society*. Indicating that the case histories naturally grow out of experiences in which persons entered therapy because of a problem, Erikson observes that "in these, as in all situations, the psychoanalytic method detects conflict; for this method was first focused on mental disturbance."[20] As he developed his theory of the eight stages of man, however, a theory that does describe the development of healthy personality, Erikson states, "I found myself implying a latent universal value system which is based on the nature of human growth, the needs of the developing ego, and certain common elements in child training systems."[21]

Erikson's turn from pathology to normative health, from a predominantly negative to a stronger quality of positive consideration, is revealed in the following statement in which he comments upon his methodology in studying both Luther and Gandhi:

> The analytic genius of Freud has bequeathed to us a certain grammar and syntax of what may be called traumatology, which makes it almost impossible, given some goodwill seasoned with more or less therapeutic intent, not to see what is basically "wrong" with somebody. In applying my traumatological metier to young Luther I have attempted to understand also the fabulous restorative energy of youth which helped his native genius to reaffirm Christian faith with new liveliness and power. In studying middle-aged Gandhi, I must try to trace indications that such a leader started to develop his singular effectiveness as well as his great concerns rather early in life, and that attempts to reduce the quality of these concerns to earlier as well as bigger and better childhood traumata is wrong in method and perhaps evil in influence.[22]

This last sentence especially notes a decided direction in Erikson's thought which will be explained more completely in the discussion of virtues.[23]

From the Individual to the Larger Milieu

Actually it is possible to begin this generalization one step prior to the individual. It has been observed that Erikson's concern is a move from the id to the ego.[24] In at least one of his books he states specifically that in Freud's early work "the focus of theorizing was the 'id,' the instinctual force driving man from within...." While he notes that Freud also considered group behavior, the primary concern in much psychoanalytic methodology is the atomistic approach. And he argues that "man alone" cannot be treated as disengaged from his contexts.[25]

Not only does the larger milieu suggest a move from the id to the ego, it demands a shift in focus from the preoccupation with infantile sexuality to a consideration of the crises of each stage in the life cycle. For psychoanalysis had, until Erikson's time, consistently concentrated upon the period up to adolescence. It was assumed that at that time rational genitality would "absorb infantile fixations and irrational conflicts or . . . admit them to repeat performances under manifold disguises."[26]

To enlarge the scope even further, consideration must be given to the generational question beyond the individual. Erikson's central concern of identity involves more than youth. The older generation is responsible for providing an ideology that youth may either accept or against which they may rebel. His interest is with more than the individual or even one generation. The cogwheeling of generations means that an enlarged area of investigation must be undertaken.[27]

To speak of generations is to introduce the whole matter of societal configurations, a central theme in Erikson and another area in which he revises Freud's interpreters, if not Freud himself. The psychoanalytic method, Erikson says, "cannot quite grasp identity because it has not developed terms to conceptualize the environment."[28] The problem is the tendency to separate the individual and his environment in a way that overlooks the fact that the environment is internalized and not just an objective reality in which the individual lives as an unrelated, isolated unit: "We never," he says, "—not even as a new born—meet any environment as a person who never had an environment."[29]

Erikson's procedure is more suggestive at this point than definitive. He sees himself as a pioneer, seeking to mold new methodological concepts, but it is not at all clear, as yet, whether such a methodology belongs primarily to "a psychoanalysis sophisticated enough to include the environment . . . (or) a social psychology which is psychoanalytically sophisticated. . . ." The real intention seems to be a uniting of both of these approaches, resulting in "a new field which would have to create its own historical sophistication."[30] Here again Erikson is the stepchild, not quite at home, but hopeful for the next generation.

Erikson's dispute, to repeat, is with an atomistic methodology. His plea is for a more inclusive approach. He speaks of a "post-Freudian position," expressing his criticism of Freud who stated that a crystal's structure is only seen as it cracks: "But a crystal, on the one hand, and an organism or a personality, on the other, differ in the fact that one is inanimate and the other an organic whole which cannot be broken up without a withering of the parts."[31]

An example of Erikson's interest at this point could be any one of his several culture studies. One might expect, for instance, that study of the Yurok Indians would attribute their trait of stinginess to "anality." Erikson accepts the Freudian interpretation as partially correct, but goes on to cite the cultural and economic factors that also contribute to this trait, refusing to reduce it to a single cause.[32]

Finally, in noting the expansion of Freudian concepts to an ever-enlarging milieu, attention must be given to Erikson's notion of the "I" beyond the mere ego. He states that "a final methodological problem may or may not point beyond psychoanalysis." He notes that Freud, in his conceptualization of the ego, "failed to analyze the role of the observer who chooses to study conflict in himself as well as in others." There is an "I" which is at "the core of consciousness." This "I" is related further to the identity crisis when "in adolescent experience . . . the 'I' can first really perceive itself as separate." There is a transcendence to the "I" that supersedes the definition of the ego, and it is for this reason, Erikson states, that he has studied religious figures where "the dilemma of existence versus politics"[33] is more squarely faced and thus deserving of exploration.

So much for the expansion of Freudian method and theory as Erikson seeks to move out from the atomistic to the larger milieu. This line of thinking is further developed in the following sections dealing with the social and historical dimensions.

From Interpretation of Dreams to Play Configurations

A third area of methodology which constitutes a shift in approach from the Freudian model has to do with Erikson's concern with play analysis. For Freud the interpretation of dreams was the royal road to an understanding of the subconscious. Erikson does not discount this method. In fact he deals quite specifically with dream interpretation. However, for him the way in which children and youth arrange play scenes is of greater interest than dream interpretation.

Again and again in his clinical practice, Erikson studied the way in which children arrange given materials. One of his more significant theoretical conclusions is reached primarily through this approach. Instead of focusing upon the assumed penis envy of women, a negative way of noting what is lacked, Erikson concludes that positively women are aware of having inner space, the womb from which the life of man emerges. Women may proudly claim this endowment which entitles them to an identity of their own rather than the more derogatory "not male" kind of identity Freudian theory has often assigned to them. Erikson's conclusion is reached through repeated experiments and analysis of the play configurations of boys and girls. Boys' interests usually indicate action, obtrusiveness, and even violence; girls' scenes communicate an interiority, protectiveness, and inclusiveness which time after time runs so true to form as to allow no other conclusion for Erikson than that a sense of inner space is a source of psychosocial identity.[34]

From Male Superiority to Female Identity

The methodological shift just described leads to a theoretical conclusion that in turn affects further methodology. Beyond Freud, Erikson might be described as moving from male superiority to female identity based on the woman's own uniqueness and not on her deprivation. Erikson calls Freud's "general judgment of the identity of women ... probably the weakest part of his theory."[35] When Erikson in turn moves beyond Freud's approach, a change in methodology is obvious.

A woman's uniqueness, creativity, and inner feeling equips her for social roles yet to be fully discovered. The responsible society will be one that recognizes the value of woman's social organization as well as her morphology. Women's creativity belongs in the leadership of science and not just in token representation.[36] And what is true for the field of science is also true in politics, as Erikson goes on to indicate.[37]

My interpretation, using the motif developed earlier of left- and right-handedness, is that Erikson is appealing for equality for the woman's native gifts of the left hand. He would not in any way deny that women can be as logical and analytical as men. However, his method has led him to conclude that the intuitive gifts of women are a helpful balance to male objectivity. When each sex is recognized for its unique gifts society will be enriched, as will formerly restricted, overly narrow sexual identities.

From Originology to Responsibility

A final way of noting the shift beyond Freud in Erikson is to describe his discontent with "originology." It was no longer sufficient to analyze the early source of problems for a patient. Erikson saw the importance of "what world image they were sharing, where they were going from where they were, and who was going with them."[38]

Erikson expresses this same conviction with reference to his study of Luther and Gandhi. The lives of great men cannot be explained on the basis of childhood traumata alone, although these are certainly to be considered. Beyond childhood determinism one must consider historical and social circumstances together with individual responsibility. It is true that we are driven, but it is Erikson's firm conviction that we also *do* something with our drives.[39]

A conclusion to this section dealing with Erikson's revision of, or at least new direction within, psychoanalytic theory is what we have called the "Second Stage." In typical Eriksonian word-sketching, he notes that Freud and those following his method had made significant discoveries and led a revolution in the study of man. Psychoanalysis "had turned *inward*" to study the unconscious; "it searched *backward*" to find the origins of mental disturbances; "and it pressed *downward*" to explore those instincts which were often denied or repressed. But for Erikson it was time for *"the second stage."* Life is more than inward, backward, and downward discoveries revealed in the clinical setting. It became Erikson's goal to enlarge his study to include those visions which lead *"outward* from self-centeredness to the mutuality of love and communality, *forward* from the enslaving past to the utopian anticipation of new potentialities, and *upward* from the unconscious to the enigma of consciousness."[40]

In sketching this enlargement of the second stage, Erikson is convinced that this had been Freud's goal also, both implicitly and in the style in which he had written and been recognized by his own generation. Here we see both Erikson's allegiance to Freud and his enlargement upon the concerns of traditional psychoanalytical thought.

Psychosocial Identity

The social as well as the historical elements of Erikson's approach have been referred to above since his interdisciplinary method obviously overlaps single categories. Some additional consideration of each of these is essential, however. There are a number of ways the social dimension might be described, but the crux of the matter centers around his very key concept of identity.

Identity is multidimensional. It may commonly be thought of in terms of a person's awareness of who he is, but it is Erikson's conviction that this awareness is impossible apart from social response, "for we deal with a process 'located' in the core of the *individual* and yet also in the core of his *communal culture*, a process which establishes, in fact, the identity of those two identities."[41]

This process is "one of simultaneous reflection and observation."[42] A person judges himself in relation to how he believes others are judging him, and their judgment of him is affected by their own self-understanding and how that self-understanding relates to their own significant identity types. In turn, the identity-seeking youth is simultaneously making the same judgment of the one judging him. This is not ordinarily a conscious process.

It is Erikson's hope that conceptual tools will be developed to deal with psychosocial reality. Traditional psychoanalysis has not done this because it has failed to include the environmental dimension. In fact, Erikson sees as quite antithetical to his approach the common way of designating environmental factors as "outer" or "objective" when in reality the environment is a "pervasive actuality." Erikson points to the introduction by the German ethologists of the word *umwelt*, which indicates an environment that is more than surrounding one; it pervades.[43]

Closely related to this view is the contention that, especially as an infant, one's experience of self is dependent upon one's social relationship with the mother. Freud had spoken of self-esteem as being dependent upon "the residue of childish narcissism, i.e., the child's natural self-love"; but it is Erikson's contention that "if a healthy residue of infantile narcissism is to survive, the maternal environment must create and sustain it with a love which assures the child that it is good to be alive in the social coordinates in which he happens to find himself."[44]

Erikson points out the positive role of society in affirming the worth of life in each developing stage.[45] It is important to see the cogwheeling, or interrelationship of person and society. The practice in thought and speech that refers to "the organism and 'its' environment . . ." is too simplistic. "Members of the same species and of other species are always part of each other's *Umwelt*."[46]

Erikson attempts to forge the tools of an interdisciplinary methodology as he elaborates upon the configurations involved in the lives of Luther and Gandhi. These both open the way to consideration of the third aspect of Erikson's approach, the psycho-historical. The method is not yet clear, but the need is obvious. "Only psychoanalysis and social science together can eventually chart the course of individual life in the setting of a changing community."[47]

Psycho-history

The Theory

Freudian psychoanalysis, revised by Erikson in the "Second Stage," and psychosocial dimensions of identity formation are two basic components of Erikson's methodology. To these a third is added—the psycho-historical. The products of this procedure are to be seen in Erikson's major works on Luther, Gandhi, Thomas Jefferson, and in many less fully treated subjects ranging from American folklore to Adolph Hitler, Maxim Gorky, and such cultural studies as those concerned with the American Indians.

The psychoanalyst is an historian in the sense of taking life histories and making life histories as a participant-observer. He also makes history as the creator of theory. But all of this does not make him an historian fully qualified in the methodological tools of a quite separate discipline. When the psychoanalyst turns his attention to an historical figure and seeks to adapt clinical methods to historical interpretations, he moves into an undefined area described by Erikson as "the hyphen" between psychoanalysis and history. He is thus designing and seeking to forge methodologically useful tools that will be less refined during the time when the new science is developing than they will be in the future. Graphically, Erikson describes this impure methodology as "the compost heap of today's interdisciplinary efforts, which may help to fertilize new fields, and to produce future flowers of new methodological clarity."[48]

While Erikson's method of writing psycho-history will need to be understood, it is also vital to note a change in his own attitude since his earlier description of it as a "compost heap." Perhaps his more recent comments indicate that the fertilizer was effective enough.

In *Dimensions of a New Identity*, Erikson has this to say about psycho-history: "I have come to use this term only with tacit quotation marks. . . . I would not wish to associate myself with all that is done in the name of this term."[49]

He goes on to say that as the combined methods of psychoanalysis and history are bridged, historians will surely be more sensitive to and accurate in reporting the psychological determinants in their study. Also, psychologists will become better historians.

Having stated his psychoanalytic presuppositions, Erikson describes the psycho-historical approach to a document such as Gandhi's autobiography as one which will fathom "the complementarity of at least four conditions under which a record emerges."[50] These are the following: 1. the *moment* when the individual (e.g. Gandhi) chose to record an event; 2. the *sequence* in the life history in which the event was recorded; 3. the *moment* in the larger context of the community; and 4. the *sequence* in that community's own history.[51]

The importance of keeping all four of these variables together is to see the relationship of life-event and life-history, the intersecting of life-history and historical period as well as the larger historical perspective.

One of the contributions that Erikson sees psychoanlysis making to a study of history is "the clarification of rigid and unconscious inner obstacles, stemming from past history, which obstruct emerging (and already strongly desired) decisions in present history."[52]

Also clear in this first set of variables is the social dimension of historical moments. The decision of an individual must be sustained by his culture for him to sense the continuity essential to psychosocial identity.

To this first essential set of variables Erikson adds another relating to the reviewer of the event. If the clinical psychoanalyst must first experience therapy himself in order to understand himself and be conscious of his own life cycle as he acts as healer to others, even so must the psycho-historian be aware of the perspective he brings to his review of an historical event.[53] Erikson suggests the same four complementarities for the reviewer of an event that were functioning for the original recorder of the event: 1. the *moment* in the reviewer's own life; 2. the *sequence* "in the reviewer's life history;" 3. the *moment* in the larger context of the communities of the reviewer; and 4. the *sequence* "in the history of the reviewer's communities."[54]

An example of what is at stake in this set of variables is Erikson's reminder to his readers that he approached his study of Gandhi having just returned from a conference on disarmament, and in that context Gandhi's life and quest for truth, especially as related to solving conflicts in society, seemed worth pursuing.

To these two sets of variables that Erikson diagrams, he adds a third dealing with a leader's followers, and a fourth dealing with other analogous historical events.

In summary, "the psycho-historian's job [is one] of specifying in all their complementarity the inner dynamics as well as the social conditions which make history seem to repeat, to renew, or to surpass itself."[55]

Erikson differentiates between psychological reality and historical actuality. To consider this subject is to recall our earlier reference to disciplined subjectivity. However, the differentiation is essential to psycho-history. While he develops this in an entire chapter of *Insight and Responsibility*, his summary in *Gandhi's Truth* is sufficient at this point. "In my clinical ruminations I have found it necessary to split what we mean by 'real' into that which can be known because it is demonstrably correct (factual reality) and that which feels effectively true in action (actuality)."[56] Here is the synthesis symbolized in the imagery of left-handed knowing.

Reality may be capable of demonstration, but actuality involves more than the demonstrable. Irrational forces within a life history or a culture's history must be reckoned with and the psycho-historian's task is to do just that.

Psycho-history Criticized

It is in the area of psycho-history that Erikson has become the object of much criticism. To begin with, "some historians have viewed biography from time immemorial as a stepchild among historical genres."[57]

Added to this basic prejudice of some historians in general is the charge by Roland Bainton, David Donalds, Lewis Spitz, and others that Erikson's historical data for his Luther book is often inaccurate.[58] Some have been more critical than others. One concession made by George Lindbeck, Professor of Theology at Yale University, is that since Erikson's writing, Roman Catholic and Protestant historians "are much closer to an ecumenical consensus on previously controverted points. This is not simply a matter of ecumenical good will. A tremendous amount of solid fresh research has been done."[59] Other historians have also agreed that the material available to Erikson at the time of his writing was far more limited than it would be today.

Ironically, many who are critical of Erikson's psycho-historical studies on the one hand (shall we say the right hand?), find value on the other. Lindbeck writes:

> . . . when I finally sat down this past year to a thorough reading of Erikson on Luther, I expected to like the psychosocial approach to the causes of the Reformation, but to be skeptical of the psychobiographical elements. Both of these anticipations were fulfilled, but what I had not foreseen was that my over-all response would be so positive.[60]

Lewis W. Spitz, Professor of history at Stanford University and an author of works on the Reformation era, is equally positive, ranking Erikson as having "creatively gone beyond Freud."[61] Later, in referring to the Luther study he states that "Erikson offers a look inside which is more than historical and has *the ring of truth*."[62]

Finally, Spitz calls Erikson's study a "great achievement" and concludes as follows: "*Young Man Luther* is a marvelous vehicle for relating in a moving parable the way an unusual youth became a great man of history, in fact, historians are in the author's debt for pointing up the great importance for history of a single man and what transpires with the 'inner court.' "[63]

This brief review of psycho-history is far from adequate for anyone wishing a complete analysis of this one aspect of Erikson's way of knowing. The book *Encounter with Erikson*, edited by Capps, Capps, and Bradford is almost totally concerned with psycho-history. Roazen has an entire chapter on the subject,[64] and the book edited by Peter Homans, *Childhood and Selfhood*,[65] has a number of chapters critical of Erikson's psycho-historical work.

Roger A. Johnson lists twenty-two "Reviews of Erikson's Young Man Luther." He also has a very helpful introduction to the book he edits. The volume reprints the Bainton and Spitz critiques. Johnson astutely observes that the historians are also in error as they interpret Erikson and he provides an analysis of their errors.[66]

It is vital to understand that for Erikson, psycho-history as it began and has developed is basically a discipline that will ultimately contribute to a deeper understanding of how great men have moved beyond adjustment to generative adaptation.[67] In this sense psycho-history is a contribution to contemporary society and the future we are forging even as we study the past.

The Right-handed Artist

While this chapter has emphasized the relation of left- and right-handedness, the intuitive and the rational, the primary concern has been with the "knowing." Another aspect to be considered is Erikson's style.

Seeing, as he does with the eyes of the artist, a left-handed activity, he nevertheless paints word pictures graphically, and verbalization is usually assigned to the right hand, a more rational, prosaic means of expression than art. In his autobiographical chapter of *Life History and the Historical Moment*, Erikson reflects upon his own early perplexity as to how he as an artist could ever fit into a scientific and verbal movement such as psychoanalysis.[68]

Erikson recalls three early impressions. First, when he began studying psychoanalysis he was still a teacher of children and as he undertook the interpretation of dreams he was also observing children at play. The play theme was referred to above as a change in Erikson's method from Freud's focus on dreams.

Second, Erikson began to realize that Freud was also (what we have called) left-handed in interest with his indomitable visual curiosity, "which sent him hurrying to Italy and through her city squares and museums whenever his work permitted. His descriptions of his patients' memories and dreams also reveal that he deeply empathized with their imagery before he entered what he had heard and seen into the context of verbal nomenclature."[69]

Finally, Erikson recalls that Anna Freud responded to his doubts about having a place in "such high intellectual endeavors . . ." with what must be judged to be a prophetic insight. "She said quietly: 'You might help to make them see.' "[70]

Readers of Erikson's writings often find themselves fulfilling that prophecy as they experience a new understanding, a kind of Platonic breakthrough of vision called "eidetic," an "Aha!" grasping of relationships formerly restricted to a more confined scheme of understanding. Erikson's interdisciplinary approach forces his readers to enlarge their vision and expand their schematic way of viewing reality.

An example of Erikson's ability to help people "see" emerges from his treatment of American identity as he recalls it from the days of his immigration here to a new homeland. Perhaps only a stepchild artist psychoanalyst could see in the American scene the picture he paints.

A nation of wealth had suffered the humiliation of financial depression. It is paralyzed. Its very identity as a self-made nation of destiny is at stake. Then, from out of those depths, there emerges a leader who is himself a victim of paralysis. In spite of his personal tragedy, he appears in public erect, as he is helped by another. His mood and his voice challenge personal and social depression. People were uplifted by his courage, and the nation "marched—behind the man in the wheelchair."[71]

The knowing which is gained through the imagery of that view of America is profound. It brings together as Erikson so often does the rational, visual, factual and emotional realities of history.

Purposeful Play

I shall conclude this treatment of Erikson's left-handed knowing by returning to his preference for play, hardly an activity of the right hand of intellectualization. However, for Erikson, play becomes a reliable way of knowing. He begins his book *Toys and Reasons*, citing a passage from Plato's *Laws* in which the great philosopher expounded upon "the model of true playfulness in the need of all young creatures, animal and human, to leap. To truly leap, you must learn how to use the ground as a springboard, and how to land resiliently and safely. It means to test the leeway allowed by given limits; to outdo and yet not escape gravity."[72]

Here the dialectic of left- and right-handedness emerges again. The rational philosopher praising playfulness. The psychoanalyst relating the purposefulness of play in learning about limits, for that is how Erikson interprets a child's playfulness. He is learning "to master reality by experiment and planning."[73]

For the adult creative genius it is the ability to play with ideas that is often productive of new ways of thinking. Erikson often cites Einstein as one who also praised playfulness. A chapter in Erikson's book *Toys and Reasons* is entitled "Einstein's Puzzles,"[74] and relates that as a child the great scientist enjoyed playing with building blocks and picture puzzles.

According to Gerald Holton, Einstein saw our ultimate understanding of life as being based upon a " 'leap of intuition.' "[75] He also reminds us that Einstein's formulation of the theory of relativity was first a hunch, a dream, and only later a scientific fact to be proven by verification.[76]

More will be said in the concluding chapter regarding this aspect of Erikson's thought. But in summarizing his ability to bring together left- and right-handed knowing, I conclude with his citing of William Blake for the title of the book quoted in this section:

> The Child's Toys and the Old Man's Reasons
> Are the Fruits of the Two Seasons.[77]

For Erikson, the significance of Blake's words is not merely in their literal truth, but in the fact that seasons repeatedly introduce each other, as do toys and reasons.

NOTES

1. Jerome S. Bruner, *On Knowing: Essays for the Left Hand* (New York: Atheneum, 1971), p. 2.
2. For further reading in the area of the brain's hemispheres, both serious and more popular sources may be consulted, e.g., Robert E. Ornstein, ed., *The Nature of Human Consciousness, A Book of Readings* (San Francisco: W. H. Freeman, 1973); Ornstein, *The Psychology of Consciousness*, 2d. ed. (New York: Harcourt Brace Jovanovich, 1977); Eugene P. Wratchford, *Brain Research and Personhood: A Philosophical Theological Inquiry* (Washington, D.C.: University Press of America, 1979); *Human Nature*, 1:5 (May 1978) (New York: Human Nature, aff. Harcourt Brace Jovanovich); and, finally, Patricia McBroom, "Are You in Your Right Mind? Or Your Left? It Can Matter," in *Today, The Inquirer Magazine*, May 20, 1979 (Philadelphia: The Philadelphia Inquirer).
3. Bruner, *On Knowing*, p. 65.
4. Ibid., pp. 59–60.
5. Portions of this chapter and those to follow are adapted from the author's earlier work on Erikson: *Responsibility as an Ethical Norm in the Thought of Erik H. Erikson* (Ann Arbor, Mich.: University Microfilms, 1973).
6. Richard I. Evans, *Dialogue with Erik Erikson* (New York: E. P. Dutton, a Dutton Paperback, 1967), p. 111.
7. Calvin S. Hall and Gardner Lindzey, *Theories of Personality* (New York: John Wiley & Son, 3d. ed., 1978), p. 108. See also Mark Edward's charge that psychoanalysis is not scientific, Peter Homans, ed., *Childhood and Selfhood: Essays on Tradition, Religion, and Modernity in the Psychology of Erik H. Erikson* (Lewisburg, Pa.: Bucknell University Press, 1978), p. 37.
8. Erik H. Erikson, *Life History and the Historical Moment*, p. 113.
9. Erik H. Erikson, *Insight and Responsibility* (New York: W. W. Norton, 1964), p. 53.
10. Henry William Maier, *Three Theories of Child Development: The Contributions of Erik H. Erikson, Jean Piaget, and Robert R. Sears, and Their Applications* (New York: Harper & Row, 1965) pp. 88ff.
11. Coles, *Erik H. Erikson*, pp. 48–49.

> It is important to note that Erikson did not at first speculate on the conceptual relationship between psychoanalysis and anthropology or history. Instead he made a series of observations, direct observations of specific people living under particular and varying circumstances. One by one he studied both individuals and the conditions of life they face, and in paper after paper he showed—concretely and specifically—how the various 'drives' we all have in common in no way prevent the development of very different people on this planet. . . . In ten years, perhaps without knowing exactly

what his overall purpose was, Erikson gradually gave psychoanalysis enough clinical information to achieve the very theoretical connection his book's title announced when it was published in 1950: *Childhood and Society.*

12. Erikson, *Insight*, p. 10. Also *Childhood and Society* (New York: W. W. Norton, 2d. ed., revised and enlarged, 1963), p. 17.
13. Erikson, *Insight*, p. 163. For other criticism of objectivism see pp. 72–74.
14. Ibid., pp. 163–64.
15. Ibid., pp. 19–46. This entire chapter, "The First Psychoanalyst," is an address "delivered at a ceremony held jointly by the universities of Frankfurt and Heidelberg, at the University of Frankfurt, on May 6, 1956," celebrating the 100th birthday of Sigmund Freud. In a number of other references he identifies himself as Freudian. See Erikson, *Life History*, Part I. It would appear that most interpreters of Erikson would describe him as revising Freud, and yet creatively moving beyond him. One writer who states flatly that Erikson is not a revisionist or a "neo-Freudian," is Peter Homans; see Homans, ed., *Childhood and Selfhood*, p. 15.
16. Erikson, *Life History*, pp. 33–34.
17. Ibid., p. 36.
18. Ibid.
19. Erikson, *Insight*, p. 76, n. 5. See also *Life History*, p. 45.
20. Erikson, *Childhood*, p. 15.
21. Erik H. Erikson, "Growth and Crisis in Healthy Personality," in *Personality in Nature, Society and Culture*, ed. Clyde Kluckhohn and Henry A. Murray, 2d ed., revised and enlarged (New York: Alfred A. Knopf, 1953), p. 186. See also Erikson, *Childhood*, p. 34; *Insight*, p. 113.
22. Erik H. Erikson, "Gandhi's Autobiography: The Leader as Child," in *The American Scholar* 35:4 (Autumn 1966), p. 634.
23. A number of other references to Erikson's discontent with the pathological orientation could be cited here. Also see Erikson, *Childhood*, p. 34; *Insight*, p. 113.
24. Maier, pp. 16, 24. Also see Coles, pp. 35, 187.
25. Erikson, *Identity: Youth and Crisis* (New York: W. W. Norton, 1968), pp. 45–46.
26. Erikson, *Childhood*, p. 277.
27. Erikson, *Identity*, pp. 29–30.
28. Ibid., p. 24.
29. Ibid.
30. Ibid.
31. Erik H. Erikson, "Inner and Outer Space: Reflections on Womanhood," *Daedalus* (Spring 1964), p. 594. The reader is referred to this section for a more complete discussion of the way in which psychoanalytic methodology has determined its conclusions, especially as relating to its interpretation

of women and penis envy. This essay was revised for *Identity: Youth and Crisis;* see p. 276.

32. Erikson, *Childhood*, p. 183.

33. Erikson, "Autobiographic Notes on the Identity Crisis," *Daedalus*, 99 (Fall 1970), pp. 756–57. This portion of the original essay was revised for *Life History*, "Postscript and Outlook," see pp. 107–108.

34. Erikson, *Identity*, pp. 261–94. Also see Coles, p. 33. This section on play is also the subject of Erikson's book *Toys and Reasons* (New York: W. W. Norton, 1977).

35. Evans, *Dialogue*, p. 43.

36. Erikson, *Identity*, p. 292. Also see *Insight*, p. 113.

37. Erikson has been criticized by the women's movement and responds in the chapter "Once More the Inner Space," *Life History*, pp. 225–47. I shall discuss this aspect of his thought in more detail in the section to follow on Erikson's ethics.

38. Erikson, *Life History*, p. 44.

39. Erikson, *Young Man Luther* (New York: W. W. Norton, 1958, 1962), p. 18. Also see Erikson, "On the Nature of Psycho-Historical Evidence," *Life History*, pp. 113ff.; *Insight*, p. 114; *Gandhi's Truth: On the Origins of Militant Nonviolence* (New York: W. W. Norton, 1969), p. 98.

40. Erikson, *Life History*, p. 39. Italics his except for phrase the "second stage."

41. Erikson, *Identity*, p. 22. Italics his.

42. Ibid., pp. 22–23. While I here attempt to reword Erikson's complex definition the reader is encouraged to reflect upon Erikson's own words in the text.

43. Ibid., p. 24.

44. Erikson, *Identity*, p. 71.

45. Ibid., p. 47.

46. Ibid., p. 219. Italics his.

47. Ibid., p. 45.

48. Erikson, *Luther*, p. 16.

49. Erik H. Erikson, *Dimensions of a New Identity* (New York: W. W. Norton, 1974), p. 12. Italics mine.

50. Erikson, *Life History*, p. 136.

51. Ibid.

52. Erikson, *Insight*, p. 206. An example would be Gandhi's childhood theft and its later relationship to the Ahmedabad event. See *Gandhi's Truth*, p. 221. Also see Erikson, "Psychoanalysis and Ongoing History: Problems of Identity, Hatred and Nonviolence," *American Journal of Psychiatry*, 122 (July 1965), p. 242.

53. Erikson expresses this thought in a book review of a work co-authored

by Freud, "The Strange Case of Freud, Bullitt, and Woodrow Wilson," *New York Review of Books*, 8 (Feb. 1967), pp. 3–8. "Freud, in being frank and clear, at least, fulfills the first rule of a psycho-historical study, namely, that the author should be reasonably honest about his own relation to the bit of history he is studying and should indicate his motives without undue mushiness or apology." Revised in *Life History*, p. 88. Another example would be Erikson's long letter to Gandhi midway in his book, stating his own personal objections to some of Gandhi's actions. See "A Personal Word," *Gandhi*, pp. 229–54.

54. Erikson, *Life History*, p. 146.
55. Ibid., p. 168.
56. Erikson, *Gandhi's Truth*, p. 396.
57. Donald Capps, "Psychohistory and Historical Genres: The Plight and Promise of Eriksonian Biography," in Homans, *Childhood*, p. 222.
58. See Roland H. Bainton, "Luther: A Psychiatric Portrait," *Yale Review* (Spring 1959), pp. 405–410; also "Psychiatry and History, An Examination of Erikson's 'Young Man Luther,' " *Religion in Life* (Winter 1971) pp. 450–78; David Donalds, as quoted by Donald Capps in Homans, *Childhood*, p. 193; Spitz, in Capps, Capps, & Bradford, eds., *Encounter with Erikson* (Missoula, Mont.: Scholars Press, 1977), pp. 33–57.
59. George A. Lindbeck, "Erikson's Young Man Luther: A Historical and Theological Reappraisal," in Capps, *Encounter*, p. 9.
60. Ibid., p. 8.
61. Spitz, in Capps, *Encounter*, p. 39.
62. Ibid., p. 53. Italics mine.
63. Ibid., p. 57.
64. Paul Roazen, *Erik H. Erikson: The Power and Limits of a Vision* (New York: Free Press, 1976), Chapter 5, pp. 73–85.
65. See Part I, Chapters 1–3, and Part II, Chapter 5, "Psychohistory . . .", by Donald Capps in Homans, *Childhood*, pp. 189–228.
66. Roger A. Johnson, ed., *Psychohistory and Religion: The Case of Young Man Luther* (Philadelphia: Fortress Press, 1977), pp. 10–18; 197–98.
67. Erikson, *Life History*, p. 145.
68. Ibid., pp. 29–30.
69. Ibid., p. 30.
70. Ibid.
71. Erikson, *Dimensions*, p. 98.
72. Erikson, *Toys*, p. 17.
73. Erikson, *Childhood*, p. 222.
74. Erikson, *Toys*, p. 139.
75. Ibid., p. 60.
76. Ibid., pp. 142ff.
77. Ibid., title page.

CHAPTER III

From Virtues to Vision

Assumptions

As indicated in the introduction, the very heart of Erikson's theory is the eight-stage development of the human organism within the womb of society. This development is predictable according to observations that Erikson has made in his theoretical study and clinical practice. They parallel in many ways the cognitive stages of growth proposed by other developmental scholars, such as Jerome Bruner, to whom we have earlier referred, and Piaget, a European scholar well known to students of developmental psychology.

Due to the complexity of the eight stages of development, it will be important to look at a number of the factors affecting them before moving on to describe each period of growth. This chapter serves as both an introduction to that description, explaining Erikson's use of the phrase "life cycle," and also offers my interpretation, which is that the virtues Erikson perceives as emerging from each developmental stage feed into an overall vision he has for healthy human beings and society.

Our task at this point is to see what Erikson means by life's developing in eight stages, sequences which out of his Freudian tradition correspond to periods of psychosexual development in the infant, child, and youth. Erikson carries these stages beyond youth to adulthood, however, thus providing us with an entire life cycle. It is to that cycle, the assumptions that he has about its development, and the ultimate emergence of virtues that lead to a vision of wholeness, to which we now turn our attention.

The term "life cycle" is Erikson's way of describing the eight-stage development of a person in society. (See the outline beginning on page 51.) The very word "cycle" may be interpreted in many ways, and if we fully understand Erikson's own definition, we will see that he does not mean cyclical in the sense of simply returning to the point of entrance. There is that kind of interplay, however, as we saw in the previous chapter. Each stage is in interaction with every other stage which does, indeed, foster a cyclical imagery. This was illustrated by Erikson's use of the child's toys and the old man's reasons. Toys and reasons, however, do belong to different stages of development, they do interact, but the overall direction is toward maturity.

" 'Cycle' is intended to convey the double tendency of individual life to 'round itself out' as a coherent experience and at the same time to form a link in the chain of generations from which it receives and to which it contributes both strength and weakness."[1]

In Erikson's view, life is not just for the living, not mere existence; it is purposeful growth and the attainment of virtue. Perhaps a word such as "spiral" would be more precise in describing Erikson's eight-stage development.[2] But this is admittedly my interpretation of Erikson and he does use the word cycle, assuming that the reader will endow it with all that is characteristic of the growth of the healthy organism.

The second part of the definition of "cycle" quoted above refers to the individual's relationship to a generation. Erikson speaks of contributing both strengths and weaknesses, but his firm hope is that the positive will outweigh the negative.

From Erikson's earliest writing to his most recent, there has been a development in the direction of ethical concern. Tracing the eight-stage development in the life cycle and noting the emerging virtues leads to a vision of a new humanity: "the strengths which potentially emerge from each developmental crisis in life can also be seen to serve the evolvement of a truly ethical sense."[3]

The final chapter of Erikson's *Toys and Reasons* is entitled "Visions and Countervisions." The polarity is significant, as we shall see. That the eight-stage development of the human organism combined with a development in the social order leads to a new vision is clearly Erikson's hope, however.[4]

We therefore precede our treatment of that which is central to Erikson's theory with this chapter, "From Virtues to Vision." Before describing the meaning of virtue for Erikson, there are a number of assumptions to consider.

Development

Erikson interprets Freud as developmental in his description of man's nature and, as discussed in previous chapters, he builds on Freudian theory, expanding upon the stages beyond childhood. "Freud showed that sexuality develops in stages, a growth which he firmly linked with all epigenetic development."[5] Erikson's interest is in more than sexual development. The entire life cycle and especially the concept of identity have concerned him, for identity is *the problem* of our rootless historical period as sexuality was in Freud's Victorian age.[6]

Erikson describes development by referring to the epigenetic principle which states that "anything that grows has a ground plan, and that out of this ground plan the parts arise, each part having its time of special ascendancy, until all parts have arisen to form a functioning whole."[7] As this principle is observable for the fetus in embryo, so is it discernible for the person in the larger womb of society. Thus, development is psychosocial as well as psychosexual.

As noted previously, Erikson's methodology, which moves beyond the pathological, leads to a description of normative health. Significantly he states, "I cannot accept the conclusion that just to be alive, or not to be sick, means to be healthy, or, as I would prefer to say in matters of personality, *vital*. I must have recourse to a few concepts which are not part of the official terminology of my field."[8] It is therefore with the entire life cycle and how it weathers its storms to achieve vitality that he is concerned. In *Young Man Luther* he speaks of character as being a goal of the ego as it transforms instinctual energies into patterns of action.[9] Freud's use of the energy concepts of his day are not to be interpreted so literally. They were a part of his historical situation, and today life is known to be more than just a balance of quantities of energy—psychic or whatever.[10]

It is thus the entire life cycle and the *quality* of life that is Erikson's focus of interest.

Interaction

Secondly, his theory is one that encompasses the interaction of the developing organism with the cycle of generations and society as a whole, referred to in the section on psychosocial identity in Chapter II. He calls his theory "a bridge from clinical experience to observations on society,"[11] and again a bridge between the psychosexual and the psychosocial. With regard to the latter and his whole purpose in writing *Childhood and Society*, he states that the "interpenetration of the biological, cultural, and psychological . . . is the subject of this book."[12]

How is his theory interactional between the developing organism and society? Erikson observes that not only do families bring up babies, but the reverse is true as well. It is here that the responsible society is seen for what it is. For each new stage in personal development there is a corresponding responsibility for the family and society. Thus he speaks of "the metabolism of generations" and not just of the individuals.[13]

The Crises of the Life Cycle

Erikson's description of the eight-stage development is structured according to the crises that he sees occurring. Crisis here means "not a threat of catastrophe, but a turning point, a crucial period of increased vulnerability and heightened potential, and therefore, the ontogenetic source of generational strength and maladjustment."[14] It is with the resolving of each crisis that the individual emerges with new strength and a sense of inner unity and social acceptance. These stages and the nature of each crisis will become more evident as the life cycle is described in the following chapters.

Jerome Bruner, in the work referred to earlier, found Erikson's concept of crisis to be a helpful way of interpreting literature. He applies a number of Erikson's crisis stages to four fictional works, adding his gratitude to the psychologist for the insight he has gained through the life crisis concept.[15]

No Achievement Chart

A word of caution is essential. Erikson often implores his readers to avoid literalizing and forcing into a rigid structure the observable sequence he describes and develops. His eight-stage theory is a kind of typology that is not to be stereotyped as an achievement chart. His purpose is to note the nature of personal development and the way in which each crisis is a kind of encounter with the environment, leading to health in persons and in society when the ratio is a favorable one. The overlapping of stages and the flexibility of interpretation of the eight stages will become apparent in the discussion to follow.[16] See the outline beginning on page 51.

For each stage there is a kind of anticipation of future stages as well as a legitimate place for regression. He develops this primarily for the identity stage, but it is applicable to each crisis. For example, before a child reaches the crisis of autonomy, that characteristic—as well as the rest of the cycle's positive and negative traits—may certainly be observable in him. Similarly, there are periods in which regression may be advisable. Erikson develops this interaction of the stages in an article on the "Life Cycle" which he contributed to the *International Encyclopedia of Social Sciences.*[17]

A Place for Polarities

Erikson is consistently dialectical in his thinking. In reference to previous consideration of his left-handed approach, however, the word "thinking" must allow for what he has observed clinically, culturally, and personally. It must include the vital ingredients of insight and imagination.

In each stage of development Erikson observes negative and positive forces at work. He often refers to "a favorable ratio of basic trust over basic mistrust." That terminology is significant, for it is not his view that trust must somehow obliterate mistrust. On the contrary, the negative element is vital to development.

In answer to those who have criticized him for being overly optimistic, as the concept of "vision" might imply, he points out that each stage of the life cycle is marked by conflict and crisis.[18]

An example of a movement that ignored mistrust is "hippiedom."

Erikson states, "These young people seemed to convince themselves (and sometimes us) that the fall from grace and the expulsion from paradise must count as overexertions of divine rigor and that basic mistrust is superfluous baggage for a 'human being.' "[19] Ultimately, however, the utopian trust of "the flower children, too, suffered—precisely because of their repression of the necessary minimum of mistrust—from the combined exploitation by microbes, drug pushers, and publicists."[20]

This necessity of recognizing the reality and purpose of counterforces is traced by Erikson in more than just the individual psychosocial life cycle. The theme occurs over and over and will often be noted in the pages to follow. For the reader interested in pursuing this theme, however, here are a few examples of Erikson's polarities:

- Identity itself may become totally negative.[21]
- The positive rituals of each stage of development have their negatives in what Erikson calls "ritualism."[22]
- The very concept of a player implies a counterplayer.[23]
- While adults may benefit by play and find it therapeutic, there is also a malignant kind of adult play found simply in playing a role.[24]
- Conscious motivation is always interacting with unconscious motivation.[25]
- Vision "remains dynamic with countervision."[26]
- Good and evil.[27]
- Sin, or senselessness, always stands over against wholeness. Erikson is clear in saying that sin is more than animal instinct. It is humanity's idiosyncrasy.[28]
- Species is a natural cultural way for persons to group themselves, but when they use their species to exclude others, isolate themselves as superior, or claim special privileges, they become a pseudospecies.[29]

This list illustrates the dialectical nature of Erikson's way of viewing and describing reality. It is essential to our understanding of the psychosocial development of the individual in his life cycle. The list is not exhaustive; it puts the psycho and the social into the picture just as we might the person and his history, or his culture's history, etc. Certainly not all of the polarities of Erikson's thought are to be interpreted as of a negative versus positive nature. They are simply part of the overagainstness of reality.

We have been dealing primarily with description. Erikson observes life developing in eight stages according to a number of assumptions: development itself, interaction, crises marking off the eight stages of development, flexibility rather than a rigid kind of achievement chart, and finally the fact that there is always a constructive tension between polarities.

But Erikson does more than merely describe eight stages. He attributes to the healthy resolution of each stage a new *quality* of life that he has chosen to describe as a "virtue," or strength. Without these virtues Erikson's work would remain primarily descriptive. With them, I find him to be prescriptive, providing a framework for an ultimate ethical vision and a foundation for a religious point of view.

Emerging Virtues

Erikson first articulated these virtues in the contribution of a chapter to Julian Huxley's *The Humanist Frame*.[30] He has since revised that essay and included it in his book *Insight and Responsibility*. He now lists the virtues along with the respective stages in the life cycle, a further indication of his growing interest in normative health and his move away from pathology.[31]

In seeking to define what he means by "virtue," Erikson notes a number of etymological reasons for his selection of the word. "In Latin virtue meant virility, which at least suggests the combination of strength, restraint and courage to be conveyed here. . . ."[32] Added to this ancestry of virtue is the old English use of it. "It meant inherent strength or active quality, and was used for example for the undiminished potency of well preserved medicines and liquors."[33] Virtue was at one time used interchangeably with spirit, which again helps to explain what Erikson has in mind—this vital element that healthy people have and that for others seems to have been drained away. Further, he reminds his readers that "the Romans meant by it what made a man a man, and Christianity, what added spirit to men and soulfulness to women."[34] Though these qualities differ, the common denominator in all uses is that of "pervading strength and strength of efficacy—not only shining, then, but 'heating and retorting heat.' "[35]

More light is shed upon Erikson's use of virtue in considering his observations of Indian culture and how it, too, seems to reflect awareness of this pervading strength at various stages of life:

> What we describe clinically as orality and anality, the Indians evaluated and emphasized according to whether these characteristics would serve to develop the kind of person the culture considered 'good.' And 'good' meant whatever seemed 'virtuous' in a 'strong' man or woman in that culture. I think this contributed eventually to my imagery of basic human strengths.[36]

This use of "good" and Erikson's indication of its contribution to his own thinking is interesting in light of his disclaimers. He does not intend virtue to be synonymous with moral virtue. He suggests that "human strength be reconsidered, not in the sense of nobility and rectitude as cultivated by moralities, but in the sense of 'inherent strength.' "[37]

The question must here be raised, "Is not Erikson attempting to restrict his uses of virtue in light of his purpose?" The inherent strength Erikson speaks of is to be kept free from moral overtones, and yet for this strength to develop it is dependent upon more than the human organism alone. It is vitally related to society, as has been noted, and the best society will offer an ideology, values, and the kind of care that will cause these virtues to emerge. Part of responsible society's fostering of these virtues is through its institutions such as religion, and the virtues in turn revitalize the institution.

What then is the source of the virtues? It is in the interrelationship of the individual life cycle and society itself. While virtue, for Erikson, may be something other than nobility and rectitude, it is something more in his own thought than the words "inherent strength" imply. Because its emergence is dependent upon society and society's task is, in part, to furnish values to each new generation, there is a closer relationship between the emerging virtues and society's values than Erikson admits.

In all of Erikson's attempts at definition and explanation of virtue, one is aware of a certain sense of frustration which has not been as apparent in his other formulations. He states, "It is not easy to admit, while speaking with some conviction of an evolving ground plan, that one does not yet know how to observe or to formulate its components."[38] It is appropriate, therefore, to note the source of his problems.

For Erikson, as a psychoanalyst, to embark upon a search for human strength is for the most part to sail an uncharted sea. He notes that in psychotherapy's preoccupation with pathology it has hardly known how to deal with health. In fact, it has avoided the subject. When recovery has been noted in a formerly ill patient, the only way that it could be explained is with a double negative: "a person whom we would declare reasonably well is relatively resistant to regression, or somewhat freer from repression, or less given to ambivalence than might be expected."[39]

Erikson is critical of his profession for its lack of interest in pursuing the source of health.[40] Further, he lays the blame at the feet of the world mood resulting from Darwin's and Freud's theories, a mood which has concerned itself too much with man's "lower nature."[41] Thus it has developed that "our theory of inner psychic economy does not tell us what energy transforms the whole appearance of a person and heightens, as it were, his tonus of living."[42] It is this source of vitality that Erikson seeks to circumscribe, an effort confounded by a lack of methodological experience within psychoanalysis.

A further difficulty for Erikson grows out of the interrelationship of a number of different systems involved. The three systems are: "epigenesis in individual development, the sequence of generations, and the growth of the ego."[43]

Individual development itself is complicated by a number of factors. In addition to the psychosocial matter to which Erikson primarily addresses himself, there is the psychosexual concern of a great area of psychoanalysis and the cognitive development that has been investigated and described by Jean Piaget.[44] So much for the complexity of the methodological task Erikson faces in seeking to describe the emergence of virtues. Of greater interest to us is Erikson's commitment to the necessity and the value that he assigns to these emerging virtues.

The strength of the virtues gives potency to the values of the society, and these in turn offer to the individual the milieu in which he can and will develop. The values become the essence of the ideology that a person must have in identity. "Man's psychosocial survival is safeguarded only by vital virtues which develop in the interplay of successive and overlapping generations, living together in organized settings."[45]

In all of this, Erikson's growing concern for ethics is evident. "I cannot conclude these developmental remarks without expressing the belief that considerations of this kind will clarify what clinical and genetic observation can contribute to a future ethics—ethics not based on the moral injunction of avoiding affront to the ideal but on the ethical capacity to provide strength in the actual."[46]

It is with this combination of ethical concern and psychoanalytic observation that Paul Roazen takes exception, especially as the integration of the two relates to the emerging virtues. He raises the philosophical red flag of the naturalistic fallacy—deriving an "ought" from an "is"—in several discussions of Erikson's ethics. Roazen does not object to moralizing, but he does feel that Erikson mixes up his methods.[47]

"The problem is that Erikson does not seem sufficiently aware of the logical dilemma in moving from empirical statements to value judgments, in inferring an 'ought' from an 'is.' "[48] Even if Roazen is correct in this analysis, the naturalistic fallacy has itself been questioned by some philosophers as to its validity. Perhaps it insists too rigidly that the right hand not know what the left hand is doing.[49]

Unlike Roazen, Don Browning interprets Erikson as contributing a vital new concept to our understanding of human development. In a sense Browning moves beyond Erikson, yet he bases his conclusion upon Erikson's theory:

> It is the integrity of the actuality and mutual activation in the sequence of the generations which determines the quality of each man's inner strength and his virtue. Virtue is the very end of ethical action—to create virtue in others and to enhance virtue in oneself. . . . Erikson's list of virtues serves as an index of moral action on the part of people and institutions.[50]

After discussing this idea of virtue's developing out of the synthesis of the person's own psychosexual development in interaction with the psychosocial and cognitive, Browning concludes that "the concept of virtue . . . is not simply an overextension of a biological principle, thereby committing the 'naturalistic fallacy' of reducing man to the impersonal laws of evolution."[51] The place of virtues in the life cycle will be discussed again as they apply to each stage. Also in our last chapters, as we deal directly with the ethical and religious connotations of Erikson's thought, we will evaluate the virtue concept in Erikson's thought.

It is to the eight stages and the specific strengths and virtues of each stage that attention is now to be given. We must remember that for Erikson there is a complementarity between individual development, the sequence of generations, and the evolving social order.

In the next chapter the caption of the polarities of the life stages duplicates Erikson's own phrasing. The complementary phrasing of the virtues in polarity is my addition, but a continuation of Erikson's motif, if not the precise way he constructs the theme. Erikson lists only the positive virtue emerging in each stage. But the lack of virtue, or weakness, is implied in his description and it is helpful to our understanding of what he means by the virtue to see it expressed opposite its corresponding vice, although he prefers not to use that word, citing malignant psychological symptoms instead.[52]

NOTES

1. Erik H. Erikson, "Life Cycle," David Sills, ed., *International Encyclopedia of Social Sciences* (New York: Macmillan Co., 1968), p. 286.
2. One writer has used this word "spiral" in a recent book. See David Belgum, *Religion and Personality in the Spiral of Life* (Washington, D.C.: University Press of America, 1979). Belgum draws heavily upon Erikson and Gordon W. Allport in an easily readable attempt to relate religion and personality.
3. Erikson, *Life History and the Historical Moment,* p. 263.
4. Erikson, *Toys and Reasons,* pp. 167–68.
5. Erikson, *Childhood and Society,* p. 65.
6. Ibid., p. 282. Italics mine. Erikson is careful in making this historical distinction to point out that such a highlighting of one problem for a particular period in history must not be interpreted simplistically. In other words, Freud's discoveries regarding sexuality apply to patients today. And similarly, Erikson's findings regarding identity are not limited to our historical period. Patients in Freud's day suffered identity crises also.

7. Erikson, *Identity: Youth and Crisis,* p. 92. Also see *Childhood,* pp. 65ff., 108; and *Gandhi's Truth,* p. 38.

8. Erikson, *Identity,* p. 91. Italics his.

9. Erikson, *Luther,* p. 254.

10. Erikson, *Childhood,* p. 64. "It was clear to him, and it becomes clearer to us—who deal with new areas of the mind (ego), with different kinds of patients (children, psychotics), with new applications of psychoanalysis (society)—that we must search for the proper place of the libido theory in the totality of human life."

11. Ibid., p. 70.

12. Erikson, *Childhood,* p. 108.

13. Erikson, *Luther,* pp. 253ff. Also see *Identity,* p. 96; *Childhood,* p. 255; and Richard I. Evans, *Dialogue with Erik Erikson* (New York: Dutton, 1967), p. 63.

14. Erikson, *Identity,* p. 96.

15. Jerome S. Bruner, *On Knowing: Essays for the Left Hand* (New York: Atheneum, 1971), p. 45.

16. Erikson, *Childhood,* pp. 92, 273; *Identity,* pp. 92–96.

17. Erikson, "Life Cycle," p. 287.

18. Erikson, *Life History,* p. 259.

19. Ibid., pp. 209–210.

20. Ibid., p. 210.

21. Erikson, *Identity,* pp. 172–79; 195–96; see also *Life History,* p. 20. This will also be developed in more detail in Chapter V.

22. Erikson, *Toys,* pp. 90, 97, 102, 106, 110, 111, and 112.

23. Ibid., pp. 44, 45, 48, 57, 72.

24. Ibid., p. 18.

25. Ibid., pp. 169–70.

26. Ibid., p. 169.

27. Ibid., p. 168.

28. Erikson, *Life History,* p. 188.

29. Erikson, *Identity,* pp. 41–42, 241, 298–99, 319; *Gandhi's Truth,* pp. 431–33, 434.

30. Erik H. Erikson, "The Roots of Virtue," *The Humanist Frame,* Julian Huxley, ed. (New York: Harper, 1961), pp. 145–65.

31. In the *Dialogue* with Evans, 1967, and in his article, "Life Cycle," *International Encyclopedia of Social Sciences,* vol. 9, pp. 286–92, Erikson includes in each caption of the eight stages the emerging virtue, e.g., "Basic Trust vs. Mistrust—Hope."

32. Erikson, *Insight and Responsibility,* p. 113.

33. Ibid.

34. Ibid., p. 175.

35. Ibid. This "heating" image is one which Erikson "plays with" based upon a title page quotation from Shakespeare. He picks the theme up again in discussing "The Golden Rule in the Light of New Insight," *Insight*, p. 232. "But orders and rules are kept alive only by those 'virtues' of which Shakespeare says (in what appears to me to be *his* passionate version of the Rule) that they, 'shining upon others heat them and they retort that heat again to the first giver.' "

36. Evans, *Dialogue*, p. 62.

37. Erikson, *Insight*, p. 111. Also see Evans, *Dialogue*, p. 30.

38. Erikson, *Insight*, p. 139.

39. Ibid., p. 112.

40. Ibid., p. 138.

41. Ibid., p. 143.

42. Ibid., p. 162.

43. Ibid., p. 135. Erikson discusses these in detail and the reader is referred to pp. 134–57 for that discussion.

44. Ibid., p. 115. Note footnotes 1, 2, and 3, especially.

45. Ibid., p. 114. Also see pp. 157 and 175; *Identity*, p. 232; and *Childhood*, p. 274.

46. Erikson, *Insight*, p. 177.

47. Roazen, *Erik H. Erikson*, pp. 119; 161–65.

48. Ibid., p. 119.

49. See Chapter II, "Left-Handed Knowing." I am indebted to my philosopher friend Jerry H. Gill at this point, who has reassured me that the naturalistic fallacy has come into question since Hume's day and G. T. Moore's formulation of the concept.

50. Don S. Browning, *Generative Man: Psychoanalytic Perspectives* (Philadelphia: Westminster Press, 1973), p. 160.

51. Ibid., p. 161.

52. It is probable that the vices corresponding to our schedule of virtues are to be found in the array of inner states which reveal themselves in psychopathological symptoms which in recent decades have been studied in so much detail. We would recognize, for example, an inner affinity between the loss of hope and the nature of delusion and addiction, between the impairment of will and the structure of obsession and compulsion. They spotlight the various ways in which ecological (or adaptive) integrity is forfeited: like the transgressions called *deadly*, the symptoms called *malignant* indicate the forfeiture of "ecological integrity" in man.

Erikson, "Roots of Virtue," p. 162.

CHAPTER IV

Becoming As Children

Introduction: Jefferson and Jesus

Erikson finds Thomas Jefferson's own version of the life and teachings of Jesus to be a provocative study. He compares Jefferson's work to what modern critical biblical scholars have done in seeking to identify the writer's place, time, and purpose in a given historical era. These facts relate to why some events and teachings are recorded and others are overlooked as simply not serving the writer's purpose. The process, on Jefferson's part as well as by the original writers of the New Testament, is perceived by Erikson as a kind of psycho-historical means of analysis.

Significantly, Erikson is delighted that Jefferson included in his New Testament version the story of Jesus' teaching that we must *become as children*.[1] The story is as follows:

> "And he came to Capernaum: and being in the house he asked them, 'What was it that ye disputed among yourselves by the way?'
>
> "But they held their peace: for by the way they had disputed among themselves, who should be the greatest.
>
> "And he sat down, and called the twelve, and saith unto them, 'If any man desire to be first, the same shall be last of all, and servant of all.'
>
> "And he took a child, and set him in the midst of them: and when he had taken him in his arms, he said unto them,
>
> " 'Whoever shall receive one of such children in my name, receiveth me; and whosoever shall receive me, receiveth not me, but him that sent me.' "
>
> (Mark 9:33–38)

Erikson is unequivocally clear in all of his writings that basic trust and the childlike virtue of hope are essential to his vision of wholeness and vital life development. Thus, Jesus' teaching that the Kingdom belongs to those who become as children is one which Erikson pointedly reaffirms.

In beginning our treatment of the eight stages of development, it would be helpful to the reader to be familiar with Erikson's outline of the life cycle. In the outline which follows, I have noted the eight stages of development and their relation to others, institutions, activities, and Freudian theory. The very fact that Erikson does not include ages in his charts is probably due to his insistence that we not confine our thinking to a rigid achievement schedule. He does discuss the ages when the crises normally occur, however, and it is helpful to note them, provided that we do not reify the schedule.[2]

At times Erikson is unnecessarily abstract if not obtuse in his wording. One critic has put it this way: "Erikson may know what he means. A reader may feel that he, too, knows intuitively what Erikson means. But how can he know that this meaning, arrived at by intuition, corresponds with Erikson's meaning?"[3]

In reading Erikson's charts, we may well feel what our critic has expressed. In the summary outline to follow, I have attempted to describe as simply as possible the way in which Erikson charts the eight-stage development of the life cycle.

I have also added the virtues that emerge within each stage. These were discussed in the previous chapter and will be noted again as each crisis is described. With these introductory comments behind us, let us look at the four stages of childhood as described by Erikson.

Outline of Erikson's Eight-Stage Life Cycle

Stage 1

The first year of a child's life is that period in which the psychosocial crisis of trust vs. mistrust is encountered. The key person to whom the child relates is the mother or maternal person. The social institution which preserves and serves the trust quality, or negatively, mistrust, is that of religion. For Freud, this period was categorized as the oral stage, but for Erikson it is broadened to more than the "getting" of orality. In getting, one also learns how to give. The virtue Erikson sees emerging in this stage is that of hope, as over against despondency.

Stage 2

In early childhood, usually ages two through three, the crisis of autonomy vs. shame and doubt is experienced. Beyond the more singular relationship with mother, both parents now become significant to the child's development. The social institution corresponding to this stage in Erikson's scheme is that of law and order, or the political and legal structures of society which define and protect each person's autonomy in relation to any other's autonomy. In Freud's scheme, this period is generally thought of as the anal stage. Erikson again expands upon Freud's sexual categories to include the holding on to and letting go of many things, such as toys and hair in addition to the bowel movement. The virtue which this stage fosters is that of will or willpower vs. impotence.

Stage 3

In the play stage, generally ages two through four, the psychosocial crisis of initiative vs. guilt is lived through. The persons of significance to the growing child expand now to the basic family. The institution relating to this stage is that of economic order, where initiative is offered its opportunity for expression. Again, comparing Erikson to Freud, the latter considered this general period as the genital stage. Erikson broadens his consideration to all those experiences of making like and of playing like. Therefore, the emerging virtue of the third stage is purpose which is found in play, purpose as over against passivity.

Stage 4

During the school years, prior to adolescence, generally thought of as ages five through twelve, the crisis of industry vs. inferiority is faced. Those of significance to the developing person now are all persons with whom relationships are established, those of the neighborhood and school environment. The institution of significance to the fourth stage is that of technology, the realm in which industry is encouraged and rewarded. Freud could only call this period between infantile sexual activity and adolescent puberty the latency period. For Erikson, it is a time of actually engaging in the process of making things, as school age children are known to do, along with others. The virtue fostered by this developing stage is competence, as over against the inability to make things.

Stage 5

Most crucial to the developing person is the adolescent stage of identity vs. identity confusion. This is the period in which the significance of peer groups becomes equal to and often greater than the family. The institution of society which corresponds to this developmental stage is that of ideology. For Freud, puberty is the sexual orientation of adolescence. Beyond Freud, Erikson sees the emergence of identity and the sharing of oneself as the mode of being in the world. The emerging virtue is fidelity vs. the vice of apathy.

Stage 6

In young adulthood the crisis faced is that of intimacy vs. isolation. Relationships which become significant in this stage usually involve those of the opposite sex with whom love relations develop, but are not limited to marriage partners. Friends, as well as those involved in cooperative and competitive pursuits, are to be included in the intimacy radius of relations. The broad institution Erikson suggests for this stage is simply that of relationships. Genitality was the word used by Freud to describe the post adolescent period, but for Erikson, the mode is broader than just the physical. Intimacy means giving oneself to another while at the same time finding oneself in a new dimension in the process of shared intimacy. Love is the emerging virtue, a strength contrasting with withdrawal and isolation.

Stage 7

In adulthood one either becomes generative or absorbed with oneself. Thus the crisis of this period is that of generativity. Those persons of significance to adults are the ones with whom labor is shared and divided. Education is the social institution by which adults provide for the development of future generations. Care is the virtue which develops with generativity.

Stage 8

Finally, in old age, the crisis of integrity vs. despair is encountered. Erikson sometimes adds the word disgust to despair and the picture becomes clear when one reflects upon those old persons in whom there is either a predominance of integrity or despair and disgust. The whole world is now significant to the developing older person, all of humanity. The social institution which fosters integrity is that of philosophy, or wisdom. One's basic posture towards the world is simply that of "being." Having developed through the eight stages, or having been, one can now simply be and face the prospect of not being. That is integrity. The virtue of this stage is that of wisdom vs. futility.

Basic Trust vs. Mistrust; Hope vs. Despondency[4]

Corresponding to Freud's oral stage, Erikson calls the infant's first crisis one of trust vs. mistrust. He extends the Freudian theory to include more than the mouth. He prefers to call it "the oral-respiratory-sensory stage," for it is his observation that the infant is receptive to stimulation in all of these zones.[5]

Whether basic trust or mistrust is experienced in this first stage is largely due to the infant's mother or mother substitute. It is definitely not a matter of quantity of stimulation as much as of quality. The manner in which care is communicated to the infant will be that child's first experience of the cosmos and will determine to a large extent whether or not he senses that the world is to be trusted. Thus Erikson calls basic trust "the most fundamental prerequisite of mental vitality. . . ."[6]

The way in which mothers respond to infants varies with cultures. There is thus leeway as to what may happen in spite of the fact that there is no question about what must happen. The baby must be fed, protected, and cared for. Beyond this there are societies that restrict freedom with swaddling, as in old Russia, and others that provide nearly total freedom.

Erikson calls the mode of this stage that of the incorporative—mainly to suck. The modality is to get and it is here where the interactional nature of development first becomes obvious. As the baby gets what is wanted, he is also learning the dimension of giving through the mother's example. This, in turn, instructs the child to be one who gives. At least in a very elemental kind of identification with the mother, the interactional nature of development is illustrated.[7]

The crisis of this stage is complicated by the biological emergence of teeth. The infant experiences loss of breast when he begins to bite, and just how that loss is experienced is part of the precarious balance of trust vs. mistrust. There are ways of withdrawing the breast without causing the child to sense loss of the mother too.

In his study of Luther, Erikson finds in Margareta Luder, Martin's mother, a person who "must have provided him with a font of basic trust on which he was able to draw in his fight for a primary faith present before all will, conscience, and reason, a faith which is 'the soul's virginity.' "[8] He believes that it was Luther's mother's singing to him, and the quality of her care that helped him later to sing and speak and identify with those necessary feminine-type characteristics of the religious mystic. This is not to say that there were not also negative elements of Luther's relationship with his mother that produced some ambivalence in his attitudes towards women.[9]

While Erikson often expands upon this stage from the point of view of pathology—the problem of not having developed basic trust in infancy—we must underscore the fact that, essentially, the first crisis of life is one of learning that all is well with oneself and one's world, the quality of basic trust. At the same time, it is essential to keep the polarity of mistrust in perspective. The precarious balance is never so resolved as to indicate a winning out of the positive over the negative in a once-and-for-all victory. As noted in Chapter III, Erikson very deliberately keeps mistrust in the picture. There are elements of the negative that are necessary to trust itself. For example, a child must learn to mistrust whatever may be harmful or dangerous.[10]

David Elkind, in commenting on the lifelong nature of the trust vs. mistrust crisis, gives this explanation and interesting example:

The child who enters school with a sense of mistrust may come to trust a particular teacher who has taken the trouble to make herself trustworthy; with this second chance, he overcomes his early mistrust. On the other hand, the child who comes through infancy with a vital sense of trust can still have his sense of mistrust activated at a later stage if, say, his parents are divorced and separated under acrimonious circumstances.[11]

To summarize, the crisis of trust vs. mistrust must be seen as including both the positive and negative elements. Also, as the example illustrates, it is essential to realize that an unresolved crisis in the infant stage may be carried over into later stages where, under proper care and perhaps therapy, basic trust is discovered or recovered.

Religion: The Social Institution

With each of his stages Erikson indicates a corresponding social institution; in this stage religion preserves and serves the sense of trust and the virtue of hope. Further development of the need for social institutions will be discussed in the chapter on ethics; it is worth noting here, however, that it is out of the sense of basic trust that faith is born. "Religion, it seems, is the oldest and has been the most lasting institution to serve the ritual restoration of a sense of trust in the form of faith while offering a tangible formula for a sense of evil against which it promises to arm and defend man."[12]

The use of the word "ritual" here, in connection with the concept of a social institution, is clarified in Erikson's book *Toys and Reasons.* There he traces the human characteristic of playfulness in each of the eight stages. For example, the mother who enters the baby's room each day, calling the child by name, raising the window shade, and smiling at the responsive infant is in fact ritualizing an everyday kind of experience. That kind of playful ritual fosters trust and becomes institutionalized in religion.[13]

Erikson, the artist, often sketches his views with figures and diagrams. One can see this "mutuality of recognition" that begins in childhood moving down through the eight stages of life, finding its culmination in the adult rituals of the numinous. The basic trust experienced in a mother's recognition is the foundation and forerunner of trust in God.

Ritualization for the eight stages is generalized by Erikson into six periods of life:

1. infancy, in which the mutuality of recognition finds its culmination in the adult sense of the numinous;
2. early childhood, in which the awakening conscience culminates in the adult sense of the judicious;
3. the play stage sense of the dramatic is literally that for the adult, a place for drama;
4. when in school one learns "rules of performance" the foundation is laid for adult rituals of formality;
5. the adolescent rituals he labels as "solidarity of conviction," and they culminate in adulthood's commitment to an ideology; and finally
6. the adult ritual of "generational sanction" sensing and exercising legitimate authority as parents and teachers is the fulfillment of all earlier rituals.[14]

True to his commitment to reality, seeing the negative forces which ever threaten the positive development of humanity, Erikson posits a counter ritual*ism* for each of the six rituals. They are respectively: idolism, legalism, role playing, formalism, totalism, and authoritism. These will be discussed in the pages to follow.

Hope: The Emerging Virtue

If the first psychosocial crisis of life is the infant's conflict with trust vs. mistrust, the virtue emerging from the crisis is hope and its vice is despondency. By hope Erikson does not mean to indicate specific hopes, but rather the capacity for Hope.[15] Hope, then, is to be understood as an essential quality of man's existence, a basic virtue that will remain lifelong though somewhat childlike in nature, having emerged out of his experience of the first stage of life.

All of the virtues, for Erikson, are as necessary as and to be compared with instincts in the animal world. Virtues assure man's survival in the world, but unlike instincts they are more dependent upon society. "Man is born only with the capacity to learn to hope, and then his milieu must offer him a convincing world view and within it specific hopes."[16]

As the psychosocial crisis helps to produce hope, so does the psychosexual, another of the three interdependent areas of development which along with cognitive maturation determines the epigenetic ensemble in development. Freud spoke of orality in this stage, and Erikson is convinced that this is a factor, but not the only factor. Social verification is of equal importance.[17]

Mothers and Mutuality: The Ritual of Recognition

As noted previously, the significant person in this first stage of development is the infant's mother; and her capacity to foster hope in her child is related to that system Erikson refers to as the sequence of generations. She must, herself, have learned hope as an infant, as well as having had that hope verified by the social order and its institutions.[18]

Mutuality is a characteristic of the process by which hope is born and sustained.[19] Hope is a given of healthy existence—given as it develops in the convergence of the psychosexual and psychosocial crisis of infancy, and religion as an institution verifies hope. Hope is not invented by theologians or philosophers. It is an essential ingredient to life itself as borne out by R. A. Spitz's study which showed that infants who lost hope due to lack of love either died or suffered from emotional disorders. Upon this basic need religions are built and hope is confirmed.[20]

In addition to Erikson's citing of Spitz's research, he also notes from clinical experience the fact that a universal phenomenon among psychotics is loss of hope: despondency. That is why I have polarized despondency as the opposite of hope. Trust may be impaired and confidence wounded and life sustained. But when hope is gone there is little of life that remains beyond being a mere organism.

Hope Fosters Faith

Hope, then, is the emerging strength of the first stage of the life cycle. It is essential to humanity's ability to envision a future, to trust a dependable universe, and to have faith. We sense again Erikson's unique combination of the rational and intuitive, the right and left hand.[21]

Without hope, personal identity will not be forthcoming, for by its very nature identity is dependent upon mutuality between the person and his milieu and fidelity to an ideology. Neither mutuality nor fidelity is possible where trust and hope have lost out to the malignant forces of mistrust and despondency in the first stage of the life cycle.

Although Erikson is credited primarily for his insightful work in the area of the identity crisis, it is perhaps only because that problem is more easily focused upon in our rootless age than how parents impart trust to children. But the identity crisis and every crisis of the other seven stages of life are integrally related to what happens very early in life. Erikson's first great work was *Childhood and Society*. It is not at all surprising that his later book, *Toys and Reasons*, returns to those themes of childhood with an even keener vision.[22]

Autonomy vs. Shame and Doubt; Will vs. Impotence

The second crisis of the life cycle that builds upon basic trust and contributes its resolution to later stages is that of autonomy vs. shame and doubt. Freud labeled this the anal stage. Again Erikson expands the mode to include the total muscular structure, describing the social modality as that of holding on and letting go. If the child in this period learns to hold on to the right things at the right time and to let go of the right things at the appropriate time, he achieves a sense of willpower and autonomy that will be a lifelong value. Contrariwise, if in this period he is shamed for actions not rightly accomplished and unduly scolded for his failures, he learns self-doubt.

With regard to his society, the child is dependent upon an environment that will provide the proper firmness to "protect him against the potential anarchy of his as yet untrained sense of discrimination, his inability to hold on and to let go with discretion. As his environment encourages him to 'stand on his own feet,' it must protect him against meaningless and arbitrary experiences of shame and of early doubt."[23] Regulation must avoid rigidity and premature expectation. Autonomy is achieved only when it develops in an atmosphere of free choice balanced with firm guidance and example.

Freud's description of this stage of life as anal provides the most obvious example of the autonomy that is to be learned by the growing child. The control of bowels and bladder is the primary task of the age, although child development offers many other examples as well, such as the holding onto someone else's hair and the letting go of toys through car windows. The primary point is that muscular control and coordination are to be helped by the child's social radius in such a way as to foster his autonomous will.

One of the problems of contemporary society is that the machine of technology has become a model so that to "function without friction" becomes an obsession and children the victims. "Thus a child becomes a machine which must be set and tuned even as before it was an animal which must be broken—while, in fact, will power can develop only by steps."[24]

Erikson stressed the precarious balance that is both necessary and yet a challenge to be faced and conquered. The results of the crisis of this period, if a favorable balance of self-control wins out, is that free will emerges. On the other hand, if there is a loss of self-control, due perhaps to overprotection on the part of the parents, "a lasting propensity for doubt and shame" is the outcome.[25]

The balance to be maintained on the other side by the responsible society is that of stamina and firmness mixed with flexibility. The example of parents who themselves demonstrate a kind of autonomy whereby they are the masters of their modalities is essential to the growing child, if he is to become "an independent individual who can choose and guide his own future."[26]

An illustration of irresponsible parenthood is Hans Luder who, according to Erikson's analysis, forced Martin into a premature autonomy and out of the needed trusting relationship with his mother. Thus, shame and doubt were two of Luther's psychic enemies until his theological solution restored a sense of trust.[27]

Will: The Emerging Virtue

Closely related to the sense of autonomy is the emerging virtue of will, or willpower as Erikson sometimes calls it. Psychosexually, will is related to the child's experience with his own sphincters, his ability to will control, the development of self-control. Psychosocially, control involves the necessary relations with others who also seek control. Will is obviously related to making decisions in a world in which fate may have already set the course of events. Yet, decision-making is essential to a sense of autonomy.[28]

Law and Order: The Social Institution

Institutionally the capacity for the vital strength called will is verified in systems of justice, notably those political and legal organizations that promise control of the wills of others as well as oneself and thus the promise of goodwill.

As indicated in our treatment of the basic trust stage, the social institution has its origin in the everyday rituals that Erikson identified as becoming the core of the institution. For example, in the autonomy stage a child early learns the pattern of limitation.

Some things are good, others bad, some are clean, and others are unclean. The childhood rituals which mark these boundaries find their culmination in the adult rituals of the judicial system. Here, in Erikson's words, "the criteria for all rituals" are seen: "Meaningful regularity; ceremonial attention to detail and to the total procedure"; and a sense of the symbolic nature of the ritual being greater than the reality in and of itself.[29]

Erikson's allusion here to the adult judiciary ritual points to the social institution in which a person's autonomy is called into question in what may be a public trial. The vision image appears again, as the person who is being tried by that which limits his autonomy, the system of justice, is placed upon the public stage of the courtroom. His life has encountered the ever-watchful eye of the law, and autonomy and individual will find their limits in the legal system.[30]

In the autonomy stage the developing person begins the practice of free will; however, he also encounters social boundaries that indicate limitations. The ritual of this experience in everyday life is institutionalized in the law and order of the social system. Negatively, the legal system may become overbearing and unreasonable in a kind of ritualism "which we may call legalism; the victory of the letter over the spirit of the word and the law."[31]

As noted previously, Erikson traces the building of each stage's ritual and its developing institution from the early thread of the religious numinousness into the ever-strengthening cord of social institutionalization.[32] Each succeeding stage joins the former, thus, on a social level, rounding out the life cycle of individual development.

In many ways will is a key virtue in Erikson's system, for it is a strength given to the ego by which it is able to control the drives sometimes described in psychoanalytic literature as though they are uncontrollable. Erikson never disavows the power of libidinal drives; however, he counterbalances them with the figure of a strong ego whose will becomes will-power, able to choose and interact in mutuality, and which in conjunction with the willpower of others creates a society where will is institutionalized in law and order.[33] Will is a vital virtue if persons are to be responsible, and in Chapter VII it will be shown that that is precisely how Erikson's ethical person is best described.

What then is the virtue Erikson labels as will or willpower? It is that characteristic which is variously described by society as pluck, self-determination, independence, or control. A person in whom will has found the ability to control will act with restraint regarding his own powers. The characteristic of independence refers more to the spirit of a person who is able to act in a way commensurate with his desires, able to choose freely and to act on that choice.

The opposite of will is impotence, which in pathology gives way to obsession and compulsion.

Initiative vs. Guilt; Purpose vs. Passivity

Often referring to this as the ambulatory stage, Erikson's point is that now the child is able to move—intrusively—in many ways. Most obviously, he initiates action by moving into physical space, the unknown, as he follows his consuming curiosity, penetrating others' ears by his voice, others' bodies by literal attack, and in imagination, for the boy, at least, into the female body.[34] The latter indicates why this is also called the phallic stage. It is a time of sexual awakening and discovery, and for Freud the period of the Oedipal complex.

Imagination is significant for the ambulatory child. His fantasies are not limited to the sexual. He also dreams of roles he might fulfill, tasks he might accomplish, and also great endeavors he might not accomplish or at which he might severely fail. For this reason the polar opposite of initiative is guilt. The intrusion of either reality or fantasy in too great a measure can only result in a shrinking back from tasks too great to handle, with the result of a sense of guilt. Erikson indicates that the child frightens himself with his own dreams.

The psychosocial modality of this stage is that of "being on the make." The sexual implications and relations to the phallic stage are obvious, but the making modality is more inclusive. In this stage in which initiative is born, there is a strong desire to make as well as to "make like" in play experience. It is thus one of the responsibilities of society and the family, especially, to provide opportunity for making, to demonstrate with care and "by patient example where play ends and irreversible purpose begins and where 'don'ts' are superseded by sanctioned avenues of vigorous action."[35] Purpose, then, as we shall see is the emerging virtue.

Other responsibilities of society at this stage include an understanding of the sexual nature of the development, allowing for a certain amount of normal exploration without undue prohibition or attention. For boys social responsibility will include avoiding fostering the feeling of somehow being repulsive with their intrusiveness. For initiators, competition will be a delight and the setting of reasonable goals by adults a necessity.

Conscience and Inner Division

During this period initiative becomes regulated by emerging conscience, and here Erikson sees an inner division occurring that will effect a radical change in the developing child: "the 'inner voice' of self observation."[36] Overburdened by adult moralists, the inner voice may become a source of self-doubt and punishment, thus being counter-productive to the morality it is intended to foster. Hence, another responsibility for the generation caring for its children—that of providing reasonable prohibitions and models for the conscience-forming child.

There are two observations which seem appropriate at this point. First, in Erikson's own developing theory it would appear that there may be more evidence that conscience develops in the second stage rather than the third than he had formerly postulated. In *Toys and*

Reasons, as he discusses the second stage of development and its relation to law and order, he says, "But this also demands the development of that inner self-watch which Freud called the super-ego, that is, literally a part of ourselves standing watch over the rest of ourselves and confronting us with detestable self-images. We thus learn to look down upon ourselves as unworthy and guilty. . . ."[37]

A second observation is that perhaps Erikson has not changed his theory at all. While in his early writings he described conscience as emerging in the third stage, it is no contradiction that he should later find evidence of second-stage development. In fact, with earlier maturation, all of the characteristics of the stages may be found to exist in earlier periods. Children are becoming youths, and youths adults, at a quickened pace. There is always an interweaving and an interplay between the stages.

While the autonomy of the previous stage tends to deal with a kind of independence and self-will, the contribution of the initiative stage is more positive, although this is not to say more valuable or essential. Initiative is essential to the planning, achieving, making person. This period in the life of the child is one of readiness to achieve. He learns quickly and is ready to share obligations preparing him for cooperative tasks in his adult life.

Purpose: The Emerging Virtue

Growing out of play experience and the child's desire to make things, purpose in its rudimentary form emerges as the virtue of this third stage of development. Erikson is eminently qualified to speak of play experience, having used it as a methodological tool to explore the unconscious as Freud used the dream. He concludes that "play is to the child what thinking, planning, and blueprinting are to the adult, a trial universe in which conditions are simplified and methods exploratory, so that past failures can be thought through, expectations tested."[38]

The play age thus offers to the child an opportunity to develop purpose, test it, and prepare himself for future roles in the larger social milieu. Now in control of his muscles, he determines what he shall do, where he shall go, and what he shall make. His development of initiative contributes to the emergence of his strength of purpose.

Gradually, then, purposefulness attaches itself to a sense of reality, to goals less in the realm of fantasy and more realistically related to life. In his play-stage training ground he has had real projects preparing him for real life. As indicated, purpose's ally is the developing conscience which informs the child as to what may and may not be attempted in thought, word, and deed.[39] Its polar opposite is passivity, that state in which nothing seems to matter and what happens will be the result of what life does to one, for no design or goal has inspired the person lacking purpose.

This play age is of special significance to Erikson.[40] In a number of previous discussions we have noted the importance he attached to a child's play. His book *Toys and Reasons* is in many ways an enlargement upon this key subject as it relates to ritualization of everyday experience and leads to adult purposefulness.

Ideal Prototypes: The Social Institution

Erikson is less clear about the precise nature of the social institution of this stage, speaking sometimes of ideal prototypes and other times of the Economic Order. When children play the roles of adults, the economic order with its variety of types offers them a sense of guidance and purposefulness in deciding what they make *like* and ultimately what they will make *of* their lives.

The institution society provides for the adult player is that of the stage. Through imagination and projection we see and hear our own inner and outer conflicts expressed and experience what Erikson calls "the catharsis of affects, both timeless and universal. Genuine drama, well played, can shake us to the bones: we know it is 'just a play,' but because of the dramatic condensation of time and space, we experience something of an intensified reality, unbearably personal and yet miraculously shared."[41]

Negatively, the ritual of the play stage for both child and adult is when playing roles and playing with prototypes becomes a kind of role-playing that is merely impersonation. Here is the ritualism which limits rather than expands, confines rather than stimulates to more personally creative roles unique to our own personhood.

In terms of development, as noted in the two previous stages, there is here the epigenetic growth of the person. Socially, the ritual thread of the numinous and judicial is strengthened by the dramatic, all elements of everyday experience, all contributing to social institutions.[42]

Industry vs. Inferiority; Competence vs. Inability

The final stage of childhood leads from initiative to industry. The dreams and ambitions of the previous stage are channeled into something less than the roles fantasied, for the industry that is to be achieved is a preparation for the grander tasks. Erikson states that in all cultures there is a school-age period of preparation, whether the school is of the formal nature common to Western culture or of the more informal home or tribal instruction.

This diversion from dreamed-of tasks is substantiated and possibly determined by what is going on in the physical and psychical nature of the school age child. Freud called it the latency period. The erupting forces of early childhood seem to subside until puberty. Having realized the limits of his own future in the family through the Oedipal conflict, the child will have to find the resolution of his initiative elsewhere in society, and for this he needs the skills and tools for his technology, thus demanding an industry related to technological preparation, one fostered by the school experience.

Socially, Erikson sees this stage as being decisive in that "industry involves doing things beside and with others, a first sense of division of labor and of differential opportunity, that is, a sense of technological ethos of a culture, develops at this time."[43]

The danger of this period, as noted in the descriptive polarity, is that of inferiority. When the child is face to face with the requirements of technology's skills and tools, the task may seem overwhelming. Thus, inadequacy, inferiority, and limitation may be the result, rather than industry.

Another danger is more likely to attach itself to a successful resolution of this crisis, an all-too-successful resolution in which industry, work, identification with tasks and only tasks becomes the child's identity. "If he accepts work as his only obligation and 'what works' as his only criterion of worthwhileness, he may become the conformist and thoughtless slave of his technology and of those who are in a position to exploit it."[44] This is what Marx called "craft idiocy."[45] Or there is the further danger of simply not enjoying work or the sense of having acquired the ability to achieve.

Responsible society will provide for industrious children in many ways. In the family, preparation will be made for school prior to school age, and during school age teachers will be upheld by the family as persons to be trusted. Also, schools and teachers will be provided for the children by responsible parents.

Looking at the larger view of society's preparation for industry, Erikson notes that "where he finds out immediately, however, that the color of his skin or the background of his parents rather than his wish and will to learn are the factors that decide his worth as a pupil or apprentice, the human propensity for feeling unworthy may be fatefully aggravated as a determinant of character development."[46]

Within schools, the responsibility of teachers for fostering a sense of industry in students is staggering.[47] In his typical polarity kind of configuration, Erikson notes two extremes to be avoided. On the one hand, there is the traditional approach that makes school life a foretaste of "grim adulthood by emphasizing self-restraint and a strict sense of duty in doing what one is told to do . . ."[48] On the other hand, there is the extreme of making school so permissive and playful that there is no direction or firmness, which frustrates industrious children.

Somewhere between these extremes as well as those of total work identity vs. total inadequacy, lies the kind of emphasis in which children may learn to be constructive and may achieve a sense of industry to be carried over into the youth and adult stages.

Psychosexually, this is the period of latency, a time when childhood sexuality appears simply to await the awakening of puberty. The child is thus free to prepare for youth and adulthood, moving beyond hope, will, and purpose which "anticipate a future of only dimly anticipated tasks . . .,"[49] to competence in which basic skills in technology are prepared for.

Competence: The Emerging Virtue
Competence is relative to the culture in its content but universal in its task. It is that strength which emerges when youth are prepared for

whatever technology awaits them. "Indians out in the forest give a little boy a little play bow and arrow. We are a literate civilization and so we show children how to read and write."[50] In mastering the skills of one's technology one is prepared for adult roles, and one feels competent. Workmanship has its roots in this virtue of competence.

Erikson indicates that ego strength is dependent upon this strength of competence or workmanship. "Without it man feels inferior in his equipment, and in his ability to match an ever-increasing radius of manageable reality with his capacities."[51]

As for the play age, society helps to foster competence by the ideal prototypes it offers school-age children. Sometimes these ideal examples are real, sometimes mythical. By whatever means, the child's social milieu is greatly enlarged in this stage, offering him new tools, whether of reason or body, by which he will be competent. The fourth in the schedule of emerging virtues, therefore, is competence. Here method is added to the former virtues of hope, will and purpose.

Technology: The Social Institution

Competence is that personal quality institutionalized in society as technology. It is the ability to complete reasonable tasks in cooperation with others as opposed to a sense of incapacity or unfitness. As noted, the malignant characteristic is best described simply as inability.

Parents, teachers, and other adults whose lives affect children, will do well to heed Erikson's warning which grows out of a lifetime of careful clinical observation, "*one* teacher can be credited with having kindled the flame of hidden talent. Against this stands the overwhelming evidence of vast neglect."[52] Thus, society is responsible for providing the kind of teachers who will foster industry and seek to alleviate accumulated feelings of inferiority.

The school age ritual that becomes the core of the technological institution is that of "methodical performance. Without this, the elements mentioned so far would lack a binding discipline holding them to a minute sequence of competent acts and an over-all quality of craftsmanship and perfection."[53]

The negative ritualism of this period is that of formalism. To work merely for the sake of work, to make the method the model instead of making it that which enables purposeful performance would be to ritualize it in a negative way.

NOTES

1. Erikson, *Dimensions of a New Identity*, p. 46.
2. This outline is a summary statement of what Erikson has in one form or another often charted. One of his first charts may be found in *Psychological Issues*, Vol. I, No. 1, 1959, Monograph 1, International Universities Press, New York.
3. Mark U. Edwards, Jr., "Erikson, Experimental Psychology, and Luther's Identity," in Homans, ed., *Childhood and Selfhood*, p. 98.
4. While Erikson deals with the eight stages throughout his writing, they are treated systematically in the following works: *Childhood*, pp. 247–74; *Identity*, pp. 96–141; *Luther*, pp. 255–63; Evans, *Dialogue*, pp. 11–58; and "Life Cycle, *IESS*, vol. 9, 286–92. In *Toys and Reasons* he relates the eight stages to rituals in the chapter entitled, "Ritualization in Everyday Life," pp. 85–118.
5. Erikson, *Childhood*, p. 74.
6. Erikson, *Identity*, p. 96.
7. Ibid., p. 99.
8. Erikson, *Luther*, p. 255.
9. Ibid., pp. 72–73.
10. Erikson, *Childhood*, pp. 273–74.
11. David Elkind, "Erik Erikson's Eight Stages of Man," *New York Times Magazine* (April 5, 1970), p. 84.
12. Erikson, *Identity*, p. 106. This theme of ritualization in relation to each institution is also developed in Erikson's *Toys and Reasons*, pp. 67–118.
13. Erikson, *Toys and Reasons*, p. 69.
14. Ibid., p. 114.
15. Erikson, *Identity*, p. 117.
16. Evans, *Dialogue*, p. 30. Also see Erikson, *Insight*, p. 142.
17. Erikson, *Insight*, p. 141.
18. Ibid., p. 152.
19. Ibid., p. 116. Also see *Toys and Reasons*, pp. 67–118.
20. Evans, *Dialogue*, p. 17. "By this I do not mean to imply that the highest Hope is 'only' a facsimile of the earliest, but that the whole plan of man's concerns develops in ontogenetic stages. And in this context, hope is the basic ingredient of all strength."

21. Erikson, *Insight*, p. 153.
22. Erikson, *Toys and Reasons*, p. 50.
23. Erikson, *Childhood*, p. 252.
24. Erikson, *Identity*, p. 108.
25. Ibid., pp. 109–10.
26. Ibid., p. 114.
27. Erikson, *Young Man Luther*, pp. 255–56.
28. Erikson, *Insight*, p. 119.
29. Erikson, *Toys and Reasons*, p. 96.
30. Ibid.
31. Ibid., p. 97.
32. Ibid., p. 98.
33. Erikson, *Insight*, p. 154.
34. Erikson, *Identity*, p. 116.
35. Ibid., p. 121.
36. Ibid., p. 119.
37. Erikson, *Toys and Reasons*, p. 93.
38. Erikson, *Insight*, p. 120.
39. Ibid., pp. 121–22. Also see Evans, *Dialogue*, pp. 24–25.
40. Erikson, *Insight*, p. 122.
41. Erikson, *Toys and Reasons*, p. 102.
42. Ibid., p. 101.
43. Erikson, *Childhood*, p. 260.
44. Ibid., p. 261.
45. Erikson, *Identity*, p. 127.
46. Ibid., p. 124.
47. Ibid., p. 125. Italics his.
48. Erikson, *Identity*, p. 126.
49. Erikson, *Insight*, p. 123.
50. Evans, *Dialogue*, p. 27.
51. Erikson, *Insight*, p. 124.
52. Erikson, *Identity*, p. 125.
53. Erikson, *Toys and Reasons*, p. 103.

CHAPTER V

Coming of Age:
Identity and Fidelity

"Who Am I?" is the question by means of which the concept of identity is usually raised. By its very wording that expression communicates a concern for self and perhaps only for self. If contemporary man is to a large extent psychologically oriented, as many have observed, then it is little wonder that identity is thought of in self-centered, if not self-serving, terms.

Psychoanalysis, by definition, is that branch of psychology which looks at a person's past history, subconscious, and conscious wishes and fears. It is natural that an automatic reaction to the subject of identity is that it is totally self-oriented. But as we begin to look at that stage of life, the fifth in Erikson's scheme, in which the identity crisis occurs, we must remember his move beyond Freud as discussed in Chapter II, that which we called the second stage. Erikson's conviction is that the interpretation of identity needs to involve far more than just the look inward, backward, and downward. He suggests that along with those three areas we need to explore the outward, forward, and upward as well.

Identity is more than the private "Who Am I?" We must ask about the "I's" environment, society, world view, and culture. The identity question relates to the future and anticipated adult roles. It seeks a vision that leads upward in hope.

Identity vs. Role Confusion: Fidelity vs. Apathy

Of Erikson's eight major books, two deal primarily with the identity crisis, *Young Man Luther* and *Identity: Youth and Crisis*. A ninth book, which he edited, is entitled *The Challenge of Youth*, and his opening chapter is "Youth: Fidelity and Diversity," an analysis of the identity crisis.

We might also classify the book *Dimensions of a New Identity* as falling into this category, although it is more of a specific treatment of identity concepts as they relate to America, its founders, and its future. I shall reserve the final section of the discussion of identity for this specific treatment: "American Identity: Jefferson to My Lai."

Why is identity so central in Erikson's thinking? Because, as we indicated in Chapter I, this particular historical period, mid-twentieth century, this revolutionary age with all its uprootedness, is a time productive of more severe identity crises than most other historical periods. "To condense it into a formula: the patient of today suffers most under the problem of what he should believe in and who he should—or, indeed, might—be or become; while the patient of early psychoanalysis suffered most under inhibitions which prevented him from being what and who he thought he knew he was."[1]

To support his theory concerning the identity crisis, Erikson offers many examples. Two of these, Erik Erikson himself and Martin Luther, already have been discussed, and along with Gandhi will continue to be a focus for our consideration. Erikson's own concentration on this subject requires us to give more lengthy analysis to it than to any of the other eight stages in the human life cycle.

The Nature of the Identity Crisis

It was noted previously that the industry stage initiates the latent period. It seems to be a time when libidinal forces are easily sublimated. It is also a time when technological society dictates that the child should enter school, causing a preoccupation with a dimension of life outside of the family. Suddenly, with puberty, the latent psychosexual forces make themselves known. Basic skills have been learned and childhood is at an end. "In puberty and adolescence all sameness and continuities relied on earlier are more or less questioned again, because of a rapidity of body growth which equals that of early childhood and because of the new addition of genital maturity."[2]

The phrase "sameness and continuities" offers a clue to the nature of identity. While Erikson prefers not to define the concept, he does indicate that in general it is that state when a person senses a sameness and continuity between his own inner self and the society in which he finds himself. It is because there is a break in this sameness and continuity in the adolescent that the crisis occurs. The break is twofold: on the one hand, a person is not the same physiologically, and, on the other hand, the world now faced is not the world of childhood. New demands are now placed upon the person to find a career and eventually to enter into the intimacy of the sexual relationship. Erikson points out the discontinuity and lack of sameness; the break is dramatically compared to that breathless moment when a trapeze artist must let go of one bar to reach another. This letting go and reaching out can only be done when trust in the process is secure.

So for the identity-seeking youth, there must be an assurance of the relatedness of past and future, and the trust that those he leaves behind, as well as those about to receive him, are reliable. Erikson goes on to say that "what the individual has learned to see in himself must now coincide with *the expectations and recognitions which others bestow on him. . . .*"[3]

The words italicized above, "the expectations and recognitions which others bestow on him," indicate yet another key aspect of the identity crisis. Suddenly adolescent youths are extremely curious and sometimes morbidly preoccupied with how others perceive them. Here sameness and continuity comes under rigid scrutiny. Do others see me as I see myself?[4]

Throughout infancy and childhood, a person forms many identifications. But the need for identity in youth is not met by these. It is something more than the sum total of all earlier identifications. It is, in part, the "sameness and continuity" which becomes evident in the choice of a career.[5]

"Career," then, is another key concept in the identity crisis. It is Erikson's conclusion that this need more than others is a source of the crisis of adolescence. Technology demands skills and commitment, and the adolescent youth is too unsure of himself to feel "himself" in the face of society's demands.[6]

The common experience of falling in love during adolescence is not so much a matter of sexual fulfillment as it is a situation of testing one's identity, giving oneself to another in order to check the reading reflected back. Erikson sees this as the reason for so much conversation in adolescent love relationships. Once again the continuity and sameness felt in oneself is being verified, or at least clarified, in the experience of a romance.

In any attempt to define Erikson's concept of identity, we face what is actually a paradox in his treatment of the subject. On the one hand he praises "Stuart Hampshire, who has stated approvingly that I 'leave (my) much misused concept of identity undefined' because it primarily 'serves to group together a range of phenomena which could profitably be investigated together.' "[7] Erikson credits Hampshire with this insight, seeing the near impossibility of defining "something that is both psycho and social."[8]

On the other hand, Erikson proceeds to follow those words of praise with an attempt to more clearly define the identity crisis by noting four meanings and again later describing "three complementarities—or are they three aspects of one complementarity?— namely, the personal coherence of the individual and role integration in his group; his guiding images and the ideologies of his time; his life history—and the historical moment."[9]

The four meanings or aspects of the identity crisis that Erikson lists are these:

1. There is that quality already noted of a person feeling a sameness and continuity in himself and paralleled in his view of the world;
2. It is both conscious and unconscious at the same time. One is aware of sensing identity but not always in touch with motivations operating on an unconscious level;
3. Identity belongs to a definite stage in development when the body, mind, and social orientation combine to make its emergence possible in a way that could not have occurred previously. This adolescent stage varies according to many factors in both the individual's life and historical period;

4. It is the product of its past stages, unique in its present orientation to a youth culture, and dependent upon the promise offered by an envisioned future of adulthood.[10]

While there is some overlapping in these descriptions of four meanings and three complementarities, as well as with other descriptions of the identity crisis that we shall discuss, we must note that Erikson offers yet a third way of describing the complexity of the identity crisis in terms of the three orders involved: the somatic, personal, and social orders.[11]

In yet other books and articles, Erikson offers succinct definitions. Perhaps the simplest formulation is found in *Toys and Reasons*, where he states: "the process of identity formation depends on the interplay of what young persons at the end of childhood have come to mean to themselves and what they now appear to mean to those who become significant to them."[12]

It is therefore little wonder that Erikson's concept of identity has been welcomed by some and considered too vague and undefined by others. Waud H. Kracke, a University of Illinois anthropologist, is critical of Erikson's identity concept. He states that

> It is a whole set of questions, not an answer: How do people integrate values and shared symbols into their personalities? How differently can two people integrate a particular value? And so on. The problem is that when such questions are embodied in a word— and particularly a catchy one like *identity*—the word very quickly becomes an answer in itself. Intended to raise questions, it is often used, even by Erikson himself, as an explanation.[13]

Kracke is also critical of Erikson's use of the term identity because of its differing prehistory in several other disciplines: sociology, psychiatry, and social psychology. He concludes his criticism by citing H. C. Rumke, who said after a conference in which the concept was considered, " 'We all felt that this 'concept of identity' was extremely important, but it was not clear what the exact meaning was, so loaded with significance was the new term.' "[14]

Our use of the stepchild imagery is one way of trying to understand Kracke's criticism. Erikson admits that his attempt to bring together the meanings of many disciplines into one interdisciplinary study is an unusual challenge. However, until and unless that struggle is attempted, identity may be described and defined, but at best will remain somewhat of an abstract concept to all who seek clear lines of objective analysis.

To return to Erikson's attempt to describe the crisis, we must note some of the negative aspects. We will also see its relationship to the four crises described in Chapter IV.

Adolescents sometimes seek to resolve the crisis by forming cliques and subcultures. They tend to polarize themselves and their needs in opposition to those they see as their enemies. The nature of their clannish behavior, while supporting to themselves, is troublesome for others in their society who may be excluded.

The identity crisis is a culmination of all that has gone before. From each of the four earlier major crises a remnant has been retained that contributes to identity in adolescence. The first stage has contributed basic trust that is now directed towards persons and ideas which can be trusted as well as trust in oneself. From the second stage autonomy has been accrued; and in adolescence the desire to freely choose vocation and associations is strong. From the initiative stage, in which imagination ran wild, the adolescent gains the desire to find imaginative people and tasks. Finally, from the stage of industry the ratio has been balanced so that meaningful work will be sought, and, if denied, then the preference may well be to do no work rather than work at any task less than a meaningful one.[15] Thus a life history is brought to an historical period, and the sameness and continuity of that life history with that historical period is the basis of gaining identity.[16]

In all of this it is essential to repeat that the crisis involves the sexual, psycho, and social areas, consciously and unconsciously. Sometimes the crisis is quite pronounced, and for others it may not be noticeable. Identity conflicts are more likely in a society in which fears, anxieties, and dreads lie beneath the surface, and "identity vacua" exist due to the apprehensions noted. These do exist in periods of decaying ideologies, revelations of new facts, discoveries, and weapons, and in periods "of an existential abyss devoid of spiritual meaning."[17]

The identity vacua Erikson spoke of in his earlier writing becomes a more persistent concern in his recent books. The breakdown of a unifying vision; the erroneous translating of relativity in science into relativism in morals; the tendency to drop out or to join the drug subculture—all these are growing dangers which appear to be expanding the vacua of our particular historical period.[18]

In revising his earlier essay "On the Revolt of Humanist Youth," Erikson identifies six qualitative changes in the perspective of youth today. A paraphrase of these will serve brevity, but the reader will do well to note the meaningful complexities of Erikson's full description. As I see it he identifies the following changes:

1. Mistrust of the adult generation which promised more than it could deliver, perhaps due to its own fault or historical determination;
2. A reorientation of the life stages due to many factors: rapid social change, the separation of sexual activity from procreation, technological demands for specialization, and the resulting loss of opportunity to acquire and affirm values which the adolescent stage formerly provided and society desperately needs;
3. Identification with oppressed peoples and emerging nations which are dwarfed by the superpowers;
4. The transference of what has historically been a respect for warfare to a more humane concern for justice;
5. The tendency of those youth who are products of our culture to rebel against it by forming subgroups with altruistic slogans and purposes;
6. A kind of suspicion of the literacy that has maintained tradition and demonstrated hypocrisy in action.[19]

This last of the qualitative changes is described by Erikson as running the Reformation "full cycle." Youth today are looking for a new ethic, a subject we will have occasion to amplify in later sections.

So much for a general description of the identity crisis. Its nature will continue to unfold as the remaining categories are explored.

Dangers of Confusion

As the polarity suggests, this stage is a crisis of identity vs. confusion, or diffusion as Erikson sometimes describes it. Actually, after pursued analysis of the crisis, he concluded that some diffusion is necessary in the expansion of boundaries, and the use of "confusion" is most accurate in noting the opposite of a true sense of identity.[20]

Erikson cites as an example of role confusion the fictional character, Biff, in Arthur Miller's *Death of a Salesman*. Biff's complaint to his mother is this: "I just can't take hold, Mom, I can't take hold of some kind of life."[21] Such confusion is often due to earlier unresolved conflicts as the demands of adult life are now to be faced. The multiplicity of choices without and the doubt within combine to create confusion, neurosis, and sometimes psychosis.

The results of confusion manifest themselves in many ways: "dropping out of school, leaving jobs, staying out all night, or withdrawing into bizarre and inaccessible moods."[22] The confusion is intensified if there have been earlier doubts as to one's sexuality. The common tendency in all confusion of this nature, however, is to compensate with an overidentification to the extent of losing one's own identity. The objects of such overidentification are often "the heroes of cliques and crowds."[23]

It is at this point that the appeal of totalitarian groups and ideologies is often evidenced. Erikson cites Hitler's appeal: defeated Germany was unsure of its future, confused as to its national identity; Hitler's totalistic demands for loyalty that at the same time excluded others was a welcome refuge.

Totalism appeals to negative identity, and as this applied to German youth of post-World War I days, so it is in evidence among the minority youth of America.[24] There is thus a conflict between positive identity and memories and accumulations of negative identities. If a sense of wholeness is not seen as possible, the appeal of totalism will find response from one's negative identity.

In a lengthy passage Erikson contrasts wholeness and totalism. It is essential to see the difference. Today, it is not just minority youth who are attracted by totalism; the popularity of the cults among majority youth is very much in evidence. There appears to be a need for the safety of the clearly defined limits of the totalism of cult mentality. Correspondingly, there is a fear of the openness of wholeness. Let us look carefully at Erikson's comparison:

To be a bit didactic: *Wholeness* connotes an assembly of parts, even quite diversified parts, that enter into fruitful association and organization. This concept is most strikingly expressed in such terms as wholeheartedness, wholemindedness, and wholesomeness. In human development as well as in history, then, wholeness emphasizes a progressive coherence of diversified functions and parts. *Totality*, on the contrary, evokes a Gestalt in which an absolute boundary is emphasized: given a certain arbitrary delineation, nothing that belongs inside must be left outside; nothing that must be outside should be tolerated inside. A totality must be as absolutely inclusive as it is absolutely exclusive. . . .   To say it in one sentence: Where the human being despairs of an essential wholeness of experience he restructures himself and the world by taking refuge in a totalistic world view. . . . This can consist of a lonewolf's negativism; of a delinquent group's seeming nihilism; or in the case of national or racial groups, in a defiant glorification of one's own caricature.[25]

In the totalism described, the basis is laid for Erikson's concept of the "pseudospecies" that excludes others and that must now in his opinion give way to a more universal species if mankind is to survive, an ethical problem Erikson often cites in his plea for a responsible world society. However, the point is that role confusion does sometimes lead to the totalistic orientation which is by nature more than mere clannishness; it is exclusive to the extent of setting boundaries and elevating itself to arbitrary positions of power and antisocial activities.

A further danger to be included in the negative aspect of the identity crisis is that of moving to "rock bottom." Actually this has both negative and positive overtones, but the danger is obvious. Erikson states, "It is characteristic of the adolescent process that the individual should semideliberately give in to some of his most regressed or repressed tendencies in order, as it were, to test rock bottom and to recover some of his as yet undeveloped childhood strengths."[26] He sees Luther making this move, and for him as for all youth who so test, the identity crisis is found here in its greatest intensity. From rock bottom one either begins to build a new wholeness, or fragmentation and confusion are the result. Rock bottom, it would appear, is most safely tested within the security of a more-or-less prescribed moratorium.[27]

Moratorium

Offsetting the dangers described above is the way of the moratorium in the face of identity confusion. The concept of the moratorium seems to have developed gradually in Erikson's thinking. In *Childhood and Society* he simply describes the adolescent as having "a mind of the moratorium,"[28] as though it were a part of adolescence itself. Later he speaks consistently of the need for the adolescent to "have" a moratorium, giving it a more categorical specification.

Erikson defines a moratorium as "a period when the young person can dramatize or at any rate experiment with patterns of behavior which are both juvenile and adult, and yet often find a grandiose alignment with traditional ideals or new ideological trends."[29]

In having a moratorium the adolescent is allowed a period of experimentation during which the identity elements of previous stages may be integrated into his growing adolescent identity as he seeks to relate to his society.

The Institution of Ideology
and the Emerging Virtue of Fidelity

A complementarity to identity is ideology. Part of the purpose of the moratorium is the search for a meaningful set of values. Negatively stated, "a moratorium without some kind of utopian design, however, can lead only to an ideological promiscuity that both adopts and disposes of the old revolutions."[30]

Youth in crisis is looking for an ideology and there will be no identity without finding one in which he may invest his fidelity, the virtue Erikson sees emerging in this key period. Erikson defines ideology in this way: "A living ideology is a systematized set of ideas and ideals which unifies the striving for psychosocial identity in the coming generation, and it remains a stratum in every man's imagery, whether it remains a 'way of life' or becomes a militant 'official' ideology."[31]

Erikson integrates his own clinical and theoretical observations with the research of Jean Piaget, whose primary concern has been with cognitive development and who confirms that it is in adolescence that a person is intellectually ready to think in ideological terms. Ideology is the attempt to make sense out of life, to see an emerging world image, or *Weltanschauung,* as Erikson occasionally describes it. But Erikson also means more than the cognitive development described by Piaget. "By ideology, in turn, I mean a system of commanding ideas held together to a varying degree more by totalistic logic and utopian conviction than by cognitive understanding or pragmatic experience."[32] Here we see a bringing together of left- and right-handed experience, of vision and reason, feelings and understanding.

Ideology as an institution of society has its ritual counterpart. The polarities of this particular crisis accentuate the kind of ritual for which youth opt.[33] In ideology, infantile trust finds its maturity in what Erikson sometimes refers to as a "solidarity of conviction." As the infant first sought mutuality in another's eyes, the identity-seeking youth searches for the response of a universe that makes sense. A new vision of a future in which the accumulations of previous levels will find fulfillment is the quest of youth seeking identity. Later we shall see how Erikson relates this mutuality experienced in childhood vision to religion's provision of a deity who "makes His face shine upon us."

To say it yet another way, "By 'ideological,' I mean here a highly charged attitude rooted essentially in a general need for a world view coherent enough to attract one's total commitment and to render forever unnecessary the upsetting swings in mood and opinion which once accompanied identity confusion."[34]

An acceptable ideology will have a compelling power worthy of fidelity. It will give meaning and structure to life. Both of these concepts have ethical and religious overtones and implications and will be treated in the chapters to follow.

Society's Responsibility

Identity is a psychosocial crisis. The social dimension is that of the community within which the adolescent seeks to find himself. While ego-identity is a way of describing the core process, the ego is never an island. It is always in interaction with generations and society. Erikson often implies a certain social responsibility for the youth experiencing an identity crisis. There is an ideal society implicit in Erikson's agenda, a society best described as responsible in the following ways.

If the youth experiencing an identity crisis is sometimes almost morbidly prepossessed with how it is seen by others, then society's attention to its youth is one of its primary responsibilities.

> In this, children cannot be fooled by empty praises and condescending encouragement. They may have to accept artificial bolstering of their self-esteem in lieu of something better, but what I call their accruing ego identity gains real strength only from wholehearted and consistent recognition of real accomplishment, that is, achievement that has meaning in their culture.[35]

The necessity of identity is here viewed within the context of the society which either provides or denies the needed affirmation.

In addition to personal affirmation, society is responsible for the provision of a meaningful ideology. Actually, society's offer of an ideology is a prerequisite for personal affirmation. "It is the ideological outlook of a society that speaks most clearly to the adolescent who is eager to be affirmed by his peers, and is ready to be confirmed by rituals, creeds, and programs which at the same time define what is evil, uncanny, and inimical."[36]

The previous discussion of youth's proclivity to totalism, and the magnetism of those societies that make such an appeal, must be considered in light of the alternative democracies that demonstrate a wholeness that involves commitment in freedom, strength balanced with tolerance.[37]

Erikson's discussion of the identity problems of minority groups closely ties in with the ideological climate of the larger society. The nature of the identity crisis for Negroes, Hispanics, and a number of other minority groups like the Indians, is related to the discontinuity they experience, as in childhood they have known sensual gratification more fully than Anglo-Saxons, but in society they find less affirmation than the latter.[38]

The complexity of the racial problem is further confounded by the totalistic and exclusivistic tendencies of youths themselves, a matter over which society may have less control but certainly does have influence. "Young people can become remarkably clannish, intolerant, and cruel in their exclusion of others who are 'different,' in skin color or cultural background, in tastes and gifts, and often in entirely petty aspects of dress and gestures arbitrarily selected as the signs of an in-grouper or out-grouper."[39] To understand this is one of society's responsibilities. The clannishness of its youth and their intolerance of others is a defense against their own lack of identity, a matter that parents, teachers, and others in responsible positions must attempt to deal with positively. For the youth

> it is difficult to be tolerant if deep down you are not quite sure that you are a man (or a woman), that you will ever grow together again and be attractive, that you will be able to master your drives, that you really know who you are, that you know what you want to be, that you know what you look like to others, and that you will know how to make the right decisions without, once for all, committing yourself to the wrong friend, sexual partner, leader, or career.[40]

In American democracy especially, the emphasis has been upon the self-made man or woman. In this situation, "a special danger ensues from the idea of a synthetic personality: as if you are what you can appear to be, or as if you are what you can buy. This can be counteracted only by a system of education that transmits values and goals which determinedly aspire beyond mere 'functioning' and 'making the grade.' "[41] Such an educational system and ideological provision is society's responsibility.

Finally, a clear responsibility which society has in regard to its youth in crisis is that of refusing to treat as final the identities with which youth will inevitably experiment during adolescent years. Over and over Erikson calls upon parents, teachers, judges, and all who are faced with the problem of youth in trouble to see the transitoriness of this stage between childhood and adulthood. To type as a final commitment the bizarre behavior of the delinquent, the gay, the gang member, or the dropout is to render a gross misservice and misunderstanding. The youth's only salvation in such cases is oftentimes the refusal of society to judge or offer pat diagnoses that will forever brand the experimenting youth. This is especially true when a negative identity has been adopted in a society in which the dominant group stands to profit by the continued exploitation of racial groups who find their only meaning and survival in adoption of the negative identity for their race as well as individually.[42]

A Prophet to the "Me" Generation

The identity crisis involves far more than the simple "Who am I?" question by which it is often caricatured and with which Erikson becomes impatient. While identity is not easily defined, its components have been described.[43] Erikson traces back to William James and Sigmund Freud his own interest in the subject, and often quotes the letter of James to his wife in which James wrote, "A man's character . . . is discernible in the mental or moral attitude in which when it came upon him, he felt himself most deeply and intensely active and alive. At such moments there is a voice inside which speaks and says: 'This is the real me!' "[44]

Moving on from that initial concern, however, Erikson has seen the complexities of finding the "real me" within the social milieu. The theme that seems best to describe the relationship of the individual and his society is sounded in a number of statements concerning the need for inner sameness and continuity to be complemented by a sense of society's confirmation of that sameness and continuity.

It must also be repeated that the identity crisis focuses upon a dynamic that begins at birth and never ends. It comes to its primary crisis in adolescence, but it continues throughout one's life cycle. Erikson's concern is to understand the source, nature, and lifelong result of the crisis between identity and role confusion.[45]

Robert Coles, a psychoanalytic thinker of high regard in his own right, has said of Erik Erikson that "through his writings on the subject of 'identity' he accomplished the single most important shift in direction that psychoanalysis required if it was to become at all useful for other disciplines."[46] This evaluation helps to put in perspective the analysis here devoted to the fifth stage in humanity's psychosocial development.

As indicated, the inherent strength of youth is fidelity.[47] Like each of the virtues, fidelity emerges because physiologically, psychosexually, psychosocially, and cognitively youth is ready. Puberty releases in the youth's body those forces leading to genital maturation in preparation for procreation. A youth may be ready for sexual fulfillment physically, but psychosocially he is in search of his own identity and not yet ready for intimacy.

In the midst of such uncertainty youth seeks for something or someone to be true to. The often restless search reveals the intensity of the desire to find an object for his loyalty. And, as noted, if society is not responsible for its youth, has no meaningful ideology to offer, no object for youth's fidelity, then the youth's devotion may well be channeled into delinquency, perversion, or withdrawal, and the vice of infidelity to highest values and compulsive loyalty to totalistic causes will result.

The common denominator of fidelity, whatever the object, is simply that of being true—to oneself and to significant others. Thus the attraction of those movements that make great demands, call for sacrifice and devotion, capitalizing and often exploiting the pervasive need of youth for something or someone to be loyal to.

Once again the presence of a certain interaction or mutuality is to be seen in Erikson's observations concerning youth and the emergence of fidelity. Society's responsibility for its youth has been mentioned, yet there is a corresponding rejuvenation that society receives from the youth for which it cares.[48]

Sometimes calling fidelity that strength of "disciplined devotion,"[49] Erikson clearly intends that sense of sincere conviction which is revealed in commitment to a cause and its values. It is that characteristic of youth which does regenerate and sometimes revolutionize society. Where it is lacking there may be either a threatening radicality or an impotent complacency, both of which are malignant forces in either a whole person or wholesome society.

Erikson's concept of identity has often been misconstrued and misinterpreted as a preoccupation with the self. Nothing could be further from his mind. "The true—and potentially malignant—danger of narcissism, then, is a tendency in adolescence and beyond, to remain totally (and bisexually) absorbed in oneself instead of losing oneself in engagements with others."[50]

In pointing back to reformers (Luther), ethical activists (Gandhi), and forgers of new identities (Thomas Jefferson), Erikson desires to highlight the virtue of fidelity, the willingness to give the self one finds in identity to the society which both offers and needs a meaningful ideology that will lead to ever new visions of a universal humanity.

American Identity: From Jefferson to My Lai 4

The "crisis of the identity crisis"[51] is a primary concern for Erikson. He examines the origin of the American identity in his book on Thomas Jefferson, *Dimensions of a New Identity*. In that great founder of our nation he finds many of the characteristics of typical American identities: "A sense of identity means a sense of being at one with oneself as one grows and develops; and it means, at the same time, a sense of affinity with a community's sense of being at one with its future as well as its history—or mythology."[52] Applying identity to early American founders, Erikson defines once again what he means by identity, using the categories of factuality, reality, and actuality, concepts we discussed earlier, but which we may understand more clearly here as they are fleshed out.

For the early Americans there seemed to be a sense of oneness even in their diversity. Here was a new land of promise, unlimited opportunity for expansion, endless resources, and a paradise for initiators who prided themselves as "self-made men." Here is one essential ingredient to identity, *factuality*, "that is, a universe of facts, data, and techniques that can be verified with the observational methods and the work techniques of the time."[53] The shared factuality of the new American identity was the fact of a new and seemingly unlimited land.

A second essential aspect of identity is "a sense of *reality* that has visionary qualities and yet energizes the participants in most concrete tasks."[54] The vision shared in common by early Americans was twofold, a release from former bondage to tradition and obligations combined with the freedom to pursue new goals.

Thirdly, Erikson states the need for *actuality* in a new identity, "a new way of relating to each other, of activating and invigorating each other in the service of common goals."[55]

His summary statement here helps us put the three aspects of identity into perspective and to understand his use of *actuality*: "Fortunately, however, the founders saw to it that this new factual world and this new concept of reality also inspired a new actuality in the form of the participation of all (certified) citizens in the life of the community and that of the communities in the hierarchies of the federated structure."[56]

He also, hesitatingly, adds a fourth aspect which he calls luck, chance, or grace. However, the first three aspects are essential if the luck, chance, or grace has provided the opportunity for the shaping of a new identity.

The vision of a new American identity faced its challenges in wars, economic depressions, and the cold war. To be free and to liberate others from bondage has been a persistent theme in the American identity. But now that the geographic frontier has reached its limit, now that natural resources are also limited and in the hands of others who are beyond our control, now that the American dream is questioned by other nations more than it is affirmed, what of the American identity? What now is the factuality and reality we face, and is the actuality of common cause still a typical American experience?

In answer to that question Erikson pleads for a new and wider identity, beyond the pseudospecies mentality that Americans have sometimes used to exclude others. While this ethical issue will be discussed in Chapter VIII, it is essential before leaving this subject of the identity crisis to see Erikson's vision as well as his realistic understanding of the negative forces that would turn the dream into a nightmare.

The nightmare, as Erikson symbolizes it in *Toys and Reasons*, was the senseless massacring of the four to five hundred people by American soldiers in My Lai 4, Vietnam.[57]

When innocent villagers died for reasons they could not understand, and soldiers killed in obedience to commands they could not justify, the American dream became a nightmare. *Toys and Reasons* is in essence an appeal for gamesmanship in every area of life. Erikson sees My Lai 4 as "an example of that deadliness which takes over when all gamesmanship has gone out of an adult scenario."[58]

And what of the adult scenario? Erikson suggests that perhaps the century of the child and of youth be merged into a new century of the adult. As we shall see, care is one of the emerging virtues for the adult stages. In using that virtue and motif to challenge his readers to a wider identity and extended care for all mankind, Erikson concludes his Jefferson book with this summary:

Care for the youth focuses upon "what you *care to do* and who you *care to be . . ."* With the move into "young adulthood you learn whom you *care to be with . . ."* Finally, in adulthood, "you learn to know what and whom you can *take care of.*" Then Erikson bids his hearers to follow the more serious implications of the greeting which is often spoken casually, "TAKE CARE."[59]

With these words Erikson's own identity as a prophet is clear. It is not a self-centered, narcissistic type of identity that he espouses, but a socially integrated and concerned commitment to others.

NOTES

1. Erikson, *Childhood*, p. 279. Also see Erikson, ed., *The Challenge of Youth* (New York: Doubleday, 1958), pp. 1–28.
2. Erikson, *Childhood*, p. 261.
3. Erikson, *Insight*, p. 90. Italics mine.
4. Erikson, *Identity: Youth and Crisis*, p. 128.
5. Erikson, *Childhood*, p. 261.
6. Ibid., p. 262. Also see Erik H. Erikson, *Identity and the Life Cycle* in *Psychological Issues*, 1:1, Monograph 1 (New York: International Universities Press, 1959), p. 92.
7. Erikson, *Life History*, p. 18.
8. Ibid.
9. Ibid., p. 20.
10. Ibid., pp. 18–19.
11. Ibid., p. 46.
12. Erikson, *Toys and Reasons*, p. 106.
13. Waud H. Kracke, "A Psychoanalyst in the Field: Erikson's Contribution to Anthropology," in Peter Homans, ed., *Childhood and Selfhood*, p. 173.
14. Ibid., p. 175.
15. Erikson, *Identity: Youth and Crisis*, p. 128.
16. Ibid., pp. 129–30.
17. Erikson, "Autobiographic Notes on the Identity Crisis," p. 733. Also see *Life History*, p. 21.
18. Erikson, *Dimensions of a New Identity*, pp. 99–111.
19. Erikson, *Life History*, pp. 197–99.
20. Erik H. Erikson, "Reflections on the Dissent of Contemporary Youth," *Daedalus*, 99 (Winter 1970), p. 162; also see *Identity*, p. 212.
21. Erikson, *Identity: Youth and Crisis*, p. 131.
22. Ibid., p. 132.
23. Erikson, *Childhood*, p. 262.

24. Erikson, *Life History*, p. 20.

25. Erik H. Erikson, "A Memorandum on Identity and Negro Youth," *Journal of Social Issues*, 20 (October 1964), pp. 34–35. Italics his.

26. Erikson, "Autobiographic Notes," p. 733.

27. Erikson, *Luther*, pp. 103, 165, 212. Also see *Challenge of Youth*, p. 4.

28. Erikson, *Childhood*, p. 262.

29. Erikson, *Life History*, pp. 199–200.

30. Ibid.

31. Erik H. Erikson, "Psychosocial Identity," *International Encyclopedia of Social Science*, vol. 7, p. 63.

32. Erikson, *Life History*, pp. 206–207.

33. Erikson, *Toys and Reasons*, p. 107.

34. Erikson, *Life History*, p. 258.

35. Erikson, *Identity and the Life Cycle*, pp. 89–90.

36. Erikson, *Childhood*, p. 263.

37. Erikson, *Identity: Youth and Crisis*, p. 133.

38. Erikson, *Identity and the Life Cycle*, p. 133.

39. Erikson, *Identity: Youth and Crisis*, p. 132.

40. Erikson, *Identity and the Life Cycle*, p. 93.

41. Ibid., p. 94.

42. Ibid., p. 132. Also see Erikson, "Memorandum on Identity," pp. 35–36.

43. A further summary of what has been described above may be found in *Identity: Youth and Crisis*, p. 211. Also see Erikson's entire article "Psychosocial Identity," in *IESS*, vol. 7, pp. 61–65.

44. Erik H. Erikson, "The Concept of Identity in Race Relations: Notes and Queries," *Daedalus*, 99 (Fall 1970), p. 147.

45. Erikson, *Identity: Youth and Crisis*, pp. 23–24, 211.

46. Robert Coles, *Erik H. Erikson: The Growth of His Work* (Boston: Little, Brown, 1970), p. 165.

47. Erikson *Challenge of Youth*, p. 1.

48. Erikson, *Insight*, p. 126.

49. Erikson, *Identity: Youth and Crisis*, p. 256.

50. Erikson, *Dimensions*, p. 56.

51. Ibid., p. 99.

52. Ibid., pp. 27–28.

53. Ibid., p. 33.

54. Ibid. Italics mine.

55. Ibid.

56. Ibid., p. 36.

57. Erikson, *Toys and Reasons*, p. 164.

58. Ibid.

59. Erikson, *Dimensions*, pp. 124–25. Italics and capitalization his.

CHAPTER VI

Maturity and Mutuality: *Adult Postures*

If children are to be born and cared for, and if youth are to have a meaningful world in which to grow up, more attention will need to be given to those who bear and rear children and youth: the adults. At the close of the last chapter we alluded to Erikson's suggestion in *Dimensions of a New Identity*. As a chapter title, he asks the question, "A Century of the Adult?"[1]

It is not that Erikson would in any way abandon childhood's needs or those of youth. One stage always merges into another, and all interact with each other and the whole life cycle. Rather, it is a matter of priority that if there is to be an adult world toward which children mature, then adulthood, too, must be better understood. Identity, with all of its importance, is not an end but a stage in the process of development.

To identify Erikson with the identity crisis is natural, inasmuch as it has been that for which he is perhaps best known. But to overidentify him with what he refers to as a "pivotal" stage, and to make identity "the teleological end of growing up," is to misinterpret Erikson.[2]

Since Erikson first moved beyond Freud's concern for children and youth, enlarging the developmental scheme to include three crises beyond that of Freud's psychosexual orientation, others have also given more attention to adulthood. Rightly, adulthood is beginning to be seen as containing its own developmental crises. It is not just one stage, but many. Perhaps Erikson's three crises of adulthood are not enough and it is true that career changes, plateaus and promotions, family dissolutions, illness, retirement, and many other changes or crises that occur during adulthood call for additional research and reflection. Some scholars are doing that, as the developmental literature bears witness.

Consciously or not, those who have turned their attention to the adult stages are responding to Erikson's own suggestion. "The Century of the Adult" may have just begun so far as developmental studies are concerned. The Spring 1976 issue of *Daedalus* was devoted to the subject of "Adulthood." The editors not only included an article by Erikson to which we have referred, "Reflections on Dr. Borg's Life Cycle,"[3] they also acknowledged their indebtedness to him for the entire idea of an issue on Adulthood.[4]

Therefore, while Erikson's writings may have given more attention in the past to childhood and youth, his perceptive mind has been intentionally turned in these recent years to the stages of life toward which children and youth are moving—with hope and not fear.

The use of the term "mutuality" in this chapter's title, as a characteristic for all three adult stages, is very deliberate. First, mutuality is the earliest experience of trust growing out of the interaction with the infant's relationship with his mother. It then culminates in the stage in which the old adult looks for that loving face beyond the cycle of life that Erikson often refers to in terms of St. Paul's "seeing through a glass darkly."[5] Mutuality is the basis, then, of the hope and faith that round out the life cycle. This theme, as it relates to religion and ethics, will be developed further in the next four chapters.

Another reason for our use of mutuality as a characteristic of adulthood is that Erikson includes it as one of his five ethical propositions. We shall discuss these in Chapter VII. Mutuality is an essential lifelong ingredient and the very key to Erikson's ethics based upon his reformulation of the Golden Rule. Erikson feels that a person "should act in such a way that he actualizes both in himself and in the other such forces as are ready for a heightened mutuality."[6] This was, in a sense, Gandhi's Truth and Gandhi is to Erikson's adult studies what Luther was to his exploration of the identity crisis.

We turn now to those three distinct crises of adulthood that Erikson discerns: intimacy vs. isolation, generativity vs. stagnation, and integrity vs. despair. We shall note again the emerging virtues of each stage: love, care, and wisdom, together with the social institutions and rituals that relate to them.

Intimacy vs. Isolation: Love vs. Withdrawal

Once identity is discovered and physiological maturity achieved, the developmental stages are less easily identified but not less significant. In terms of structural changes in mind and body, however, there is less to be described.

Erikson reminds his readers that a part of the developmental process is the daring to risk the achievements of the previous stage as one enters the next. Thus when identity has been achieved (and achievement must always be recognized as a relative, not a fixed accomplishment)[7] the test comes in the challenge of intimacy. Is one willing to risk losing oneself in another—sexually, or in any other kind of partnership?[8]

The polar opposite of intimacy is sometimes referred to as self-absorption and at other times as isolation. When the ratio does not favor intimacy, the young adult is unable or unwilling to risk loss of identity. There is therefore a retreat into oneself and an absence of either cooperative relationship or competition in one's social role.

When isolation is preferred to intimacy, the young adult tends to seek "highly stereotyped and formal interpersonal relations (formal in the sense of lacking in spontaneity, warmth, and real exchange of fellowship)," or he finds himself seeking intimate relations with others "in repeated attempts and repeated failures."[9] When this is the case isolation is only reinforced and intimacy made less possible. Isolation inhibits further development and is oftentimes symptomatic of fear of the next crisis, which involves offspring and the need to care for future generations.[10]

In Erikson's treatment of Bergman's Dr. Borg, we find a perfect example of a man who lost in love and withdrew (the polar vice of love) to become proficient in his profession. His longing for that lost love becomes an unresolved crisis for Isak Borg, although he himself is an honored and revered physician.[11]

Another danger of this period is "man's readiness to fortify his territory of intimacy and solidarity by exaggerating small differences and prejudging or excluding foreign influences and people."[12] Erikson calls this both a counterpart and a danger to intimacy, and it would appear that the latter has increasingly become his final position. Perhaps his concern with ethics, with the need to move from subgroups or pseudospecies to universal ethics, is in part responsible for this revision in his thinking. Intimacy and distantiation are inevitably related, but genuine maturity will not allow youthful prejudices and exaggerated differences to outweigh the emerging larger concern for mankind over my kind.[13]

It is only in this stage of intimacy that true genitality develops. The maturity of youth is only physiological. Confusion over identity in the fifth stage precludes the kind of mutuality characteristic of complete genital achievement that is achieved in stage six, intimacy.

The virtues discussed thus far have not accentuated sexual differences. On the contrary they have been rather intersexual in nature. With the sixth stage of life, however, when identity has been sensed, the polarization of the sexes results and the emerging strength, or virtue, of this stage is love.

Related to the psychosexual stage of genitality, love is that ability to give oneself fully to another, to risk the identity sought for and found and fuse oneself with another. This love is not only sexual, however, it is the virtue of friendship and other patterns of cooperation as well. Its primary exhibit is to be found in that shared experience of a combined identity and mutual commitment.[14]

All of this is not to say that all claims to love are of the selfless, mutually beneficial nature. "Love can also be joint selfishness in the service of some territoriality, be it bed or home, village or country."[15]

More positively, Erikson seems to be describing a virtue that combines a contemporary understanding of eros—sexual fulfillment, and agape— that giving kind of love that moves beyond self-satisfaction to concern for the other. His use of love is more in keeping with Rollo May's description of classical eros.[16]

Erikson feels that Freud's "love object" terminology has been misused by those who would limit love to erotic pleasures alone; for Freud, love was more than his interpreters have assumed. Erich Fromm's description of love is also closely related to Erikson's description of love as a virtue.[17] It includes care, respect, responsibility, and knowledge and is thus a virtue of value to all social relationships. Love finds its greatest fulfillment, however, in the intimacy of marriage, whereby procreation is its creation and the giving and losing of oneself in another results in receiving not only a mutual satisfaction but a new generation in which love may continue to find fulfillment.

Love, as a virtue, will not emerge fully if one has not become sure of one's identity. Only fear and withdrawal from truly intimate relationships will result where the life cycle has not sufficiently produced maturity.

While Erikson has less to say about love as a virtue than might be expected, he draws heavily upon it as a counterpart to mutuality, as will be seen in the discussion of ethics in the chapter to follow.

Ritual and Institution

As in each of the previous stages, we have noted Erikson's perception of everyday experiences that become the basis of rituals and social institutions; so, for the intimacy stage, he notes the marriage ceremony, which provides "for the young adult the 'license' to enter those new associations which will transmit a way of life to the coming generations."[18] All patterns of relationship are the institutional counterpart of the sixth stage. This category is unfortunately less developed by Erikson than his earlier institutions.

In fact, while adulthood is a new focus of interest for Erikson, it is obvious that currently it lacks the theoretical description of the other stages. Adulthood becomes the fulfillment of earlier stages, but Erikson fails to inform us about it as fully as he has the earlier rituals and institutions. He calls the "adult element in ritualization . . . the generational. It includes such auxiliary ritualizations as the parental and the didactic, the productive and the curative, and so on."[19]

The negative ritualism for the adult stage is twofold. When authority becomes oppressive and irresponsible, Erikson labels it authoritism. When the final stage of integrity with its virtue of wisdom is overplayed, then the ritualism is that of sapientism, the pretense of being wiser than in reality one may be.[20]

Of course, the institutions of the earlier stages now become the responsibility of the adult and for that reason there is perhaps less of a development of the institutional complementarity for each adult stage. The earlier stages become the shared rituals and institutional responsibility of both childhood and adulthood.

Generativity vs. Stagnation; Care vs. Rejectivity

Many other words might describe the achievement of this stage—parenthood, creativity, or productivity. But Erikson prefers generativity for its dynamic emphasis. It is true that parenthood is deeply involved in generativity, the desire of two persons "to combine their personalities and energies in the production and care of common offspring."[21] However, more is involved than a single offspring. Generativity is the creation of a new generation and as such it involves a desire to guide and to teach as well as to produce.

Admittedly, some in society are not privileged—either by circumstances or choice—to share the parenthood nature of generativity, but they, too, participate through their creativity, altruistic contributions, and productivity. However, central to Erikson's concept of this crisis is the idea of procreation and one's responsibility for the next generation.

Where the crisis of this stage is not resolved, there is a turning inward comparable to the isolation of the previous stage. When this happens, "regression from generativity to an obsessive need for pseudo intimacy takes place, often with a pervading sense of stagnation and interpersonal impoverishment. Individuals who do not develop generativity often begin to indulge themselves as if they were their own one and only child."[22]

As noted previously, the earlier stages of the human life cycle emphasized that society had its responsibility for each stage. Less can be said about society's responsibility for the adult stages by the very nature of the fact that dependency is a characteristic more common to children and youth than adults. Erikson does make the point, however, that generativity does have its mutuality between generations.

"The fashionable insistence on dramatizing the dependence of children on adults often blinds us to the dependence of the older generation on the younger one. Mature man needs to be needed, and maturity needs guidance as well as encouragement from what has been produced and must be taken care of."[23] Thus the responsibility of society for adult as well as childhood stages of development is underscored.

The seventh stage logically leads to that time in the life cycle when the emerging virtue will be care.[24] As identity leads to intimacy and procreation, generativity develops in the psychosocial crisis of young adulthood. A part of the generative responsibility is that of caring for and teaching those entrusted to one's care.

Whatever man generates requires care, whether his offspring are children or ideas and works. He is to be responsible for his creations, and care and responsibility are closely related in Erikson's thinking. Irresponsibility is the word I have used to describe the absence or the malignancy of care. Only in his most recent work has Erikson dealt with the polar opposite of care. He uses the word rejectivity.[25]

When Erikson was writing *Toys and Reasons* in 1975, he reflected upon his own attention to generativity vs. stagnation and realized that he had not enlarged enough upon the negative pole of generativity: stagnation.[26]

Erikson is particularly concerned with the ethical issues of stagnation. When generativity is lacking there is a kind of rejection of all that is not already within one's " 'kind'—that is, the particular human subspecies or value system one wishes to propagate."[27]

When stagnation overbalances generativity, then instead of caring about offspring and society, Erikson notes a cruel destructive malignancy resulting in undue harshness towards children and rejection of outsiders. His words ring true in contemporary society as the themes of literature and media often depict. The narcissism of the parent generation that stagnates in self concern not only does not care for its offspring but expresses disdain, disgust, and often rejection of anything challenging the values of the adult generation. Children are tolerated rather than loved, endured rather than playfully enjoyed.

While I cannot concur with Don S. Browning that the "stage of generativity is the normative center of his (Erikson's) thought," I do, of course, accept the rest of that sentence, "that the concept of generativity has great general significance for all of his writing."[28] Again, just to make Browning's thesis clear, we hear him say that "the grand final synthesis" is generativity.[29]

My reasons for rejecting Browning's hypothesis in its entirety are twofold. First, if there is any "grand final synthesis" in Erikson's thought, my understanding would favor mutuality combined with generativity, a theme that will be seen more clearly in the chapter on Erikson's ethics. Erikson calls his baseline for ethics the reformulated Golden Rule, as described above. That includes both mutuality and the idea of generativity or activation.

However, more basically, it seems to me that the selection of any one emphasis in Erikson's scheme is to do a disservice to the remaining elements of an intricately and determinedly holistic system. It is true that some strengths and some virtues are highlighted by Erikson as more basic, and thereby of greater significance than others. But the cycle in its very interaction is skewed when the balance is lost by making one element "normative" for all the rest.

Having said that, let me express my support of Browning for the work he has done in *Generative Man*. It is a highly significant interpretation of Erikson's work, and to study and analyze the thought of such influential thinkers as Philip Rieff, Norman Brown, and Erich Fromm, and conclude that it is in Erik Erikson's vision of generativity that we find the best prescription for a new model of man, or for a new ideology, is certainly a high tribute to Erikson on Browning's part.

In the process of Browning's analysis of the scholars mentioned and the social conditions of today, he has made a rich contribution to the integration of psychoanalytic thinking with our intellectual heritage. He develops the generativity theme most thoughtfully. However, one must finally ask, "If generativity is 'the grand final synthesis,' what of Erikson's final stage of development, integrity, with its emerging virtue of wisdom?"

Erikson's final stage suggests a purposeful regression to the first, basic trust, without surrendering the strengths of all the other stages. It is, therefore, vital that no one stage be considered normative, but that we give the full range of the eight stages their freedom to suggest the grand multiplicity of many strengths and virtues.

One final word regarding Browning's development of generative man. Elsewhere I cite Freud's succinct summary of life's purpose, "to love and to work." My feeling is that generativity tends to leave too unattended the virtue of the prior stage, love, even though Erikson does make care the virtue of the generative stage. In any event, Browning's book will help students of Erikson's thought continue to flesh out the meaning of generativity.

Education as the Institution

The virtue of the sixth stage is love. It includes more than physical erotic characteristics and moves toward agape. In the seventh stage of generativity, the emerging virtue of "care" is agape's full equivalent. Care gives to society, and especially to the new generation entrusted to it. Care teaches and its institutional counterpart in society is education. Where care is lacking, the vice of irresponsibility or rejectivity will cause erosion of educational institutions and all those structures of society by which children, youth, and adults are aided in their psychosocial development.

In the section on Societal Responsibility, Chapter V, we noted the importance of parents who provide quality educational institutions. We also saw the importance of teachers who care. The institutional counterparts for the adult stages, as mentioned previously, are less developed than for childhood in Erikson's thought.

It is time now to note that stage which is the culmination of the previous seven periods. We move from the child's toys in stage one to the old man's reasons, from basic trust to the wisdom that finds renewed hope in looking back and letting go, looking ahead and experiencing hope.

Ego Integrity vs. Despair; Wisdom vs. Futility

The final period of the eight-stage development brings to culmination the conflicts and challenges of a life of triumph and disappointment. Erikson speaks of the fruit of previous stages ripening at this time. Integrity and wisdom round out the cycle in this interesting way: Erikson discovers that Webster defines trust as the ability to rely upon another's integrity, thus connecting the first and last crises.

Finding integrity difficult to define, Erikson describes its attributes, and these, too, seem to have ripened with his age. He includes order, meaning, a love for the human ego which is more than narcissism, one which includes a sense of "some world order and spiritual sense." As noted previously, integrity accepts one's own life cycle as destined, and therefore includes "a new, a different love of one's parents."[30]

A decade later Erikson is to include in his description the statement that integrity is "an acceptance of the fact that one's life is one's own responsibility."[31]

Integrity is more than this, however. Erikson's list includes a kind of "comradeship with men and women of distant times and of different pursuits who have created orders and objects and sayings conveying human dignity and love."[32]

The danger of this stage is that of despair. When ego integration has not achieved acceptance of one's life cycle, there will be fear of death, panic will give way to hopelessness, and despair will be expressed oftentimes in disgust. Disgust is basically lack of acceptance of oneself, but it is often expressed in chronic complaining and disgust with everything.

This negative aspect of the integrity stage is illustrated by Bergman's character, the mother of Isak Borg, in the motion picture *Wild Strawberries* to which I have already referred. After meeting Marianne, Borg's daughter-in-law,

> she learns that Marianne has no children and announces that she has had ten; all are dead now, except Isak. None of the twenty grandchildren ever visit her, except Evald. And she has fifteen great-grandchildren whom she has never seen. "I am tiresome, of course ... and I have another fault. I don't die." They are waiting for her money. ... And then, painfully echoing Isak's opening monologue at his desk, she concludes: "It doesn't pay much to talk. Isn't it cold in here?" and, looking at the darkening sky in the window, "I've always felt chilly ... mostly in the stomach."[33]

Isak Borg is himself representative of the integrity stage, a combination of integrity and despair. Bergman's presentation of him, and Erikson's analysis shows both the positive and the negative. And while there is a trace of the positive in Isak's mother, it is only a trace when he kisses her and finds her skin to be soft in spite of her coldness; she represents, for the most part, that imbalance of despair and disgust instead of the hoped for integrity.

There is an interesting addition to Erikson's later thought at this point. In *Childhood and Society* he notes that the one and only life cycle must be "accepted as the ultimate of life."[34] A decade later, when tracing the same eight stages, he implores each reader or study group to "develop in his or its own terms what I have gropingly begun in mine."[35] When yet another decade has passed, and he again describes integrity, he adds a dimension that very likely could be traced to his associations with theologian Paul Tillich, and is of interest to us because of the religious implications.

Noting that wisdom is the virtue of the integrity stage, he adds that wisdom is never evolved on its own but is related to a tradition.[36]

Not wanting to divorce himself from his primary concern for the human life cycle and its responsibility for civilization, Erikson nevertheless expands the interests of integrity to what he calls "a new edition of an identity crisis," the inclusion of ultimate concerns.[37] He has pointed out that "if there is any responsibility in the cycle of life it must be that one generation owes to the next that strength by which it can come to face ultimate concerns in its own way—unmarred by debilitating poverty or by the neurotic concerns caused by emotional exploitation."[38]

Whatever one's philosophy or theology, the strength of wisdom is tested by its ability to face death without despair. In a later work, Erikson confessed to some misgivings in his choice of the word wisdom, "because to some it seems to mean a too-strenuous achievement for each and every old person."[39]

Wisdom also, it seems to me, has the connotation of intellectual or rational abilities. It is often equated in casual thought with knowledge. We have seen that Erikson's approach is not limited to the cognitive, but includes the full range of left-handed intuition, aestheticism, emotion, and the right-handed proclivity for rational structuring. Erikson would probably concur with Rollo May's reminder: "Socrates was not naive when he said that knowledge is virtue but he meant knowledge which goes deep into the person's emotions, involving both rational and irrational experience, so-called 'unconscious' material, ethical decision, and so forth."[40]

Wisdom for Erikson is, in a sense, the embodiment of all eight stages as long as an element of willing resignation is also present; that is, that old persons willingly give up what is no longer theirs to occupy.

Philosophy as the Institution

We again find Erikson's institutional counterpart far less developed than in the earlier stages. Wisdom and philosophy are used somewhat interchangeably. Wisdom accepts its responsibility at the same time it is willing to let go and entrust its world to another generation. It has about it a sense of wholeness that accepts ends as well as beginnings or, even better, considers ends to conclude in beginnings which thereby preclude despair or panic in the face of death.

Where this vital virtue of wisdom is lacking there will be a sense of futility in old persons, an unwillingness to let go, possibly even an anxious grasping for diminishing life. There will be a lack of the serenity characteristic of Eastern religions, a comparison Erikson often makes with our success-oriented Western way of life that drives toward success as though there were no end.

The concept of wholeness perhaps best connotes the sense of wisdom as Erikson envisions it. The life cycle thus closes in a way that is meaningful, complete, and strong even in its demise.

Summary

An understanding of the foregoing is essential to an appreciation for any aspect of Erikson's thought. The total view which demonstrates concern for the entire life cycle and its overall meaning, balanced by an understanding of the place each part has in the whole, is a part of Erikson's great significance. The fact that life is a series of crises that pose a danger while promising a new potential, together with the insight that each stage draws upon past accruals of favorable ratios and promises to future stages its own achievements, is a view that gives significance to each stage while simultaneously communicating an implicit meaning in the whole life cycle. The individual as a body and a personality is seen in relationship to social structures as related to historical realities. Together these observations with their theoretical conclusions have provided a basis upon which the ethical and religious implications of Erikson's thought may now be further considered.

With regard to the emergence of the virtues, Erikson states: "We have attempted, in a psychosocial frame, to account for the ontogenesis not of lofty ideals but of an inescapable and intrinsic order of strivings, which, by weakening or strengthening man, dictates the minimum goals of informed and responsible participation."[41]

Thus the "inescapable and intrinsic order of strivings" is accounted for. But it is not clear to what extent the order itself "dictates the minimum goals of informed and responsible participation," and to what extent man is responsible for the order. Clearly there is a reciprocity between the evolving organism and the responding society. As such, the inherent strengths are dependent upon the responsible society as noted throughout the previous discussion. The responsible society is in turn dependent upon its virtuous members, who by their maturity and strength guide the social order in its responsibility for its developing generations.

While Erikson chooses to classify the eight virtues themselves as inherent strengths and not moral values, it is questionable, as was suggested previously, whether that line can be drawn quite so clearly. A combination of these virtues in any specific person reflects the care of a society which has been responsible to that person in each stage of development. The individual, however, is also called upon to be responsible in choosing the positive ratio in each stage, particularly the latter end of the stages, in order to assure the emergence of the respective strength. Such responsibility for the individual is a trait of character, a definition of what it means to be a healthy person, and as such it is a moral value.

The virtues, then, may be for Erikson the capacities for values rather than values themselves; however, to assure the emergence of the virtues, society must offer a meaningful ideology, and values that will foster the emergence of the virtues. Responsibility in society is in this sense a value itself.[42] On the other hand, inasmuch as persons within the society are responsible for these values and the structure of an adequate society, responsibility as an ethical norm is the sense of Erikson's usage. We now turn attention to Erikson's ethical interests.

NOTES

1. Erikson, *Dimensions of a New Identity*, p. 121.
2. Erik H. Erikson, "Reflections on Dr. Borg's Life Cycle," in *Daedalus*, 105:2 (Spring 1976), p. 25.
3. Ibid., pp. 1–28.
4. Ibid., v–vi. Also, as noted earlier, this issue of *Daedalus* has been expanded and revised in a later book edited by Erikson entitled *Adulthood*.
5. Ibid., p. 24.
6. Erikson, *Gandhi's Truth*, p. 413.
7. Nowhere does Erikson say this more succinctly about each of the stages than in this comment: "Nobody in this cast, however, nor, indeed, in life is neatly 'located' in one stage; rather, all persons can be seen to oscillate between at least two stages and move more definitely into a higher one only when an even higher one begins to determine the interplay." Erikson, "Reflections on Dr. Borg's Life Cycle," pp. 24–25.
8. Erikson, *Childhood*, p. 263.
9. Erikson, *Identity and the Life Cycle*, p. 95.
10. Erikson, *Identity: Youth and Crisis*, p. 137.
11. Erikson, "Reflections on Dr. Borg's Life Cycle," pp. 8–9.
12. Erikson, "Life Cycle," *IESS*, 9, p. 291.
13. The reader is invited to compare Erikson's treatment of Intimacy and Distantiation vs. Self-Absorption in *Identity and the Life Cycle*, pp. 95–97, with *Identity: Youth and Crisis*, p. 136, and his latest contribution on the subject in his "Life Cycle," *IESS*, 9, p. 291. In *Identity: Youth and Crisis* he specifically states that the "ethical sense" takes over from the more youthful ideological convictions and limitations.
14. Erikson, *Insight*, p. 128.
15. Ibid., p. 130.
16. "Eros is the drive toward union with what we belong to—union with our own possibilities, union with significant other persons in our world in relation to whom we discover our own self-fulfillment. Eros is the yearning in man which leads him to dedicate himself to seeing arete, the noble and good life." Rollo May, *Love and Will* (New York: W. W. Norton, 1969), p. 74.
17. Erich Fromm, *The Art of Loving* (New York: Bantam Books, 1956), p. 22.
18. Erikson, *Toys and Reasons*, p. 110.
19. Ibid., p. 111.
20. Ibid., pp. 111–12.
21. Erikson, *Identity and the Life Cycle*, p. 97.
22. Ibid.
23. Erikson, *Childhood*, pp. 266–67.

24. As noted previously, Erikson summarizes the care motif in the close of his *Dimensions of a New Identity*, pp. 124–25.

25. Erikson, *Insight*, p. 132. Also see Evans, *Dialogue*, pp. 50–51. In his revision of "Reflections on Dr. Borg's Life Cycle," for *Adulthood*, Erikson suggests rejectivity as a counterpart to care. See pp. 7, 15–18.

26. Erikson, *Toys and Reasons*, p. 59. Italics his.

27. Ibid.

28. Don S. Browning, *Generative Man: Psychoanalytic Perspectives* (Philadelphia: Westminster Press, 1973), p. 24.

29. Ibid., p. 180.

30. Erikson, *Childhood*, p. 268.

31. Erikson, *Identity and the Life Cycle*, p. 98; also see *Identity: Youth and Crisis*, p. 139.

32. Erikson, *Identity: Youth and Crisis*, p. 139.

33. Erikson, "Reflections on Dr. Borg's Life Cycle," p. 12.

34. Erikson, *Childhood*, p. 269.

35. Erikson, *Identity and the Life Cycle*, p. 98.

36. Erikson, *Identity: Youth and Crisis*, p. 140. Italics his.

37. Ibid., p. 141. Also see "Life Cycle," *IESS*, vol. 9, p. 291, in which Erikson, as he often does, leaves ultimate concern to the philosophers and theologians.

38. Erikson, *Insight*, p. 133.

39. Evans, *Dialogue*, p. 53.

40. Rollo May, *Psychology and the Human Dilemma* (Princeton, N.J.: D. Van Nostrand, 1967), p. 149.

41. Erikson, "Life Cycle," *IESS*, vol. 9, p. 292.

42. In technical ethical terms, responsibility here would be called a nonmoral value. The student of ethics is referred to the distinction made by William K. Frankena, *Ethics*, (Englewood Cliffs, N.J.: Prentice-Hall, 1959). This concise but clear definition of ethical terms has been relied upon and developed regarding Erikson's use of responsibility in my earlier book *Responsibility as an Ethical Norm in the Thought of Erik H. Erikson* (Ann Arbor, Mich.: University Microfilms, 1973).

PART TWO

Ethics and Religion

CHAPTER VII

Patterns of Responsibility:
Personal

We now conclude that portion of this book which has focused upon Erikson as a person, his bridging of left- and right-handed methods, and his eight-stage theory of the life cycle. Throughout these six chapters I have alluded to Erikson's significance for ethics and religion. In this chapter I shall examine his ethical theory as it comprises morality, ideology, and responsibility for the individual. In the chapter to follow, the social dimensions will be developed.

Perhaps the primary contribution to a theory of ethics highlighting responsibility has been H. Richard Niebuhr's *The Responsible Self*.[1] One who is indebted to Niebuhr and has continued his emphasis upon responsibility is James M. Gustafson.[2] For both of these ethicists there has been an intentional turning away from what has often been primary in ethical thinking, the concentration upon morality as rules of behavior, or ideology in terms of theories of the ideal life. These two basic elements of ethical thinking have not been ignored by Niebuhr or Gustafson; rather they have attempted to integrate these former emphases in the theory of responsibility.

In *Christ and the Moral Life* Gustafson writes, "Christian ethics as an intellectual discipline has to pay more attention to what forms the *self* than it has in recent history."[3] His reason for saying this is that contemporary culture is relying less upon rules and more upon what is sometimes referred to as "man come of age." More specifically,

Gustafson notes that we are more concerned with "the 'liberty of conscience' rather than rules to govern behavior."[4] This makes the formation of the conscience and "what forms the self" subjects of extreme significance. It is Erikson who, more than almost anyone else, has given attention to this subject.

It is my suggestion to the serious student of ethics that Erikson be read in the context of those who have also wrestled with these key concepts.[5]

Responsibility is the word that best describes what Erikson means by the ethical sense. He uses responsibility together with, and sometimes even as synonymous with, a number of other words, such as caring, householding, and generativity, but none of these is as comprehensive as the word responsibility. An ethics that does not get beyond rules of behavior, morals, and law is recognized by Erikson as inferior to adult ethics that encompasses but moves beyond morality as a rule orientation. Also, although adults need ideals, goals, and a concept of the ideal, such an intellectualization of ethics does not adequately allow for the realities of involved living experience. Facts and reality are never enough for Erikson, as we have seen. "What is actual?" is his persistent question.

Ideology is essential to adult ethics as a step in the process of developing maturity in the individual and in society, but ideology, like rules, is superseded and encompassed by a higher classification, that of responsibility. How the individual arrives at the stage in life in which he is ready to become responsible and what that means both for him and society will be demonstrated in this chapter and the next. We shall draw heavily on the book that clarifies Erikson's ethics and uses the key words that describe his method and his ethical orientation, *Insight and Responsibility*.

The Life Cycle and the Contribution of the First Five Stages to the Emergence of Responsibility

Early Infancy's Premorality

Approaching Erikson's ethical propositions or principles chronologically, we have already observed that an essential ingredient of responsibility is mutuality. This will become evident especially in the later discussion of Erikson's reformulation of the Golden Rule. Mutuality has its roots deeper than the ideology of adolescence or the morality of childhood. Like basic trust, it is one of the earliest developments of the newborn, and its presence in the life experience of each person is essential to mature ethics, and a religious perspective, as indicated in our previous discussion of the first stage of development. There is a reciprocity of value in mutuality. The adult is strengthened in his or her own identity as he or she strengthens the growing awareness of a trustworthy world in the infant. For the child, earliest maternal experiences of mutuality enlarge to widening circles with other adults, contributing proportionately to all participants in the degree to which care is demonstrated.[6]

While mutuality is an essential experience for the infant and contributes to later values, it is fallacious to entertain utopian concepts of ever returning to this lost paradise of trust. As noted previously, Erikson observes that this seemed to be the quest of hippiedom in which there was a desire "to live like the proverbial lilies of the field with trusting love as their dominant demand and display." Such a "re-enactment of the premoral stage" had its refreshing contribution to make to technological society; however such simplicity was soon revealed to have overlooked negative forces that must be kept in tension with the positive.[7] Such regression then is not fully possible, but that it is attempted in various ways does demonstrate our innate desire to find mutuality in its pure form once known to all in infancy.

As we saw in the previous chapter, mutuality becomes one of the five basic propositions that constitute Erikson's ethical theory.[8] He lists it as fourth in order because it is required by the developmental, ideological, and generative principles. It is in a sense activated in the adult attempt to put into practice the application of the Golden Rule. It is in the early premoral stage, however, as infant strengths of hope and trust are developed that mutuality has its origin. It will be further discussed in the context of adult ethics.

Erikson's Five Ethical Propositions

Having introduced mutuality first because chronologically it *is* first, I hasten to state clearly my interpretation of Erikson's five propositions. My reasons will become evident as we proceed to note that what is first chronologically is fourth in my list. What I interpret as second, ideology, is not listed as a proposition by Erikson at all. He calls it an amendment to his first proposition, the developmental one. He consistently treats ideology, however, in the same manner as the other propositions and therefore it appears to me essential to call it an ingredient of Erikson's ethical position equal to his four propositions. I therefore suggest this scheme for the five ethical propositions:

- First, the developmental – moral rules.
- Second, the ideological – ideals.
- Third, the generative – emerging responsibility.
- Fourth, mutuality – responsibility in interaction. (Erikson treats this proposition as first chronologically, but as adult in adoption.)
- Fifth, active choice – responsibility choosing the ethical sense.

This summary of what is to follow should prove helpful. To repeat, the two confusions I am attempting to clarify are these: mutuality emerges first, chronologically, but is listed as an adult ethical proposition by Erikson; I expand Erikson's own list of four propositions to five because I believe ideology deserves full status in light of Erikson's own thought, and to leave it as a mere amendment to development clouds its essential ethical importance.

Early Childhood and Morality

The mutuality of smiles, touch, and feeding experienced by the infant and the adult benefactor soon gives way to less happy experiences in which the will of the infant finds something other than accepting response. It meets the will of the adult whose purpose inevitably collides with that of the child, and a whole new dimension of living develops, leading to a basic concept of morality—the rights and wrongs of life.

The Development of Conscience[9]

It is the conclusion of Erikson's clinical observation that anger and dividedness appear to originate in the period of teething. As we noted previously, Erikson allows for possible earlier experiences of unpleasantness, yet it nevertheless seems clear that the pain of erupting teeth, combined with the social experience of needing to bite to alleviate the pain and in turn having the breast withdrawn by an angry or hurt mother, or actions by other persons who respond angrily due to the biting, leads to the child's first experience of evil in a hitherto trustworthy, affirming world.[10]

The newly expressed anger of the child may be turned masochistically against the pain-provoking teeth, against his impotent anger, and also sadistically against his environment. Such confusion leaves "the general impression that once upon a time one destroyed one's unity with a maternal matrix."[11]

While Erikson does not enlarge at length upon his observations of this very early development of conscience, he does show how it is in the entire period of dependent childhood that conscience is created, the internalization of external prohibitions, threats, and punishments. This dependence is essential, for it in turn teaches the child to depend upon himself and to be dependable; "and only when thoroughly dependable in a number of fundamental values (truth, justice, etc.) can he become independent and teach and develop tradition."[12]

As always, Erikson is here clearly integrating the biological development and the social milieu. The family plays an essential role in the development of conscience in all of the childhood stages, when will meets will, and elementary law and order are first experienced, when initiative is met by approval or rebuke, and when finally the industrious child begins to make things and develop competence or again be turned back by a sense of inferiority. In all of this, society and the child interrelate in their combined contribution to the development of conscience.[13]

The Value and Limits of Morality

There is a precarious balance to be maintained between the positive and negative development of conscience. The dependent child needs the rules of the adult world of do's and don'ts. Childhood is a stage to be lived through during which the superego demonstrates the limits of life to the ego. The danger of an overbearing and overly restrictive superego in neurotic adults, however, is one of the familiar observations of clinicians.

For the most part moral rules are enforced by threats and resulting fear of punishment. "These may be outer threats of abandonment, punishment and public exposure, or a threatening inner sense of guilt, of shame or of isolation. In either case, the rationale for obeying a rule may not be too clear; it is the threat that counts."[14]

The danger is always present that the superego will become cruel and derisive, leading to debilitating self-doubt.[15] Thus beyond the morality of childhood, an ethical system requires incorporation of the essential childhood period into a higher manner of dealing with self and societal regulation. It is in this sense that Erikson concludes that "moralities sooner or later outlive themselves, ethics never. . . ."[16]

In summarizing this precarious balance between the positive and negative place of morality in ethics, the distinction might aptly be made that morality *per se* is essential to man's developing ethics, but excessive moralism is an example of misuse in childhood and regression in the adult. Here is the foundation upon which Erikson's ethical sense is to be built. He does not begin with principles and develop an intricate ethical system, but, rather more in keeping with the true etymology of ethics, a framework is developed within which limits are set and direction indicated.[17]

Erikson illustrates the overbearing moralistic sense in the lives of a number of persons, most pointedly Martin Luther and Mohandas K. Gandhi. For the former, the negative conscience is related to a concept of God as an overbearing parent not unrelated to his own childhood experience with a harsh father, Hans. Whether Erikson is right about Luther's own parents or not, the harsh morality of Luther's historical period is a fact. It was in part from this negative conscience and rigid morality that Luther sought to extricate himself and mankind in the Reformation.[18] For Gandhi, the story is not so simply summarized, but it will be more appropriately developed in the following section.

The Danger of Fixation, Closure, and Regression

Whether in childhood moralism or adolescent idealism, there is always the danger "that man's way stations to maturity can become fixed, can become premature end stations, or stations for future regression."[19] While a study of the life of Gandhi was undertaken by Erikson primarily to understand the factors of greatness that combined to produce the originator of militant nonviolence, it was inevitable that a psychoanalyst would begin with an exploration of childhood and the development of a moral sense that stayed with the Mahatma throughout his life.

A study of Gandhi's life reveals a propensity for scrupulosity, purity, and an undying quest for truth. He is described by biographers as wishing to remain untainted and unsmudged. His experiments with truth began in childhood. As Erikson sees it, "he experimented, so he means to emphasize . . . with the devils of shame and doubt, guilt and inferiority: he challenged them and won."[20]

Gandhi is seen by Erikson to have had a very special relationship with his father, one in which the younger was almost superior rather than equal or subordinate to the elder. His precocious conscience made him an adult as a child, and the fact that he was not present at his father's death seemed to be unforgivable to Gandhi's overly scrupulous conscience, a curse much like that which Søren Kierkegaard assumed for himself.

Gandhi's moral strength is further revealed in his trip to London as a youth, vowing to his mother and himself to abstain from sex, meat, and wine. This vow would be the precursor of many later vows that would involve far more than diet or biological needs.[21]

Gandhi's moral fervor is well illustrated in his own words which both express his reason for rejecting Christianity and the depth of his moral quest: " 'I do not seek redemption from the consequences of my sin. I seek to be redeemed from sin itself, or rather from the very thought of sin. Until I have attained that end, I shall be content to be restless.' "[22]

Midway in his book on Gandhi, Erikson, following his own clinical manner of confrontation and truth telling, writes a letter to Gandhi, a technique appropriate to psycho-historical writing in which the author must clearly state his own historical and existential position. In this letter, criticism of Gandhi's obsessive morality becomes a primary objective. He notes that he senses untruth behind Gandhi's professed truth, uncleanness in protestations of purity, "and above all . . . displaced violence where nonviolence was the professed issue."[23]

The truth believed in by the psychoanalyst cannot allow the denial of reality so easily adhered to by Gandhi and others of his era. Life is not so simple. Freud's discovery of truth that eludes man has led society into understandings of deeper truths. It is Erikson's desire to reveal a number of Gandhi's oversights in his morality, but especially he objects to Gandhi's relationship with his wife and family. Naturally, Gandhi would be unaware of the Freudian revelation and development of ambivalences, but Erikson explains to him in his letter: "Ambivalence means, of course, that an act, which is seemingly guided by one conscious emotion is, at the same time, unconsciously codetermined by the opposite emotion: an act of love by hate, an act of kindness by vindictiveness."[24]

Later, after pointing out a number of illustrations of Gandhi's misuse of supposed truthfulness, Erikson returns to the theme of the need to recognize ambivalence and shows how Freud, on another level, was also an experimenter with truth.[25]

In Freud's system the inner enemy is confronted nonviolently, and it is only when this truth is combined with Gandhi's Satyagraha— militant nonviolence—that real truth and mature ethics can emerge, superseding the moralistic approach of Gandhi.

All of this is not to say that Erikson did not greatly respect the true ethical sense revealed by Gandhi as he applied a Golden Rule approach to his adversaries in his many campaigns of militant nonviolence. More will be said about Gandhi's mature ethics later. However, the point of this discussion has been to illustrate the danger of closure, fixation, and regression that is often found in persons who overly emphasize rigid morality.

The Developmental Proposition: The First of Five

While mutuality has its roots in the premoral stage, it comes to fruition in adulthood as explained above, and is therefore Erikson's fourth proposition. His first is called the developmental proposition. It is simply that morality is the developing child's first experience of an ethical dimension to life. Morality is the foundational layer of an emerging ethical orientation.[26]

The precarious balance between moralism and a legitimate moral sense has already been discussed. The important thing to see here is that the moral stage and its contribution to adult ethics is essential though limited. That is what is meant by developmental, "where it is to be suggested that one item precedes another in such a way that the earlier one is necessary to the later ones and that each later one is of a higher order."[27]

Adolescence and Ideology

Morality is learned by the child as he internalizes the prohibitions and sanctions of family and society. For the adolescent, however, a period of life is entered into in which ideological experimentation replaces and encompasses the moralities of childhood. It is in his search for an adequate ideology that youth begins to sense his own identity.

Identity, Moratorium, and the Search for Ideology: the Second Ethical Proposition

Intended only to be the subject of a chapter in a book on youth in crisis, Luther proved to be too complex and challenging to fit within such confines. Thus a full-length book was the result of Erikson's research on the reformer. The elements of adolescent identity crisis, experience of a moratorium, and the search for an ideology are easily identifiable in Luther.

As we have seen in Chapter V, the very period of youth is productive of the identity crisis as a time when the individual stands between childhood and adulthood, needing to face the requirements of repudiation of one stage of life and acceptance of and devotion to the new. It is a time of discovering new inner resources of adaptiveness and creativity. A new person is born as identity is experienced, "and with this new person a new generation, and with that, a new era."[28]

Society, recognizing the transitory nature of this period, should grant to the developing adolescents a period for experimentation that has already been referred to, a moratorium, "a span of time after they have ceased being children but before their deeds and works count toward a future identity."[29]

Moratoria differ according to cultures and periods of history. For Erikson, in his personal life, it was the wandering artist. In twentieth-century technological culture it may be the period of college education, or for others a dropout experience in a counter culture, or even delinquency. Also, "psychiatric treatment today has become a sanctioned form of moratorium in some countries and classes. . . ."[30]

For Luther, it was the monastery that provided his moratorium. Like Gandhi, Luther had a relationship with his father that involved a lifelong struggle. Unlike Gandhi, Luther's relationship involved more struggle and repudiation of parental dominance than the unusual experience of the precocious child Gandhi. Erikson develops the struggle in Luther's experience of having to decide between obedience to his earthly father or his heavenly Father. Here the repudiation-devotion theme emerges as productive of an identity crisis. The crisis came clearly in Luther's vow to become a monk during a frightening thunderstorm as he was returning from his home to continue his father's lifelong ambition for him, his graduate law studies at Erfurt. The crisis led to the monastery and a period of reflection and experimentation identified by Erikson as delayed moratorium leading to identity.[31]

It was in the celebration of his first Mass that Erikson sees Martin Luther facing "the Great Divide of his life. . . ."[32] With his earthly father in the congregation behind him and his heavenly Father now to be approached without any mediator in the Mass before him, the struggle of his childhood and youth reached its culmination. Some historians document the fact that he would have fled the scene and avoided the choice were it not for the restraining action of a superior. In any case, this moment of truth, combined with a commotion caused by his father at the banquet following the Mass in which he is reputed to have suggested that Martin's call to the monkhood was possibly the voice of the devil, resulted in a kind of repudiation of childhood ways and a movement toward a new identity on Martin's part, which would come only after a period of confusion and soul struggle.

This time of identity diffusion led gradually to a new sense of identity as Luther found a friend and father in Staupitz, his superior at the Augustinian monastery in Wittenberg, where his studies would reveal to him answers to his quest for justification, a God who lovingly accepts sinners through a more human kind of Christ than Luther had previously understood. As Staupitz forced Luther to teach and preach, he found in his own verbal ability an affirmation of worth he had not previously thought imaginable. Such personal satisfaction combined with a fidelity to a new-found ideology marks the discovery of identity.

This is a brief presentation of what Erikson takes pages to elucidate, but it serves the purpose of illustrating the basic components of the adolescent experience of crisis, moratorium, identity diffusion, and its resolution through fidelity to an ideology. The genius of the budding reformer was in Erikson's words, the fact that he could mean what he said. "Meaning it, means to be at one with an ideology in the process of rejuvenation. . . ."[33]

For Gandhi, the ideological stage is more succinctly stated, though equally complex in Erikson's treatment. As already noted in the discussion of Gandhi's moralistic nature, his vow to abstain from women, meat, and wine, while in England, afforded him a kind of moratorium.

Gandhi brought with him to London "his soul's baggage" of "lasting identifications: Mother, Father, and Evil Other."[34] (The latter is the immoral friend Gandhi had sought to reform in India, a kind of self-appointed test of his own moral strength.) In London Gandhi was free to experiment with these images, to test himself as to his true identity, and experiment he did.

Upon returning to India in 1891, at the age of twenty-two, Gandhi learned of his mother's death on the very day he met Raychandbhai, "a deeply philosophical young man who came as close to being Gandhi's guru as anybody ever did . . ."[35] A man only a few years older than Gandhi, Raychandbhai represented the Indian faith of Gandhi's mother. A deep friendship resulted and "Rajchandra (Gandhi's affectionate form of the name) succeeded in translating for him the highly personal commitment of his vow into the ideological terms of the Jain community."[36]

This acceptance of Jain ideology did not include "any dogma or ritual whatsoever."[37] For Gandhi, an ideology must include action, and his final identity and ideology would be uniquely his own. Gandhi could not accept the other-worldliness of Rajchandra, nor his submission to the caste system, but he had been greatly helped by his friend in his quest for an ideology.[38]

It was in South Africa that Gandhi's identity was finally formed. A twenty-year stay in that land resulted in Gandhi's first use of his Satyagraha method, a nonviolent militant stand against the racial prejudices of that land and correspondingly an affirmation of the truth that Asians in Africa deserved equal rights.

The identity experience came on a night when Gandhi was traveling first class by rail from Durban, Natal, to Pretoria. When a white man objected to sharing a compartment with Gandhi, an Asian, Gandhi was ordered to third class. He refused to move and was subsequently deposited on the station platform, his baggage confiscated. He resolved to become the Indian reformer in Africa. "There is every reason to believe that the central identity which here found its historical time and place was the conviction that among the Indians in South Africa he was *the only person equipped by fate* to reform a situation which under no conditions could be tolerated."[39]

Such a conviction would find lifelong counterparts in the struggle for truth whether in Africa or India. He was a lawyer by training but more importantly a reformer by vocation. To discover the truth and to act upon it was his commitment for life, an identity to be tested and challenged by many forces, not the least of which would be the British Empire.[40]

In the case of Luther and Gandhi, the place of ideology, commitment to an ideal, leads not only to reformation but to revolution as well. In fact Erikson states clearly that it is in ideology that social groups find the very stuff of revolution. He applies this to an analysis of contemporary youth, citing the need for society to understand the roots of dissent, in which an adequate ideology has often been denied the younger generation by a confused and irresponsible adult world. The quest for identity will usually require allowance for a moratorium and always the offer of an adequate ideology. A quotation cited earlier is helpful to repeat here: "A moratorium without some kind of utopian design ... can lead only to an ideological promiscuity that both adopts and disposes of the old revolutions."[41] And again, "By ideology ... I mean *a system of commanding ideas* held together more (but not exclusively) by totalistic logic and utopian conviction than by cognitive understanding or pragmatic experience."[42] Here is another reminder of Erikson's attempt to bridge rationalism and lived experience.

The Limits and Dangers of the Ideological Stage

The last quotation of the above section uses the word "totalistic" in a somewhat constructive sense. We have seen how Erikson also defines, in his theory and application to the great and not so great men, the danger of a total*ism* that excludes diversity and thereby precludes development of a true ethical sense. This is the primary limitation of any ideology that in turn makes it only a "stage on life's way," to use a Kierkegaardian phrase, that makes it essential for the ideological era to be subsumed in a larger, more adequate, adult ethic.

The danger of the totalistic fixation is described by Erikson in Luther's case in a chapter entitled "Allness or Nothingness."[43] The young monk in his moratorium interim was experiencing the inner struggle that was, by contrast with what was yet to come, the quiet before the storm. The very fact that within a decade he would emerge a leader of such dynamic proportions indicates that more was happening than the external historical account reveals.[44]

History's outstanding example of pathological totalism is Adolf Hitler.[45] The point of mentioning the totalistic limitation, however, is not so much to type historical personages as it is to indicate the precarious balance that faces all adolescents in their inner and outer struggle with somehow seeking an ideology by which they may become everything, lest, failing in this quest, they become nothing.

Yet the polarization between allness and nothingness is still not the point of Erikson's reason for seeing the ideological stage as only a transition to a higher form of adult ethics. Whether one moves totalistically in the regressive, destructive direction, or holistically toward the progressive, constructive, more mature posture, in either case there is the danger of exclusiveness that does not allow for diversity, and this is the primary limitation of the ideological stage. As

Erikson has said so graphically, "Fidelity without a sense of diversity can become an obsession and a bore; diversity without a sense of fidelity, an empty relativism."[46]

Fidelity, loyalty to an ideology, is an essential ingredient for adult ethics. It is *the* contribution of the ideological stage. It is a virtue maintained ever so precariously, however, especially during late adolescence when the temptation is to limit and set boundaries, to become totalistically inclusive and exclusive rather than holistically committed yet tolerant of diversity within the whole.

The Middle Ethical Term

To summarize, in Erikson's ethical theory, the ideological stage becomes a middle term between childhood morality and mature adult ethics. He amends his first proposition, which he called the developmental proposition, to allow for this middle term of adolescent ideology, "for between the development in childhood of man's *moral* proclivity and that of his *ethical* powers in adulthood, adolescence intervenes when he perceives the universal good in *ideological* terms."[47]

Thus, while Erikson makes the ideological stage only an amendment to the developmental proposition, it is a vital link in which the "ethical view is approximated, but it remains susceptible to an alteration of impulsive judgment and odd rationalization."[48]

The contribution of this stage must be seen in balance with its danger. Constructively it is the stuff of revolutions, the rejuvenating power of the prophetic dreams of youth. Destructively, it is the specter of fanaticism and totalistic arrogance that excludes diversity.

The Responsible Adult

As indicated in Chapter VI, Erikson describes three stages in adulthood just as there are four in childhood, separated by the fifth stage of adolescent identity. With regard to his ethical theory, it has been noted that the all-important adult principle of mutuality finds its origins in the premoral period of childhood. Morality, then, is learned in childhood, and ideology in adolescence.[49]

In adulthood, Erikson suggests, there are three ethical propositions: generativity, mutuality, and active choice. They combine with the reformulated Golden Rule that Erikson calls his baseline to constitute the foundation and structure of his ethical theory, which is summarily described by the word responsibility.

There cannot be as sharp a distinction between the stages within adulthood as there is in adolescence and childhood.[50] Thus generativity, mutuality, and active choice are not so easily assigned to just one particular stage within adulthood, although there is a continual degree of maturing between the first stage of young adulthood and the final stage of integrity. The degree of maturing must be balanced in one's thinking with the reality of overlapping.

Young Adulthood

Erikson describes the young adult as one in whom the childhood morality and adolescent ideology have developed into what he calls a "true ethical sense." In this stage there is a concern for both "intimate relationships and work associations by which man can hope to share a lifetime of productivity and competence."[51]

In this way Erikson both summarizes the previous contributions to ethics and introduces several attributes of adult ethics. In his description of the adult stages he has noted that once identity is sensed, and only then, the young adult is ready for intimacy that in turn opens the way to mutuality and generativity.

Intimacy

Erikson includes the sexual experience in his treatment of intimacy but it is not limited to that physical relationship. Intimacy has wider ethical implications. Prior to identity, genuine relationships with others tend to present the risk of losing one's tenuously held identity and will be avoided. Luther is a good example of this. His father had wanted him to marry and had made all of the arrangements when Luther aborted the plans with his "call" to the monkhood. He was not ready for intimacy and it was only much later when his identity had been more firmly grasped that he could move into the intimate relationship of marriage. For Luther, identity and intimacy blend into a single stage, more so than is normally observed.

Once identity is sensed there is the ability and desire to risk fusing oneself with another. This comes both in sexual relations and in commitments to vocations, affiliations, and other objects of fidelity. At least two of Erikson's books introduce into the discussion on intimacy a conversation Freud is reputed to have had about the goals of human endeavor. Freud defined them as "to love and to work."[52] Erikson believes that what Freud meant by love was more than genital love; it included the larger dimension of intimacy. Thus, intimacy is seen to include but mean much more than sexuality.[53]

The Beginning of Responsibility

It is my contention that Erikson's use of "the ethical sense" is in reality what the word responsibility as a moral quality denotes. He uses the term "ethical sense" as being the adult quality which builds upon the two earlier layers of childhood morality and adolescent ideology.[54]

The Danger and Limitation

On the individual basis, the intimacy of the young adult is polarized with isolation. Where there is a fear of taking chances with one's identity, intimacy will not be entered into and there will be no procreation requiring care.

The negative pole of isolation is also carried over into normal maturing intimate relationships in the form of what Erikson calls "the territorial defensiveness of one who has appropriated and staked out his earthly claim and who seeks eternal security in the super-identity of organizations."[55] We would add to this totalistic tendency the present youth culture's search for security in the cults.

Once commitment is made, limitation is inevitable. The way in which that limitation is expressed and the degree to which it is insisted upon is the difference between a balanced fidelity with diversity and a fanaticism that excludes any possibility of diversity. Intimacy by its very nature can become exclusive and brand all outside the intimate relationship as enemies of another species. Such pseudospeciehood must of necessity give way to a wider identity if mature ethics is to prevail. This concept of the pseudospecie has been discussed and will be further developed.[56] Let us be clear, however, that for Erikson, "The Black, the young, and the female have one experience in common: They have been the others, where the adult white male has been 'it.' "[57]

Adulthood

As Erikson discusses the contribution of morality and ideology to adult ethics in one of his journal articles on youth, he defines adult ethics as follows: " 'ethical' meaning a universal sense of values assented to with insight and foresight in anticipation of immediate responsibilities not the least of which is a transmission of these values to the next generation."[58]

Here the issue of generativity is seen clearly as one of the vital aspects of adult ethics. While the generativity principle for the individual cannot be ultimately separated from societal responsibility, it will be helpful to distinguish the differences of their meaning as the following sections attempt to do.

The Parent-Child Relationship

Thus far, much has been said concerning the child-parent relationship, but primarily from the developing child's perspective. He or she experiences the affirmation that comes in mutuality. He learns basic trust, hope, and faith as he responds to the caring adult. It is time to examine more closely what is meant by the ethically caring adult.

As usual, Erikson observes this phenomenon in all its complexity and interrelatedness. Childhood in contemporary studies has been rediscovered for its significance to the mature adult—his own childhood, the child within. Yet there continues to be a lack of attention given to the childhood of great men. Actually, Erikson sees two extremes emerging: treating the childhood of great men as meaningless, or becoming overly concerned about one's origins.[59]

Between these two extremes, Erikson offers a significant alternative, "a new truth, namely that the collective life of mankind, in all its historical lawfulness, is fed by the energies and images of successive generations; and that each generation brings to human fate an inescapable conflict between its ethical and rational aims and its infantile fixations."[60]

It is then with the responsible adult who has gained identity, intimacy, and generativity that responsibility for the next generation is seen as of utmost importance. Therefore, to consider the childhood of great men and whether or not they developed basic trust is impossible without considering, correspondingly, the sense of responsibility on the part of the child's parents and their society.[61]

Erikson suggests that "the chosen unit of observation must be the generation, not the individual."[68] Thus, generativity is the third proposition in Erikson's ethical formulation, the first of the three adult stages.

The next adult proposition Erikson considers is that of mutuality. This has already been introduced as having its roots in the infant's premoral development. However, it is in the intimacy of adulthood that it comes into its own. Especially will it be seen to be of vital importance in the discussion that is to follow concerning the Golden Rule. Erikson makes his suggestions as to the importance of mutuality in the form of an open-ended question: "Should we, then, endow the Golden Rule with a principle of mutuality, replacing the reciprocity of both prudence and sympathy?"[69]

Finally, Erikson's fifth proposition is that of active choice. Active choice is "a (consciously and unconsciously) active and giving attitude, rather than a demanding and dependent one."[70]

Throughout his description of Luther and Gandhi, as well as in his general description of the mature adult, Erikson has used the term "activate." Responsible adults activate in those to whom they relate a quality by which they are enhanced, while at the same time the actor too is helped. This leads then to the necessity of considering Erikson's baseline to the five propositions upon which his ethical theory is constructed, the Golden Rule.

The Golden Rule

Reminding the reader that identity is his "general orientation," Erikson goes on to add that such a person who so activates and has been activated "will also acquire the experience that *truly worthwhile acts enhance a mutuality between the doer and the other—a mutuality which strengthens the doer even as it strengthens the other*. Thus, the 'doer' and 'the other' are partners in one deed."[71]

It is essential that this reformulation of the Golden Rule be seen in the light of the knowledge that has been gained through the ages regarding human development. "This means that the doer is activated in whatever strength is *appropriate to his age, stage, and condition*." Thus the rule is reformulated to say that "it is best to do to another what will strengthen you even as it will strengthen him—that is, what will develop his best potentials even as it develops your own."[72]

Beyond the parent-child relationship to which much discussion has already been given, Erikson goes on to expand consideration to include how such an ethical principle applies to relationships between the sexes, doctor and patient, labor and management, and finally nations in the arena of international relations.[73] With the opening of the discussion to this broader field, it is appropriate to move into a consideration of responsibility that includes society and not just the individual.

NOTES

1. H. Richard Niebuhr, *The Responsible Self* (New York: Harper & Row, 1963). The four elements of responsibility for Niebuhr are: response, interpretation, accountability, and social solidarity. His definition is as follows: "The idea or pattern of responsibility, then, may summarily and abstractly be defined as the idea of an agent's action as response to action upon him in accordance with his interpretation of the latter action and with his expectation of response to his response; and all of this is in a continuing community of agents," p. 65.

2. James M. Gustafson and James T. Laney, eds., *On Being Responsible* (New York: Harper & Row, 1968). In other books Gustafson has continued to develop the concept of responsibility.

3. James M. Gustafson, *Christ and the Moral Life* (New York: Harper & Row, 1968), p. 263, n. 20. Italics mine.

4. Ibid.

5. In *Responsibility as an Ethical Norm in the Thought of Erik H. Erikson*, I document the interest in responsibility in these others beyond Niebuhr and Gustafson: Albert R. Jonsen, Abraham Maslow, Erich Fromm, and Rollo May. More could be added to this list.

6. Erikson, *Insight*, p. 231.

7. Erikson, "Reflections on Dissent," p. 167. See also essay as revised in *Life History*, pp. 193–224.

8. Ernest Wallwork, "Erik H. Erikson: Psychosocial Resources for Faith," in Johnson, Wallwork, Green, Santmire, and Vanderpool, *Critical Issues in Modern Religion* (Englewood Cliffs, N.J.: Prentice-Hall, 1973), p. 359, n. 27, makes this statement: "Mutuality is the central value in the ethical

theory that Erikson joins with his psychosocial theory." Because Erikson locates mutuality in early childhood but then lists it as his fourth ethical proposition, not all interpreters have viewed it as a key concept. As we saw earlier, Browning considers generativity to be more pivotal.

9. An unpublished doctoral dissertation which is a comprehensive discussion of conscience in Erikson's thought is by Michael F. Glessner, O.S.A., S.T.L. (Rome: Academia Alfonsiana, 1977).

10. Piediscalzi is correct in observing that Erikson fails to deal with the fact that many babies are bottle fed, and withdrawal of the breast could hardly be the source of an awareness of evil. He overlooks the fact, however, that Erikson places equal emphasis upon the reality that cutting teeth in itself is painful, and that the child's will is opposed by the wills of others than just the mother when teething on the wrong object or person is objected to. He is correct, nevertheless, in suggesting that this area needs far more development as the source of evil in Erikson's theory. See Nicholas Piediscalzi, "Paul Tillich and Erik H. Erikson on the Origin and Nature of Morality and Ethics" (Diss. Boston University, 1965), p. 462.

11. Erikson, *Childhood*, p. 79.

12. Ibid., p. 405. In his treatment of conscience, typically, Erikson warns against either extreme of rigidity or dismissal, leaving underdeveloped a very comprehensive view of conscience.

13. Erikson, *Insight*, pp. 121–22. In *Dimensions of a New Identity*, p. 65, Erikson takes issue with B. F. Skinner. He contrasts our founding fathers' emphasis upon the initiative of the self-made man with Skinner, who has a cosmology, according to Erikson, "in which the 'environment' takes over the function of 'the inner gatekeeper,' namely conscience."

14. Erikson, *Insight*, p. 222.

15. Ibid., p. 223.

16. Erikson, "A Memorandum on Identity," p. 42.

17. The Greek word for ethics, *ethos*, literally means stall or framework. "What was originally referred to animals as giving stability and security to their existence came also to be applied to human relations. So, the ethos of a society denotes that which gives stability and security; that without which it cannot hold up, cannot be a society at all." Paul L. Lehmann, "The Foundation and Pattern of Christian Behavior," *Christian Faith and Social Action*, John A. Hutchison, ed. (New York: Charles Scribner's Sons, 1953), p. 97.

18. Erikson, *Luther*, p. 195.

19. Erikson, *Insight*, pp. 225–26.

20. Erikson, *Gandhi's Truth*, p. 107.

21. Erikson, *Gandhi's Truth*, p. 152.

22. Ibid., p. 169.

23. Ibid., p. 231.

24. Ibid., p. 235.

25. Ibid., p. 244.

26. Erikson, *Insight,* p. 222.

27. Ibid., pp. 224–25.

28. Erikson, *Luther,* p. 20.

29. Ibid., p. 43.

30. Ibid., p. 100.

31. Ibid., pp. 130–31.

32. Ibid., p. 140.

33. Ibid., p. 210.

34. Erikson, *Gandhi's Truth,* p. 145.

35. Ibid., pp. 157–58.

36. Ibid., p. 162.

37. Ibid.

38. Ibid., p. 163.

39. Ibid., p. 166. Italics his.

40. Throughout his writings Erikson develops the complexities of the identity crisis and the place of ideology for a great many leaders of civilization: Freud, Darwin, G. B. Shaw, and many others, as well as fictional characters such as Hamlet.

41. Erikson, "Reflections on Dissent," p. 158.

42. Ibid., p. 164. Italics his.

43. Erikson, *Luther,* pp. 98–125.

44. "We can only account for this fact by assuming a fierce, if as yet quite dumb struggle in him between destructive and constructive forces, and between regressive and progressive alternatives—all in balance at this time." Ibid. p. 99.

45. See Erikson, *Luther,* pp. 105–110 for the development of the Hitler theme.

46. Erikson, *The Challenge of Youth,* p. 13.

47. Erikson, *Insight,* pp. 224 and 226. Italics his.

48. Ibid., p. 225.

49. One needs only to reread Erikson's own words about the necessity of ideology to see the logic of giving it an "identity" of its own: Erikson, *Insight,* pp. 224–25. It hardly seems possible that Erikson should confine the ideological proposition to an amendment of childhood morality when he has devoted so much of his efforts to exploring identity that is so dependent upon and interrelated with a meaningful ideology.

50. For example, in *Identity,* pp. 91–141, Erikson treats the first four stages in considerable detail, leading up to the all-important fifth stage, identity. He then blends the last three stages into one single section labeled "Beyond Identity." Also, as noted in Chapter VI, he is presently giving more attention to the adult stages.

51. Erikson, *Insight*, p. 226.
52. Erikson, *Identity: Youth and Crisis*, p. 136. Also see *Childhood*, pp. 264–65. One also recognizes here Erich Fromm's possible indebtedness to Freud, whether conscious or not, for his two major productive orientations— love and work, or thought.
53. Erikson, *Childhood*, p. 266. Erikson here expands on the theme of intimacy by listing the goals of genitality as follows:

    1. mutuality of orgasm
    2. with a loved partner
    3. of the other sex
    4. with whom one is able and willing to share a mutual trust
    5. and with whom one is able and willing to regulate the cycles of
        a. work
        b. procreation
        c. recreation
    6. so as to secure to the offspring, too, all the stages of a satisfactory development.

54. Erikson, *Identity: Youth and Crisis*, p. 136.
55. Erikson, *Insight*, p. 226.
56. Erikson, *Identity: Youth and Crisis*, p. 136.
57. Erikson, *Dimensions of a New Identity*, p. 114.
58. Erikson, "Reflections on Dissent," p. 164. This journal article is one of the more significant contributions of Erikson to the entire discussion of ethics.
59. Erikson, *Insight*, p. 44.
60. Erikson, *Insight*, pp. 44–45.
61. See Erikson, *Young Man Luther*, pp. 164–65; p. 255; and Erikson, *Identity: Youth and Crisis*, p. 103.
62. Erikson, *Identity: Youth and Crisis*, p. 177.
63. Ibid., pp. 29–30.
64. Erikson, *Insight*, pp. 132–33.
65. Erikson, *Insight*, pp. 133–34.
66. Erikson, *Childhood*, p. 267.
67. Ibid., p. 269.
68. In addition to all of the evidence to be found in human history, Erikson calls to his support the experiments of Professor Harry Harlow with monkeys. See Erikson, *Insight*, pp. 228–29.
69. Ibid., p. 231.
70. Ibid., pp. 232–33.
71. Ibid., p. 233. Italics his.
72. Ibid. Italics his. This concept of the Golden Rule is discussed again in Chapter X, "Erik H. Erikson: Homo Religiosus?".

73. Erikson is especially fond of Gandhi's principle: "That line of action is alone justice which does not harm either party to a dispute." Erikson, *Insight*, p. 239.

CHAPTER VIII

Patterns of Responsibility: *Social*

Certainly one of the contributions for which Erik H. Erikson is most often credited is that of combining the three areas of physical, psychological, and societal considerations. One cannot concern oneself with physical development in isolation. The interaction of the developing organism with its social environment and the complex interrelationship of both organism and society with developing ego must all be kept in proper perspective in consideration of any one of the three elements.[1]

Responsibility for Childhood and Youth

As previously developed, Erikson's earliest interest was directed toward children and the responsibility that society has for them. He suggested in his *Childhood and Society* that "societies create the only condition under which human growth is possible."[2]

In that same book, which so firmly established Erikson as an original thinker, he maintains that society is responsible for preparing its children for parenthood as well as for "[taking care] of the unavoidable remnants of infantility in its adults."[3]

The child with his or her prolonged period of dependence upon the adult society will either learn to trust, to have a sense of his own ability and willpower to realize purpose and competence, or his society will adversely foster mistrust, shame, and doubt, guilt and inferiority. All of this is related to the developing conscience discussed above, an ability to depend upon the world and thus oneself.

Further, Erikson sees one of the problems as that of keeping in balance the relationship between society's responsibility and childhood's development.[4] The complexity of this problem is enormous, but Erikson has opened the way at least to begin to analyze its elements and see the problem in all of its dimensions.

It is in his consideration of societal responsibility that Erikson has most often been critical of existential thinking which "shirks the responsibility for the generational process. . . ."[5]

An adult ethics, then, will be responsible to the generations, to childhood entrusted to its care, and to youth.[6]

If society provides the necessary period for childhood dependence and learning of morality, it finds its responsibility even more diversified for the developing youth. Now its ward is in quest of identity and all of the independence that goes with it. Yet the individual is never independent, even though for youth, especially, this is the sought-after goal. And society must provide the matrix in which the youth can seek to discover that which he will never completely find. This is a task for society requiring the utmost responsibility.

Erikson has required of society, in thinking of its responsibility to the youth, that it allow for a moratorium, that it offer an ideology to which there may be either acceptance or rejection, that it refrain from absolutizing transitory states, and that it accept from the youthful generation the needed correctives to its own imagined achievement.[7] The responsibility of society is not to grant thoughtless and normless permissiveness, but rather to provide that "ethical guidance" which will include morality, ideology, and responsibility.[8]

Responsibility for the Sexes

The inclination here is to consider only society's responsibility for women, inasmuch as this is a concern for both Erikson and contemporary society. To consider one sex, however, is always to involve the corresponding effect such consideration has upon the other, and so it is best to look at society's responsibility to both sexes in this section.

In Chapter II consideration was given to Erikson's theory as it affected women and inner space. Now, from the social perspective, the question arises how society can truly be responsible for fostering an equal place for women.

Erikson sees the whole question clouded by any thought of men's granting equality to women as though it were within man's prerogative to be so benevolent. The image a man grants is his own and this is not equality, for it has already been determined that woman's image differs from man's. Must woman fit man's typologies? "In other words, even where equality is closer to realization it has not led to equivalence, and equal rights have by no means secured equal representation in the sense that the deepest concerns of women find expression in their public influence or, indeed, their actual role in the game of power."[9]

Erikson has much to say about the contribution women have to make to society. Their somatic "inner space" equips them with more than a physical uniqueness. There is a corresponding psychological differentiation that endows woman with a capacity to include, to household and care in a special way that civilization, if it is to survive, desperately needs. One cannot speak of the contribution women might make to society, however, without simultaneously seeing the need for that society to foster a new role for womanhood.

As an example, Erikson pursues the question of what contribution women have to make to science with their special endowments for creativity, sensitivity, and caring. The computer is sexless or suprasexual, but the human being doing the programming is not.[10]

If society becomes responsible to women and for women, they have a contribution to make that may save civilization from its present course of violent encounter.[11] A new appreciation for the physical, psychological, and societal contributions of women is the order of the day. Erikson attacks Gandhi for his male chauvinism with regard to all women, appreciating at the same time the fact that Gandhi took upon himself a kind of womanly disposition to household and care not only for India's disenfranchised, but, in effect, for all mankind.

This, then, indicates a new role for the male, a discovery of his femininity as well as his masculinity. He need not by anatomical determinism be destined to a phallic intrusiveness that leads only to aggression and violence. As society accepts the contributions of psychoanalysis at this point, that there is a truly human dimension which transcends both sexes' contributions and proclivities, it will in turn foster the kind of maturity in its youth which will lead to a new humanity.

Erikson feels that the women's liberation movement has misunderstood his position, and in response to their objections he includes a chapter in his recent book *Life History and the Historical Moment* entitled "Once More the Inner Space."[12]

In this more recent essay, he admits that he has been affected by the new concept of womanhood. However, he feels that with a few qualifications of style and use of words, his basic premise remains unchanged. Women, by anatomy, differ from men and therefore have a different contribution to offer to society. This contribution is greatly needed. Men have exercised authority over women in an unreasonable way. In *Toys and Reasons* Erikson admits that women have made us face the fact that ritualized male authority has often become that malignant form of the ritual experience, authorit*ism*.[13]

Erikson's overall emphasis, as I see it, is that society will be richer when it accepts the characteristics of womanhood that it has long overlooked or denied. He reminds us that he never defined generativity merely in terms of procreativity.[14]

His larger concern is for a new vision of humanity granting equality to both sexes, all races, and subgroups. For this to happen, women must be regarded in terms of equality, not in any way limited by anatomy, but rather endowed by anatomy and identity to accomplish purposes unique to their position in society. He concludes his response to those who have been critical of his position with the words, "I cannot see how such an adulthood could evolve except through an equal involvement of women and of their special modes of experience in the over-all planning and governing so far monopolized by men."[15]

Society and a Wider Identity: The Possibility of Peace

What does Erikson mean by a wider identity and universalism? One must answer that question by describing what Erikson sees as the present problem, that of restriction bounded by the pseudospecies. Man's individual identity is in a sense established when he commits himself to an ideology and feels a continuity between himself and his society or subgroup. From primitive man's identifications with a tribe to contemporary identification with social, economic, racial, or national subgroups, the pseudospecies has evolved.[16]

Behind Erikson's plea for a wider identity is his conviction that humanity is not necessarily destined to violent defense of life and territoriality. He cites and then counters Freud's letter to Einstein: " 'Conflicts between man and man are resolved in principle by the recourse to violence. It is the same in the animal kingdom from which man cannot claim exclusion.' "[17]

Erikson's objection to Freud's assumption is based, in part, upon the research of Konrad Lorenz who has demonstrated that in the animal kingdom there is also to be found a kind of ritualization that preserves life over against the commonly accepted hypothesis referred to by Freud, above.[18] This ritual of pacification, which is multiplied in Lorenz's research, is to Erikson evidence of the fact that perhaps the instinct mythology of Freud needs to be questioned, if not corrected. "There may be resources for peace even in our 'animal nature' if we will only learn to nurture nature, as well as to master it."[19] For Erikson, man is more than another animal driven by instincts, but Lorenz's research regarding pacification in the animal world is nevertheless significant.[20]

The pseudospecies into which humanity has chosen to cast its group identities need not be the only possibility in terms of social existence. If Gandhi could include his opponents in his plans and achieve a new, wider identity beyond the labor-management and beyond the Indian-British (for it was his vision to have an Indian identity within the total British Commonwealth identity), there is hope in other spheres such as racial tensions and ideological divisions for society to experience wider identities than it has known.

To appreciate this one must recall the dynamic quality of identity, the polarity always assumed by Erikson. In normal, positive identity, there are always to be kept in tension those elements of the negative identity. As this is so in the individual who finds it possible to move towards maturity and a greater balance of positive over negative factors, so, too, is it possible within society for the negative forces of exclusive totalism and pseudospecies to give way to the more inclusive, wider identity.

However, the fact that Erikson does not mean by a "wider identity" a totally utopian kind of humanity without any subgrouping is well illustrated in the book *In Search of Common Ground: Conversations with Erik H. Erikson and Huey P. Newton.* He points out that there are limits to the wideness of identity, lest it become "formless, ineffective, and lost...."[21] Concrete communalities may have both definition and an appreciation for the wider identity.

Nevertheless, it is time to see the lie in many social identities, to see the "pseudo" nature of many commitments that by their very nature are exclusive and excluding of others. The responsibility is everyone's and it is society's.

In the area of race, the responsibility begins with parents of children who have given them their first experience of a world to be trusted or feared. "Man is born only with the capacity to learn to hope, and then his milieu must offer him a convincing world view and within it specific hopes."[22] The milieu begins in family but is extended beyond homelife. Society's responsibility is much more than just a generational one. It is responsible for its stereotypes of people and races. "The systematic exploitation of the Negro male as a domestic animal and the denial to him of the status of responsible fatherhood are . . . two of the most shameful chapters in the history of this Christian nation."[23] That society continues to project the image of an "absent" Negro father is a part of its responsibility for the racial problem in America.

Erikson sees a close relationship between the kind of totalism in Nazi Germany that excluded the Jewish culture and its counterpart in America in the totalism of the Ku Klux Klan or the Black Muslims. In all cases where pseudospecies becomes a totalistic exclusion of other identities, the responsibility is to be placed at the feet of more than just the leaders of the subgroup. A society is responsible for such developments.

> The difference between a Hitler and a Gandhi is (in this context) that Hitler's violent methods were tied to a totalistic reinforcement of a pseudospecies (the German race), the fiction of which could only be maintained by villifying and annihilating another pseudospecies, the Jews. Gandhi's nonviolent technique, on the contrary, was not only tied to the political realities of his day, but

also revived the more inclusive identity promised in the world religions.[24]

Hitler and Gandhi were individuals, to be sure, but they found support in the societies that allowed them to move in the direction of either totalistic exclusion, resulting in a narrowly exclusive identity on the one hand, or the more inclusive wider identity of Gandhi that included even his opponents in a new wider identity, on the other hand.

The wider identity that moves beyond the territorial defensiveness of the pseudospecies has its historical antecedent in the *Pax Romana*. Here, by process of unification, many diverse groups were embraced. Today, technology is uniting the world economically, disarming our fears of pseudospecie limitation by means of the wider identity of interdependence.[25]

These examples have inevitably led to consideration of leaders— Hitler and Gandhi. It is clear that society either responds positively and fosters such leaders or it never allows them to emerge. Thus it is responsible, but to what extent and how is problematical. In discussing this same issue with regard to individual development, Erikson states in one paragraph: "Human strength, then, depends on a total process which regulates at the same time the *sequence of generations* and the *structure of society*. The ego is the regulator of this process in the individual."[26]

This leaves unanswered the complex problem of societal regulation of responsibility. It is one of the serious deficiencies in Erikson's theory. That there is such a thing as societal responsibility is clear and understandable to the extent to which he has explored the interrelationship of the individual and his milieu. But the line between personal and societal responsibility is ill-defined at this stage and in need of exploration.

Let us nevertheless give Erikson the credit he deserves for pointing out our lack of a wider identity, wherever the responsibility may lie: ". . . it can no longer escape us that in all his past man has based his ideologies on mutually exclusive group identities in the form of 'pseudospecies': tribe, nation, caste, region, class, and so on."[27]

Responsibility and the Institutions

Institutions cannot be separated from emerging virtues, as we noted in Chapters IV, V, and VI. Erikson states this unequivocally: ". . . virtue in the individual and the spirit of institutions have evolved together, are one and the same strength."[28] Religion is the institution about which Erikson has the most to say, and more attention will be devoted to it in the chapter to follow. Erikson relates other institutions to emerging virtues, however, some with more elaboration than others.

Erikson's observations of the institutions and how they relate to the life cycle were stated in *Childhood and Society*. He was dealing with how societies either "raise the corresponding infantile ego value to highest collective endeavor,"[29] or exploit infantile fears and foster regression.

Historically, institutions or organizations have evolved that have corresponded to individual needs and as such have tended to enhance and strengthen the individual. As those same organizations have outlived their needs, however, as they seem to do, they have had to resort to exploitation of infantile anxieties in order to survive.[30] Erikson concludes that the negative factors, the price paid for exploiting institutions, has been too high, but such consideration he again leaves to the philosophers.

To review, the institutions that complement each stage of development and the emerging virtues are these: religion; political and legal organization; the economic order; technology; social stratification; relationship patterns; education, art, and science; and, finally, philosophy.[31]

Erikson calls for a more careful study of how these institutions relate to one another, but he is especially concerned with how the institutions affect individuals and, in turn, how the successive generations revitalize the institutions. The societal responsibility for generativity is directly related at this point to a consideration of how that responsibility is focused in its institutions.

Finally, while Erikson is clear in stating the reciprocal importance of the virtues and the institutions, that each are vital to the other, he does urge caution in making any institution too specific. "There is no one-to-one connection between single virtues and single institutions, such as churches, law courts, or economic establishments."[32]

Summary and Evaluation

In this chapter, and the previous one dealing with personal elements, the essential ingredients of Erikson's ethics have been outlined. His five propositions are built upon the baseline of the Golden Rule. This is to him a "mysterious meeting ground between ancient peoples separated by oceans and eras, and has provided a hidden theme in the most memorable sayings of many thinkers."[33] Its genius is that by its very content it relates the individual, who is all too prone to think of himself in isolation, to the larger milieu of the entire world. The five propositions are related to his developmental perspective, and development is his first proposition.

The second proposition relates to the developing youth who is cognitively ready "to envisage the more universal principles of a highest human good."[34] The adolescent is ready to make a commitment to an *ideology*. But this state is not final. There is a certain tentativeness about the adolescent's commitment which makes his development to this point only an approximation of the ethical view.

Erikson's third proposition is that of *generativity*. The maturing adult will be concerned about more than his morality and ideology. He begins to care, to sense his responsibility for the next generation. He becomes more than a holder of life; he transmits life, and his concern broadens to the generational issue from its more individual preoccupation.

The fourth proposition is that of *mutuality*. Actually, Erikson's first three: the developmental, concerning morality; the ideological; and the generational concern are all dependent upon the fourth, mutuality, which begins in early infancy, in the stage he identifies as premorality. Mutuality, however, becomes the responsibility of the more mature adult who puts into practice the interaction of the Golden Rule, doing for the other as he would have done to himself.

Active choice is Erikson's fifth proposition. Built upon mutuality and epitomized in the prayer of St. Francis, it states that ethical man will actively choose to do to others and not just receive from others the right and the good of the previous propositions, the moral and the valuable.

Beyond the identification of these propositions and their baseline, the Golden Rule, primary attention has been given to the adult stages of development, for it is with adulthood that ethics attains its true sense, having evolved from the moral and ideological to the responsible. It is only in the adult whose identity has been sensed in late adolescence that intimacy and relationship with others and the world is possible. Intimacy naturally involves mutuality, and leads to generativity by procreation as well as in the larger concerns of providing for society's coming generations. Beyond that, adult ethics finds its culmination in integrity, viewing the entire life cycle with a certain wholeness that endows coming generations with a model of trust.

From the individual and generational issues, interest turns to the society in which the individual finds himself and to which he is responsible. That society is in turn responsible for the individual. Issues, among others that intersect the personal life cycle and the societal concerns, are the role of the sexes, race, labor-management, and international relations. Erikson's ethical view is that in all of these areas there is need for a *wider identity,* moving beyond provincial and pseudospecies to a more inclusive world view that, in the spirit of the Golden Rule, cares about both sides of issues traditionally pitted against one another. It is for a new universalism, a new humanism and wider identity that Erikson makes his appeal.

Finally, attention has been given to a theme only partially developed by Erikson, that of societal responsibility as represented in the institutions. He sees the latter as corresponding to the eight stages of the individual life cycle and dependent upon the corresponding virtues that emerge. It is his observation that, parallel to each stage of development, society has created an institution to foster and enhance that stage and its values. These institutions, however, are constantly in danger of attempting to absolutize and thereby cause regression rather than development. The social institutions that parallel the eight stages are these: religion, legal and political organization, economic order, technology, ideology, patterns of relationship, education, and, finally, philosophy.

Having given this basic summary of Erikson's ethics, we can now try to evaluate the contribution he has made as a psychologist to ethical theory and religion.

An evaluation of Erikson's theory must consider the eight stages of the life cycle and their central notion of identity. Their primary significance for ethics is to be found in the explication of virtue. This is described as a move from pathology to its very opposite—health and wholeness. For Erikson, merely not being sick, or just being alive, is not enough. He seeks to discover the mysteries of vitality that in turn lead to the ethical sense. Thus his own vocation has always been multiple in nature, including the work of clinician, researcher, theorist, and teacher. Character development and not mere adjustment is the goal of the ego. In his concern for health and vitality Erikson offers a framework for a deeper understanding of psychosocial development and the heights attainable when persons will be responsible for life in a community of responsible others with whom they interact and without whom responsible development is not possible.

Interaction, or the cogwheeling of the personal with the social milieu, is an indispensable aspect of development. The person can only become responsible when those within his social radius, beginning with earliest parental figures and extending to every relationship, have been and are responsible in those areas in which interaction is involved. This cogwheeling of the individual, related generations, and the entire society expands ethics from a simple concentration upon atomistic "selves" and forces theorists to include the social dimensions.

A criticism of Erikson's theory at this point is that it is circular. A person will not develop character unless other persons in his social milieu are responsible to and for him. Society, on the other hand, is dependent upon responsible persons if it is to be regenerated by emerging life cycles and thus be responsible. Perhaps anticipating this criticism, Erikson simply observes that this is the way things are. It is not a case of which comes first. What develops is an ensemble with many parts. Basic to the ensemble, however, is the input of responsible persons and a pattern of responsibility at some point, and this proclivity for dialectical progress is an assumption that Erikson makes without attempting to resolve it in any systematic fashion.

Erikson does note the presence within the process of psychosocial evolution of gifted persons such as Luther and Gandhi, who seem to transcend the circular pitfall and, in spite of irresponsible parents or rigid ideologies, rise to new heights and offer the needed input for freedom from a kind of predetermined restriction.

The dimension of giftedness, while highlighted in persons such as Luther and Gandhi, is actually a matter of degree, and elements of strength are to be found in a great many persons other than the very gifted. It is by these persons that generations become vital and regenerating. Here is the very point of Erikson's discussion of the virtues. The persons in whom virtues emerge to greater degrees in turn regenerate society insuring new opportunities for greater development in forthcoming generations. These persons, having rejected provincial totalism, have gained a sense of wholeness.

In Erikson's description of healthy persons, considerably more enlightenment is offered concerning the nature of health.[35] Erikson often calls it a sense of wholeness which in all its unity also includes diversity in the process of developing coherence. In each stage of the life cycle there is a tension, a negative and positive element, the very first being trust vs. mistrust. Allowance for polarities and creative tension is integral to development. It is where tension is not tolerated, where boundaries become exclusive and absolute, that a kind of totalism defeats wholeness and development is blocked. On the social level totalism easily becomes a pseudospecies, a group, tribe, race, or nation that delineates absolute boundaries and allows for no deviation.

This is not to say that diversity is to be valued to the exclusion of unity. It is simply that a sense of wholeness will be found where a proper balance is maintained, and Erikson describes this balance in each of the eight stages and in society in terms of ratios where, for example, trust properly outweighs yet still tolerates elements of mistrust.

Erikson concludes his own treatment of the virtues: "True *adaptation*, in fact, is maintained with the help of loyal rebels who refuse to adjust to 'conditions' and cultivate an indignation in the service of a *to-be-restored wholeness* without which psychosocial evolution and all of its institutions would be doomed."[36] The sense here is that gifted people march to the beat of a different drum, a more wholesome approach to life than is to be found in average conformity, and that by their presence the virtues are endowed with new strength resulting ultimately in a more vital society.

An assumption behind all of this is that human and social development, while prizing and seeking coherence or wholeness, will at the same time understand and allow for those polarities which observation indicates are basic to health. For the polarities to result in creative development, however, they must exist within a larger framework of wholeness that will ultimately be maintained by religion or ideology. Religion is an institution by which society restores that sense of basic trust first experienced in childhood. Particular historical periods will have particularly meaningful ideologies. Where wholeness has been lost or where ethical bonds have been broken, new ideologies must be found to restore the wholeness essential to development of both persons and social order. This is a responsibility of persons and societies that is difficult to prescribe but can be described, as Erikson has done, with the lives of great men. In fact, as we have often noted, Erikson finds in religious persons subjects who lend themselves to investigation and who then become examples of the kind of wholeness he prizes, a coherence inclusive of creative diversity.

Further to understand the healthy person who is responsible for his or her life as it includes generational and social dimensions as well as personal development, one may note what Erikson observes as irresponsible traits of character. Any totalism which by its definition rules out diversity to the exclusion of a single viewpoint or kind of person is in Erikson's view contrary to and a refuge from a more constructive wholeness. Mothers who possess children, rather than allowing them to assume an appropriate measure of self-responsibility, or who themselves are inconsistent yet demand consistency from their families, are irresponsible because they do not offer to their children or families what they in turn demand. Here, then, is an indication of a vital element of responsibility—*sameness* between the person and interacting society. Erikson's definition of identity, as much as he allows identity to be defined, is to be found in this formula, as noted in Chapter II, that there is a continuity and sameness between the individual, his life cycle, and his environment.

Other examples of irresponsibility would include teachers who do not foster industry in the children entrusted to them; therapists who impose their own values upon patients; judges who project standards of adult maturity upon immature, identity-seeking youth; and old people who offer nothing in the way of a meaningful ideology to those who look to them for meaning in the face of death if they, the younger generation, are to find meaning in life.

Finally, Erikson has formulated five propositions relating to ethics in relation to what he calls his baseline, the Golden Rule. The ethical sense is best summarized as "being responsible." Especially in the adult ethical stages of generativity, mutuality, and active choice the emphasis is upon a basic responsible disposition that is the opposite of passivity.

Man is never only the helpless victim of forces—personal or impersonal, biological or historical—acting upon him. He is not the servant of rules or ideologies, although both have a place in his ethics. Man is the responding being who at his best chooses to act responsibly. He is a person, then, as well as a biological organism and an historical product. He is responsible for his own personal psychosocial development as well as for his response to the social order in which others are to become persons. He is to act according to a pattern of responsibility, to the end that responsible persons may develop and that a responsible society may emerge with a sense of wholeness embracing the inevitable diversity of human existence, and which will thereby provide the framework in which persons may become responsible.

NOTES

1. Erikson, *Identity: Youth and Crisis*, p. 289.
2. Erikson, *Childhood*, p. 277.
3. Ibid., p. 405.
4. Ibid., p. 406.
5. Erikson, *Identity: Youth and Crisis*, p. 42.
6. See Chapter V.
7. For additional discussion of society's responsibility for its youth, see Erikson, *Identity: Youth and Crisis*, p. 157. Also see *Young Man Luther*.
8. Erikson, "A Memorandum on Identity," p. 41.
9. Erikson, *Identity: Youth and Crisis*, p. 262.
10. As we have indicated previously, the left- and right-handed methods of knowing relate to the gifts of female and male personalities and Erikson would bring together that interrelationship rather than further polarize it.

Women are not limited to just the intuitive, nor men to the rational. We have absolutized these designations and they need reinterpretation without neglecting the special giftedness in some areas for both sexes.

11. Erikson, *Identity: Youth and Crisis*, p. 293. Also see *Insight*, pp. 234–36.

12. Erikson, *Life History*, pp. 225–47.

13. Erikson, *Toys and Reasons*, p. 111. Italics his.

14. Erikson, *Life History*, p. 243.

15. Ibid., p. 247.

16. Erikson, *Identity: Youth and Crisis*, p. 299. See also *Dimensions of a New Identity*, pp. 76ff; 27–28, and 30–31.

17. Erikson, "Psychoanalysis and Ongoing History," p. 243.

18. Lorenz's research is extensive and only one example will be cited here: "When two wolves happen to get into a fight, there comes a moment when the one that is weakening first bares his unprotected side to his opponent who, in turn, is instinctively inhibited from taking advantage of this now nonviolent situation." Erikson, "Psychoanalysis and Ongoing History," p. 244.

19. Erikson, *Insight*, p. 230. Erikson, however, questions Lorenz's idea that peace might also be instinctual. Erikson feels that there is an element of intentionality, although he does not use that word, in the very process of selection. Two stags who enter the ritual choose in each other only a partner of equal strength. All of this is merely to question the whole area of instinct mythology and is not to imply an equivalence in man and animal behavior, but to point to a phenomenon other than aggression in the higher animals while keeping man and his behavior in another category. "But human aggression and human inhibition are in a different order." "Psychoanalysis and Ongoing History," p. 245.

20. Ibid., pp. 245–46.

21. *ISCG*, p. 57.

22. Evans, *Dialogue*, p. 30.

23. Erikson, *Identity: Youth and Crisis*, p. 311.

24. Evans, *Dialogue*, p. 71. Also see "Psychoanalysis and Ongoing History," p. 250.

25. Erikson, *Gandhi's Truth*, p. 433.

26. Erikson, *Insight*, p. 152. Italics his.

27. Erikson, *Life History*, p. 47.

28. Erikson, *Insight*, p. 155.

29. Erikson, *Childhood*, p. 277.

30. Erikson, *Childhood*, p. 278.

31. Ibid., pp. 278–79. Erikson uses social stratification here, where his more common phrasing is ideology.

32. Erikson, *Insight*, p. 156. This entire section, pp. 152–57, reviews the institutions

first discussed in *Childhood*. Also see *Identity: Youth and Crisis,* pp. 138–41.

33. *Insight,* p. 220.

34. Ibid., p. 225.

35. Many other words and concepts than can be discussed here are used to describe the kind of health that leads to responsibility: caring, householding, judiciousness, etc.

36. Erikson, *Insight,* p. 156. Italics his.

CHAPTER IX

The Religious Dimension

Erik H. Erikson is not a theologian nor does he claim to be a philosopher, and that is precisely what makes his interest in religion so significant. For Erikson, the religious dimension emerges out of life. For example, in and through the relationship of mother and infant, basic trust—one important element of the religious dimension—emerges.

Religion is not foreign to human experience, but is inextricably bound up in it. So that in observing and describing development, Erikson is forced to conclude that there is something More.[1]

What is the religion dimension? Only as Erikson sees it actually in the process of living, in observable ritual, and in the institution of religion is he willing to describe it. Yet it is there, and our task now is to attempt to explicate that which is integrally related to life, albeit an elusive dimension.

Why Religious Dimension?

Erikson himself dismisses the exclusively rational approach to reality as being too restrictive. He calls it the "Cartesian straight jacket."[2] In contrast to Descartes Erikson says, in effect, "I relate to social others, therefore I exist. I am acted upon and I respond, therefore I exist. I have a history, a family, and a culture into which I am born, and therefore I exist. I have a future toward which I am being driven (Freud), but which I also choose to redirect, and therefore I exist." In other words, there is more to life than thinking, though obviously rationality is an essential ingredient of life.

We have repeatedly noted Erikson's appreciation for both art and theory, intuition and scientific observation and verification. In a passage in his book *On Knowing: Essays for the Left Hand,* Jerome Bruner describes intuition as "the act of grasping the meaning or significance or structure of a problem without explicit reliance on the analytic apparatus of one's craft. It is the intuitive mode that yields hypotheses quickly, that produces interesting combinations of ideas before their worth is known."[3]

It seems to me that this is an apt description of much of what Erikson has done, not that his approach is exclusively one of intuition. It is not. The meanings have emerged, however. Inductively, the hypotheses have been yielded, and one of them is the meaning of religion.

Bruner goes on to say that this can only happen when there is a "playfulness" on the part of the observer. Yet that playfulness is within the bounds of certain rules. Intuitive does not mean irrational. It is not, after all, left-handed knowing that we have been suggesting as the only way, but an integration of the subjective and objective as they come together, a bridging of the hemispheres of the brain, and the production of a holistic view of life.

It is in Bruner's word "playfulness" that I take heart. For years I have struggled both inwardly and in college and graduate religion classes with explaining the place of religion in Erikson's thought. Erikson, himself, provided the release I needed from my own rational preconceptions when in *Toys and Reasons* he made his appeal for a greater playfulness in our approach to reality. The reader of this chapter is therefore invited to play with some very serious "toys and reasons," experiences of childhood and reflections of old age.

Shall We Dance?

Dancing is purposeful playing. Erikson begins *Toys and Reasons* with an observation about Plato, who saw "the model of true playfulness in the need of all young creatures, animal and human, to leap."[4] Then Erikson concludes the book: "Let me come back to Plato's suggestion that the leap is the model of playfulness, and let me wish us all great leaps—and firm landing."[5]

To explore the religious dimension in Erikson's scheme is to play, to leap, to dance. In my introduction I acknowledged my indebtedness to a friend who also happens to be an artist and a philosopher, Jerry H. Gill. One way of defining terms, and to indicate my direction in this chapter, is to refer to an article published by Gill, "On Knowing the Dancer from the Dance."[6] He has this to say:

> For meaning, or significance, always seems to transcend the empirical particulars that comprise it, but in a way which systematically eludes definition. There is no melody apart from notes, but melody is certainly more than what can be said about notes. A painting is comprised of line, shape, and color, but what is experienced by the viewer is not exhausted by an account of these factors. No matter how thorough the analysis of terms, meter, and syntax, the meaning of a poem is not fully explained. In each case the meaning is inextricably bound up with its particulars and yet it transcends them as well. The dance *is* the dancer, yet it is also *other* than the dancer.[7]

For Erikson, religion is inextricably bound up in the mutuality of trust. Religion is an institution which restores that trust, in part, through meaningful ritual. Yet religion is more than the sum of the particulars. The particulars point to a richness that cannot be explicitly defined, yet is tacitly understood. As a dimension of life, religion is interrelated with all of life. It interacts with, participates in, and yet is not exhausted by lived experience, which Erikson calls "the actual" as over against the real and the factual.

In all knowledge there is more known than can be said. There is an intangible, yet cognitive, element that demands explication while at the same time remaining inexplicable, or ineffable. Grasping this last point is vital as a safeguard against reductionism.

We shall begin exploring the religious dimension as we review the eight-stage development of the life cycle, concentrating upon those periods that are especially significant for the religious dimension. In the next chapter we shall review Erikson's own place as a religious person, and, finally, how we might use the Eriksonian term "Wholeness" to describe the religious dimension and to see the place religion has in the life of modern persons.

Signals of Transcendence in the Cycle of Life[8]

Erikson does not hesitate to use the word "transcendent." As we have mentioned and will continue to observe, precisely what he means by transcendent is not as clear as we might wish.

In Erikson's discussion of Jefferson's view of the Bible and Jesus, we read on the one hand that Jefferson wrote,

> "To the corruptions of Christianity I am, indeed, opposed; but not to the genuine precepts of Jesus himself. I am a Christian in the only sense in which he wished anyone to be; sincerely attached to his doctrines in preference to all others; ascribing to himself every human excellence; and believing that he never claimed any other."[9]

Here the humanity of Jesus without the traditional view of his divinity is obviously Jefferson's point of view. Jefferson considered himself a religious person by his commitment to the human excellence of Jesus. Later, however, Erikson himself writes of Jesus in these terms: "At the end, so it seems he felt, only the final agony of the crucifixion could verify his transcendent identity. Jefferson excludes the story of the resurrection, but it is clear that he believed in the singular presence of Jesus among men."[10]

Is "the singular presence of Jesus among men" what Erikson means by transcendence? In this instance, the answer is, "Perhaps." Yet he uses other terms that point beyond what one might call the "influence" of Jesus as the meaning of transcendence.

One of Erikson's most recent writings, to which prior reference has been made, is his "Reflections on Dr. Borg's Life Cycle." As one reads Erikson's interpretation of another artist (Bergman), the question quite naturally arises, to what extent does Erikson see himself in the elderly doctor's reliving of the life cycle? In fact, Erikson says "there is a 'connection' between the movie and my childhood, for Lund lies on the Ore Sund, on the Danish side of which (only twenty miles away) I spent the sunniest summers of my early years visiting my uncle's country houses and being taken for boat rides."[11] Here is an interesting bit of autobiography not found in Erikson's other books.

Dr. Borg, in Bergman's film, is retracing his life cycle. His primary companion is his daughter-in-law, Marianne, pregnant by his son,

Evald. She is thus symbolic of the new cycle of life about to begin, traveling in the company of the one living in the integrity vs. despair eighth stage of life. From an early discomfort from each other's presence (Borg refuses to let her smoke and they bicker about such minor matters as the weather) they grow into a cordial, meaningful relationship.

One scene involves an argument between two of the three young riders Borg and Marianne have picked up along the way. The two are male antagonists. All three are of the age in which some Fidelity is sought for in resolution of the identity crisis. One of the antagonists is a defender of God, a ministerial student; the other intends to be a doctor and he "plays the atheistic rationalist."[12]

When an argument centers on the question of how death should be approached, the scientific medical student interrupts Dr. Borg's reverie by asking him if he doesn't think that biological death should be faced very directly. Erikson reflects on what he sees in the film and writes:

> But Borg has been musing; and as Marianne lights his cigar for him (he, who had refused to let her smoke her cigarette), Isak (Borg), instead of offering an opinion, recites a poem: "Where is the friend I seek everywhere?/ Dawn is the time of loneliness and care . . ./ When twilight comes . . ." He asks Anders (the future minister) for help, but it is Marianne who continues: "When twilight comes, I am still yearning." And as Sara (the third youth), moved to tears ("for no reasons at all") says: "You're religious, aren't you, Professor?" Isak continues: "I see His trace of glory and power,/ In an ear of grain and the fragrance of a flower," and Marianne concludes, "In every sign and breath of air,/ His love is there."

Erikson continues,

> The poem, the setting, the tone seem to confirm the sense in which every human being's Integrity may be said to be religious (whether explicitly or not), namely, in an inner search for, and a wish to communicate with, that mysterious, that Ultimate Other: for there can be no "I" without an "Other," no "We" without a shared "Other." That, in fact, is the first revelation of the life cycle, when the maternal person's eyes shiningly recognize us even as we begin to recognize her. And it is the hope of old age, according to St. Paul's promise.[13]

Here a rational, critical question is answered with an aesthetic, religiously sympathetic poem. The claim is made clear, by Erikson, that there is a search in the developing human life cycle for that which transcends, "that Ultimate Other: for there can be no 'I' without an 'Other,' no 'We' without a shared 'Other.' "[14]

The Ultimate Other is significant for Dr. Borg in his crisis of old age and we must remember from our earlier chapter that wholeness has been missed, in part, by Dr. Borg, who lost his first love, and to compensate for that loss buried himself in his profession. There is no real sense of identity, the "I" without an "Other," a shared "Other," and for the first stage of life, there is the need for that "Other" who looks upon the infant, communicating a source of hope.

We shall retrace the life cycle here, in order to inquire into the religious dimension to be found in development. As indicated, not every stage lends itself as completely to the endeavor as the ones mentioned in Dr. Borg's experience. Where it is appropriate, however, I shall pause to elaborate on the significant ways in which the religious dimension is inextricably bound up in the cycle of life.

Everything Is All Right: Basic Trust

By way of review, let us recall Erikson's claim that the infant who is first securely held by a mother or parent substitute is in that very moment experiencing the cosmos in the only way possible. The primary first awareness of life will not be sight or sound (although these could be startling possibilities to the infant, e.g., the loud bark of a dog, etc.) but being held, supported; and the closeness, the warmth of the human mother (or father) who will love and care in partnership with another who has generated this new life. The depth of that love and care is communicated in various degrees of quality and it is experienced mutually by infant and mother.

In developing the ritual procedure beyond merely being held, Erikson describes the early morning greeting, the voice, the smiles, or possibly the absence of these, which introduces the very real possibility of mistrust.[15]

Erikson calls this ritual "a small but tough link in the whole formidable sequence of generations." Here mutuality begins. Both need the other, and that mutuality has already been described as a basic ingredient to ethical life. The need for recognition born in infancy is lifelong. It is perhaps at its most crucial juncture in the identity stage.

Erikson uses a number of religious terms to describe the mutuality of mother and infant. The child finds a sense of hallowed presence in the security of the mother's care. And this presence is of a quality of numinousness, a term usually reserved for deity. And that is precisely what Erikson means. The religious dimension is first experienced in and through the love and care of the mothering parent.

The ritual of lived, basic trust is institutionalized by society in its religions. This institution alone provides for those experiences of the numinous in which the believer expresses a sense of childlike dependence and is rewarded by the responding smile of deity. Separateness, transcendence, and "distinctiveness confirmed," are all included in religion's sense of the numinous. Therefore, Erikson concludes, we have in the religious institution "the very basis of a sense of 'I,' renewed (as it feels) by the mutual recognition of all 'I's' joined in a shared faith in one all-embracing "I Am.' "[16]

Is this a Freudian psychoanalyst? Yes, Erikson has identified with Freud, as we have seen. Unlike Freud, however, he does not see religion as regression that cripples the ego's ability to cope with anxiety. On the contrary, the ego, according to the above description of the ritual of basic trust, finds its confirmation and renewed strength in its experience with the numinous.

Freud was convinced that, in the religious regression to childlike dependency, guilt would be reawakened and thus further anxiety rather than renewed strength would develop. Perhaps Erikson's Luther study is partly responsible for his more favorable outlook on the type of religious experience that is wholesome and not used to exploit or manipulate. We see this clearly in his conclusion to *Young Man Luther*.

Erikson asks if it is really regression if in returning to one's early experience of basic trust there is renewed strength to face the future. Rather, he suggests that this kind of regression is actually a creative experience whereby "in retracing firmly established pathways, (one) returns to the present amplified and clarified."[17]

In a footnote at the end of this observation, Erikson refers his readers to "Ernst Kris' concept of a regression in the service of the ego."[18] Here it would seem that Erikson has no quarrel with the kind of regression experienced in the rituals of religion as long as the "I" is strengthened by means of the experience.

Another way of describing this basic trust is to say that there is an order in the universe which may be trusted. Any number of discussions could be cited in which Erikson expresses his belief in an orderly universe. Trust, hope, and faith, all qualities emerging in the very first stage of life, or growing out of it, are based upon an assumed order.[19]

A contemporary sociologist who has also written of trust and order is Peter Berger. His book *A Rumor of Angels* is subtitled *Modern Society and the Rediscovery of the Supernatural.*[20]

We have previously explored Erikson's approach to reality, noting his dissatisfaction with a rational, empirical, factual kind of exclusiveness in contemporary research, ignoring the intuitive. We have identified the intuitive throughout this book with Bruner's "left-handed knowing." Berger expresses a similar anxiety concerning modern man's supposedly sensate nature which is closed off to the possibility of experiencing the sacred. He says that those for whom the reality of the supernatural is meaningful today are in a "cognitive minority."[21]

Berger explores the options open to those who have this "minority" kind of knowledge, this awareness of the supernatural. These options are developed more clearly in his later book *The Heretical Imperative.*[22] The threefold possibility for those who are open to the religious perspective today is that of the "deductive, reductive, and inductive options."[23] The last of these is the one for which Berger opts in all of his writing. Out of the realm of everyday living there is the possibility of experiencing the supernatural.

While it is not our purpose to explore Berger's options in depth or even his inductive approach, it is significant for our interest to see how Berger identifies *signals of transcendence* in everyday life and how they relate to Erikson's thought.

Of the five signals that Berger describes in *A Rumor of Angels,* three relate clearly to the stage of basic trust. He contends that there is an argument from ordering, from hope, and for a moral universe, what he calls the argument from damnation.[24]

> By signals of transcendence I mean phenomena that are to be found within the domain of our "natural" reality but that appear to point beyond that reality. In other words, I am not using transcendence here in a technical philosophical sense but literally, as the transcending of the normal, everyday world that I earlier identified with the notion of the "supernatural." By prototypical human gestures I mean certain reiterated acts and experiences that appear to express essential aspects of man's being, of the human animal as such.[25]

Berger's human gestures are very similar to Erikson's rituals. One example from Berger will suffice. In the middle of the night a child awakens from a frightening dream, a nightmare. The room is dark and the dream has shaken her trust in reality. She cries out for her mother. "It is hardly an exaggeration to say that, at this moment, the mother is being invoked as a high priestess of protective order."[26] Hope is restored by her coming.

The mother's very presence helps the child to trust that all is well. This is communicated by what she does: taking the child into her arms, turning on the light, her words of comfort, and especially the implication, either spoken by the mother or assumed by the child, that now "everything is all right." Here is the argument from order. This *is* a trustworthy universe. Chaos and nightmares are its enemies, real though they may be. All of this is not said by the mother, of course, but here is a signal of transcendence Berger sees in an everyday kind of experience.

Berger is not alone in exploring the religious dimension in the common experiences of life. Langdon Gilkey has described what he calls "the dimension of ultimacy in secular experience."[27] "God, who transcends the secular, can yet be said to be apprehended in the secular in the sense that every significant joy and every compelling anxiety of ordinary existence reflect an apprehension of this dimension of the unconditioned, and the awareness of his presence or his absence."[28]

These two, Berger and Gilkey, are representative of those persons of other disciplines, Berger a sociologist and Gilkey a theologian, who are attempting to make sense of life from human experience, who see the religious dimension inductively as Erikson does. Both imply a basic trust posture toward existence and in that very trust find a basis for religious discourse.

Mistrust

But what of the negative pole of this first stage of life, mistrust? Is there a religious dimension experienced here as well? The answer is yes. The reality of the need in life to mistrust that which is harmful is certainly essential. And mistrust of that which is harmful, e.g., an uncaring mother, one who herself may not have been cared for and therefore never learned the mutuality of love, may religiously be interpreted as a form of evil.

Humanistic psychologists have often been accused of undue optimism. Abraham Maslow, for one, appears to chart a schedule leading to utopian peak experiences without the continued counterbalancing, as Erikson has insisted upon, of the negative.[29]

Erikson's insistence upon the negative polarity in everyday experiences and in every stage of life reveals an understanding of existence which parallels the religious understanding that both good and evil are present in our lives. If the positive experience of religion comes to us in and through the particulars of everyday living, so do the negative experiences. One does not sense a dualism in Erikson. Rather he has a holistic interpretation of reality in which good and evil interact dialectically. These forces are then responsibly directed into a sense of wholeness that includes both positive and negative realities.

Both poles, trust and mistrust, interact in any given situation, but to experience trust and to find the virtue of hope leading to faith, the child will need the care of the adult and the society committed to generating trusting children. Society will do just that when the religious institution fosters wholeness rather than being exploitative.[30]

When the institutionalized religion of any given society or era fosters mistrust, fear, and oppression, then, as in Luther's case, there is need for change in the religious institution of that society. In his "Epilogue" to *Young Man Luther*, Erikson cites three objects of quest of religious man. One object is that of the eternal provider; the second "is the paternal voice guiding conscience, which puts an end to the simple paradise of childhood and provides a sanction for energetic action."[31] Thirdly, man seeks "the pure self itself, the unborn core of creation, the—as it were, preparental—center where God is pure nothing. . . ."[32] This is the mystic self that is higher than the one needing provision or moral guidance. "These three images are the main religious objects. Naturally, they often fuse in a variety of ways and are joined by hosts of secondary deities."[33]

Religion as an institution revitalizes a person and a generation when it is at its best. When religion as an institution has itself regressed, however, or become stagnant and oppressive, then the institution itself will need revitalizing by a new generation, perhaps led by an innovator such as Luther.

It was in Gandhi that Erikson happily found a person who moved beyond ascetic-type religion and combined it with politics, seeing the two unequivocally related.[34] Gandhi is an example *par excellence* of a person who revitalized an institution, endowing it with the generativity that is essential for its value to succeeding generations. "The religious actualist . . . inevitably becomes a religious innovator, for his very passion and power will make him want to make actual for others what actualizes him. This means to create or recreate institutions. . . ."[35]

The Virtue of Hope

That the religious dimension is essential to Erikson's scheme is seen by the virtue which he designates as essential to the first stage of life: hope. In *Insight and Responsibility* he says: "What begins as hope in the individual infant is in its mature form faith, a sense of superior certainty not essentially dependent on evidence or reason, except where these forms of self-verification become part of a way of life binding technology, science, and new sources of identity into a coherent world image."[36]

As noted in discussing the virtues of the trust stage in Chapter III, it is not so much specific hopes that Erikson intends, but the capacity for hope. This is a significant differentiation to make because hopes are not unlike ungrounded wishes. Erikson does not seem to mean wishful thinking, although his words in some instances do sound that way.[37]

But Erikson means by hope that basic stance or posture toward life which feels assured, because of what it has learned (to trust), that it may face the future with confidence. It *is* the child's identity, if we take literally these words: "The shortest formulation of the identity gain of earliest childhood may well be: I am what hope I have and give."[38]

Thus, where trust finds a favorable ratio over mistrust, hope emerges as a strength, a virtue, and together these become the capacity for faith.

Inasmuch as it is religion that guarantees the trust and hope, in Erikson's theory, it is well to recall that St. Paul said that our knowledge, speech, and prophetic insights would all pass away, but that there are three great lasting qualities (called the virtues of the Christian faith), faith, hope and love, and that the greatest of these is love.[39] While love will be discussed at a later stage, let us consider the significance of Erikson's findings and Paul's claim, as they apply to hope and faith.

Hope is so dominant a theme in the Judeo-Christian religion that whole theologies have been centered around it.[40] The other enduring virtue cited by Paul is faith. According to Erikson, there is an ability to have faith only for that person in whom trust and hope have developed. "Hope is the ontogenetic basis of faith, and is nourished by the adult faith which pervades patterns of care."[41]

Again, we can only pause before this concept of faith which finds its origins in the capacity for trust and hope. Faith is, in a sense, synonymous with religion and a theme so vast that all we can really do at this point is to observe that here, in and through the particular qualities of trust, hope, and faith in the human child, the religious dimension emerges. In theology, faith relates to God as provider for humanity's needs and is generally treated under the theme of Providence. In the Judeo-Christian religion faith is a personal trust in God that Erikson found to be intriguing in *Young Man Luther*. That faith, for Luther, in spite of doubts, guilt, and the mystery of God's ways, liberated him from all bondage to religious institutionalism. Thus faith, as a personal relationship to God, is supported in Erikson's thought as the product of trust and hope.

Donald Capps has developed the relationship between each of Erikson's stages, the virtues, and the comparable theological themes developed by Paul W. Pruyser. The following chart lists these and serves as a suggestion for those who are interested as to how the religious dimension may be further developed:

CORRELATION OF THEOLOGICAL AND PSYCHOSOCIAL THEMES[42]

Theological Themes	*Psychosocial Themes*	*Human Virtues*
(1) Providence	Trust vs. Mistrust	HOPE
(2) Grace or Gratefulness	Autonomy vs. Shame and Self-Doubt	WILL
(3) Repentance	Initiative vs. Guilt	PURPOSE
(4) Vocation	Industry vs. Inferiority	COMPETENCE
(5) Faith	Identity vs. Identity Diffusion	FIDELITY
(6) Communion	Intimacy vs. Isolation	LOVE
(7) Vocation	Generativity vs. Stagnation	CARE
(8) Awareness of the Holy	Integrity vs. Despair	WISDOM

For the religious person the life of faith is never a final achievement. Again, we cite St. Paul, who expressed it most vividly in the words, "I do not do what I want, but I do the very thing I hate."[43] The life of faith is a struggle, and I would include this, too, as a signal of transcendence, found first in the daily existence of infantile life. To point to this fact is also to remind ourselves of Erikson's insistence that the stages be seen in their true polarization and not as a Pollyanna achievement chart. I quote again from "Dr. Borg's Life Cycle":

> If Hope is the first and fundamental human strength, emerging from Primal Trust versus Primal Mistrust, it is clear that the human infant must experience a goodly measure of mistrust in order to learn to trust discerningly, and that there would be neither conviction nor

efficacy in an overall hopefulness without a (conscious and unconscious) struggle with a persistent temptation to succumb to hopelessness.[44]

As noted in discussing the virtue of the trust stage, it is not so much specific hopes Erikson intends, but the capacity for hope. This is a significant differentiation to make, because hopes may be interpreted in a way sounding like the ungrounded wishful thinking of a Santa Claus mentality.[45]

Erikson is speaking of a stance, a basic posture toward life, one in which trust has found a favorable ratio over mistrust, and therefore hope emerges. In this first stage of life, Erikson identifies the three components of trust, hope, and faith. Here we find signals of transcendence, hints, or dimensions of ultimacy. This is an interpretation of the meaning of life that does not content itself with rational explanation. It demands an understanding which transcends, and in so doing signals a higher order than the biological development of naturalistic science. The religious dimension emerges in the particular events and experiences of infant existence.

Childhood: Free Will and Play's Transcendence

The three stages beyond basic trust vs. mistrust may be grouped together—autonomy, initiative, and industry—or to use the corresponding virtues that relate more precisely to religious themes—will, purpose, and competence.

Erikson identifies elements in each of these periods in terms applicable to what we have called the religious dimension. The problems of the will, of free will, and willfulness are human to be sure. They have long been the subject of religious discourse as well, however. In Capps' chart, above, he lists Grace or Gratefulness as the theological themes that relate to a child's possible overextension of autonomy in which the legitimate will of another is violated. Or, if autonomy has lost out to shame and doubt, only the kindness and giving of another will restore a sense of self-worth.

Erikson introduces the religious dimension at this stage when, in *Toys and Reasons*, he notes that the social institution of law regulates the interference of one will with another. Our court system assures us of the limits to which we may extend our willfulness and it protects us from the intrusions of others.

This sense of discrimination between the right and the wrong in terms of will begins in the autonomy stage and ends, in Erikson's words, in "the Last Judgment."[46] However literally we may choose to take Erikson's use of the idea of the Last Judgment, the point is that there is a religious significance and parallel that gives meaning to everyday experiences, a signal of transcendence.

Gleason discusses the relationship of this stage to toilet training. That experience affects a child's sense of worth, and may foster either autonomy or shame. It ultimately introduces the authority question. Erikson and all Freudian psychologists relate this stage to toilet training, but Gleason's point is that we have here more than an everyday experience of life. Authority is accepted, rejected, or bargained with in some degree of negotiation in lifetime experiences. In religion also, the question of authority is a paramount one, relating to the issue of free will and the autonomy of persons in relationship to deity.[47]

We can only hint at the many directions the religious dimension of this stage offers for development: We could begin with the story of humanity's primal removal from the Garden for its sin of allowing its will to supersede that of God's; the institution of the law; or the story of the willful prodigal exercising his autonomy but ultimately coming to himself and finding Grace, the theological theme Capps relates to this stage. While Erikson calls identity the central neurosis of our time, others have focused upon this matter of the will. Rollo May, in his books, and especially in *Love and Will*, points to the religious significance of will. He writes, "Indeed, the central core of modern man's 'neurosis,' it may be fairly said, is the undermining of his experience of himself as responsible, the sapping of his will and ability to make decisions. . . . It is this inner experience of impotence, this contradiction in will, which constitutes our critical problem."[48]

Erikson comments on the relationship of theology and the biological-psychological points of view regarding will in *Young Man Luther*.[49] It is a theme he treats a number of times in that book. He finds the reformer's honesty about human willfulness, especially sexuality, to be refreshing and a contribution to the total reformation and liberation that Luther led. In fact, the freedom that Luther championed religiously for all mankind in his discovery of a gracious God as over against the stern demanding God of the pre-Reformation era is compared by Erikson to the inner freedom Freud contributed to our thinking with his formulations.

Emerging conscience in childhood introduces the psychological and theological themes of guilt, dividedness, alienation, and restoration. Concerning Luther, Erikson writes, "Conscience is that inner ground where we and God have to learn to live with each other as man and wife."[50]

We must also recall that childhood is the time for play. Real play, to be sure, but play that finds purpose in discovering freedom to imagine and pretend, to adopt roles, and to suspend even childhood responsibilities. Erikson's own propensity for playfulness with words and ideas is one of the things that makes his writings delightful for many of us.

Berger has called play itself another signal of transcendence in everyday life. It is a time when we bracket off the seriousness of time and work. We literally suspend the rules in order to experience other dimensions of life. "Joy is play's intention. When this intention is actually realized, in joyful play, the time structure of the playful universe takes on a very specific quality—namely, it becomes eternity."[51]

Here, and elsewhere, Berger sounds much like Erikson as he notes that adult play restores a sense of the hope and trust of childhood. He does not use those precise words, but the idea is clear, and so is the signal. The capacity to play points to a dimension of life transcending the regularity and responsibility of pedestrian plodding. Play is a signal of transcendence.

The development of the school age in which a sense of competence emerges relates to humanity's whole sense of vocation, of being endowed with special gifts, and called to fulfill a role and a purpose for which he or she alone was created.

The theological theme of vocation, the vast literature on the Protestant work ethic, the question of man's purpose answered by Freud, as noted previously, to work and to love, all of these introduce dimensions of ultimacy, pointing to meanings transcending the arena in which they are daily played out.

The stage about which Erikson has written most and is so widely quoted, however, is that of identity. Are there religious dimensions here, and if so, what are they?

Youth: Search for Meaning and Commitment

The interrelationship of identity, ideology, and fidelity precludes a simple dealing with one without bringing in each of the others. I shall attempt to organize the following discussion according to those categories, however. Previously, in discussing identity, we have noted the contemporary social situation and Erikson's reason for discerning the identity crisis to be crucial for our time. In considering the religious dimension of the identity vs. identity-confusion stage, a different perspective will be the starting point.

William James's classic Gifford Lectures were given in the years 1901–02 at the University of Edinburgh, and later published as *The Varieties of Religious Experience*. James was an American pioneer in the field of psychology of religion. He, too, approached the subject inductively. In his work, however, he cites another American psychologist, E. D. Starbuck. Starbuck's research showed that adolescence was *the* time in life when most religious conversions occur. Contemporary society's awareness of the appeal of the cults to youth would also seem to support that claim. Erikson's theory provides a reasonable answer to anyone who would question why conversion of a religious nature tends to be so prevalent among youth.

Emerging from childhood dependence, the protectiveness of the family and society, the structure of school, and the assurance that being a child is OK, the physically changing youth begins also to face changes in social and economic expectations. He looks both inward and outward in asking the question, "Who Am I?"

As the youth in the identity-crisis years asks that question, he hears many responses from his environment. How can these be sorted out? Which are authentic and which are not? Is there any one authoritative, transcendent answer? Is there one meaningfulness transcending the many meanings? Is there an ultimate purpose to which he may give himself with the kind of finality and completeness symbolized by the word Fidelity?

I personally feel that it is significant that Erikson selected for his prime case study of the adolescent, the Protestant reformer Martin Luther. But this is not the only reason we perceive a religious dimension in Erikson's fifth stage of development.

Let us move directly to the core question raised above: Is there an ultimate answer to youth's search for social verification? We see a number of instances in which Erikson indicates the seriousness of that issue. Perhaps his discussion of Jefferson, in one of his latest books, is a place to begin. The Founding Fathers had before them, according to Erikson, the choice of two identities. The choice in that historical period had eternity as one of its poles. All historical identities have that transhistorical dimension which "relates man to what is forever contemporary, namely, eternity."[52]

The choice before Jefferson and all the colonizers was between identities symbolized in the mottos "kill and survive," or "die and become."[53] It is the first motto which represents the empires of history. It is always the temptation of any nation to exclude all opposition in staking out its claim to existence. The obvious example of opposition for Jefferson and the founders of this nation is the Indian who occupied the land before its "discovery" by the white man.

Over against the motto of "kill and survive" is "the other, the transcendent effort at insuring salvation through conscious acceptance of finiteness."[54] This is more akin to Erikson's wider identity than is the motto "kill and survive," but it is not the whole story. In the end there must be an accommodation between the two extremes. Yet, to further flesh out the religious identity, let us hear Erikson's description: "This way of identity is personified by the great religious leaders who in their own words represent the naked grandeur of the I that transcends all earthly identity in the name of Him who *is* I Am. The motto of this world view could be said to be 'die and become.' "[55]

The point of Erikson's description of these two identities, one committed completely to space and time and the other including transcendence, is to note his conclusion that a middle ground is possible. We find it in Mahatma Gandhi. In Erikson's words, "It bespeaks Jefferson's, the nation builder's, classical sense of balance that he attempted to accommodate the postrevolutionary and the dominant religious identity to each other—for the sake of a new actuality with infinite possibilities."[56]

The ethical question to which this identity issue leads in his book *Dimensions of a New Identity* is whether America in our time will adopt the "kill and survive" motto, or see its way through difficult negotiation and commitment to a "die and become" motto. The latter would lead to a wider identity inclusive of opposition, inviting the counterplayers to participation in a new vision.

The religious dimension of identity is clear in this historical example. Jefferson, who saw Jesus as his example and model, attempted to forge a new identity for Americans in accommodating "die and become" with "kill and survive." Another way of expressing the pole of eternity and historical realities as they relate to identity is to note that, for Erikson, Jefferson was an example of Protean man. This is a favorite symbol for many today who would espouse a kind of relativism without commitments. But for Erikson this is just the point concerning mythological Proteus. He could change his many appearances only because he had a core identity from which he could move.[57]

This brings us to a second component of identity, equally significant for the religious dimension, that of ideology. There is no real sense of identity without a meaningful world image to which the self relates.[58]

That ideology is not monopolized by political parties is hardly an endorsement of religion as an ideology. It is Erikson's contention for persons such as Luther and Gandhi, however, that religious faith provided them with the necessary ideological ingredients.

In *Young Man Luther* he defines ideology in terms inclusive of a religious orientation. It is "the tendency at a given time to make facts amenable to ideas, and ideas to facts, in order to create a world image convincing enough to support the collective and the individual sense of identity."[59]

According to Erikson, Luther found "his identity in the act of lecturing," and out of those lectures came a new concept of "man's relation to God and to himself."[60] What Erikson then describes is a kind of passivity on Luther's part. Certainly lecturing cannot be separated from Luther's study of the Bible in order to lecture. There is a surrendering of self to God in prayer, and Luther is reborn "out of the matrix of the scriptures."[61] In lecturing on the Bible, Luther is feeding students as a mother feeds her children. The Bible, like a mother, feeds him and he in turn feeds others. In both the feminine imagery and Luther's receptivity, a passive side of Luther's new identity is clear.[62]

The signal of transcendence here for Luther is that his identity and ideology are inseparably related to his religious discovery. His identity was reborn "out of the matrix of the scriptures." He knew himself to be the person he was as he discovered a new concept of God as a loving Father.

We can therefore see that theology, for some, may become, as it did for Luther, the core of a new ideology. This is not to equate theology and ideology as identical. Comprehensive theology does include, however, more than doctrine about God. It has to do with life, creation, nature, society, guilt, forgiveness, acceptance, and certainly the need for a return to the basic trust of childhood, believing that there is an ultimate order and that, in spite of evil's reality, life makes sense. Without that return to basic trust there can be no positive identity. In Luther's case, religion provided the necessary ingredients for a new ideology.

Peter Homans, in his essay "The Significance of Erikson's Psychology for Modern Understandings of Religion,"[63] discusses this very theme. He is not uncritical of what Erikson has done. He sees a reductionism on Erikson's part, but also an affirmation of theology. He does, however, indicate the way in which theology may relate to ideology:

> On the one hand, Erikson reductively interprets Luther's theology as ideology. Luther would not accept the view—nor do Lutherans or Protestants accept the view—that theology is "really" ideology. On the other hand, Erikson also affirms theology, for ideology is said to be a necessary ingredient in the formation of a stable identity.[64]

The degree to which ideology and theology relate to one another is perhaps a debate that will continue for some time. Ultimately it becomes dependent upon our definition of terms. My point is that there is a sense in which the adolescent youth, according to Erikson, must have an ideology, and that theology offers a world view for contemporary youth just as it did for Luther.

Finally, let us note the third element in addition to identity and ideology: fidelity. To return to the contemporary scene, we cite two authors who support the need for this quality in our youth culture.

In the work of the late J. F. T. Bugental, a humanistic psychologist, synonyms for fidelity are loyalty and devotion. Bugental feels that devotion, especially, is a desperate need for our historical era. In his book *The Search for Authenticity*, he says: "By devotion I mean the aware decision to orient one's being as fully as may be possible toward the expression of some value experienced as centrally significant to one's being."[65] Later he elaborates on this need: "Devotion is a choice to focus one's being in a certain way, to bring one's faith, commitment, creativity, and love into coordination with a particular value and purpose."[66]

Like Erikson, Bugental has sought for an answer to the question, What does it mean to be healthy, vital, and alive? He indicates that his orientation is less that of therapist for the sick than that of—as the title of his book makes plain—one who is searching for authenticity. His emphasis upon devotion is similar to Erikson's observation that those sensing clarity about their identity will also be characterized by qualities of loyalty, or fidelity.

Another contemporary author who has been widely read is Victor Frankl. The title alone of his major work suggests the need for fidelity if life is to make sense, *Man's Search for Meaning.*[67] It was his devotion to love that gave him meaning and the ability to survive the life threats of existence in a Nazi concentration camp. It is Frankl's will to meaning, the emphasis upon intentionality which reminds us of that essential ingredient to identity, fidelity.

An illustration from the protest era of the '60s will perhaps be helpful in tying together the importance of fidelity in identity, of being, as Erikson described Luther, one who means what he says and is at one with his ideology in his commitments.

A young man who was nominally religious joined the Poor People's March on Washington in 1967. In a sense he took his identity from the crowd as much as from his own inner convictions. He was with his church group and they held banners and signs, but he let others do the carrying; he was content to be in the march.

As the group moved toward the Lincoln Memorial they were "eight abreast," excited, happy, and enthusiastic. And then he looked up and saw the TV cameras. He did not want that public recognition and quickly made his way out of the line of marchers. In his words, "I was in the march for as long as it didn't count, but when I was about to be identified with it, I slipped out."

At the end of the day, as he reflected upon his own actions, he did not feel like an authentic person. He had not been at one with his commitments, he had been a deserter, and the occasion led him to a new resolution to begin to mean what he said and say what he meant.[68]

Fidelity is a concept with religious overtones. It has about it the sense of ultimate concern and commitment that Paul Tillich, the theologian, has explicated. As with the concept of hope, theologians have built entire systems around fidelity. It is a theme we find in the writings of Gabriel Marcel.[69] Perhaps J. H. Oldham expresses it most clearly in the title of one of his significant books on the meaning of Christian faith, *Life is Commitment*.[70]

Certainly no one can read the Gospels without sensing that to be a disciple of Jesus is to leave all else in order to pledge fidelity to him alone. H. Richard Niebuhr called Jesus the "One in the Many," and spoke of "faith as confidence and fidelity."[71]

We would not deny the possibility that other ideologies may also call for such fidelity. Certainly Marxism has demonstrated that sense of identity in its followers. When an ideology makes that demand, however, it is a religion if we accept Paul Tillich's concept that true religion is that about which we are ultimately concerned, that to which we have pledged our fidelity.

Trust and hope are inevitably related to the fifth stage in all of Erikson's discussions of identity. If they are signals of transcendence earlier, they are reinforced by identity's needs. In Erikson's own words, "In adolescence, the quality of *fidelity*, the capacity to be loyal to a vision of the future, incorporates such infantile trust, while the capacity to have *faith* emerges as a more focused hope tuned to an ideologically coherent universe."[72]

To summarize, I turn not to Erikson or his interpreters, but to writing by a college student from a religion class that was struggling with Erikson's concepts. The student wrote as follows:

"Trust"

First, there was the coming . . .
some of us for the first time
some of us for the last time
but all of us knowing
it was only passing through
and the moments of anticipation
of sensing how big was
the world
that we were somehow
to make of this year
together
and the moments of doubt
and of wondering
"will we all come out looking the same?"
and the moments of thinking
we finally had it all figured out
how it would be
and then . . .
having to settle back
in the not knowing.
That is the context
of
all
trust[73]

Adulthood: The Bridge to Transcendence

As noted in developing the eight stages of the life cycle, Erikson has less to say about adulthood than of childhood and youth. While admitting the need for more research, it is also necessary to recall that implicit in understanding the earlier stages is the role of adult parents, educators, the generators of the social institutions that are the product of the rituals of childhood and youth. Therefore, adulthood has not been ignored.

If children experience the religious dimension in the hallowed presence of the mother's face, then there is obviously a numinous quality in the maternal person. Erikson has clearly indicated that in this mutuality both mother and child are activated and enlivened by the very quality of the love relationship, which participates in transcendence.

Love is the virtue of the sixth stage, intimacy vs. isolation. Once identity is more favorably sensed than identity confusion, the young adult is secure enough to give away what has been precariously gained. Such love is more giving *of* self than demanding *for* self. Such love is suggestive of the agape of Christian tradition, love which gives because that is its nature rather than because of the worthwhileness of the object loved. Christian faith defines God as love and states that we are only able to love because we have been the objects of divine love.[74]

In Christianity, love is the highest of all virtues. In Erikson's highlighting of love for that stage immediately following the maturing of self in the identity stage, and in his emphasis upon mutuality, one could easily make a case for another signal of transcendence or a dimension of ultimacy, to use either Berger's or Gilkey's terminology.

Erikson's stress upon mutuality often reminds me of the works of another artist, the poet-philosopher Martin Buber. For Buber it is only in the mutuality of the I-Thou experience that reality is known. In fact Buber uses the word mutuality to describe the I-Thou relationship. The Other of an I-Thou relationship is a Thou and not just an It precisely because the quality of mutuality exists. And God is experienced where there is the depth of mutuality of an I-Thou encounter.

In his book *Between Man and Man* Buber writes:

> Above and below are bound to one another. The word of him who wishes to speak with men without speaking with God is not fulfilled; but the word of him who wishes to speak with God without speaking with men goes astray.
>
> There is a tale that a man inspired by God once went out from the creaturely realms into the vast waste. There he wandered till he came to the gates of the mystery. He knocked. From within came

the cry: "What do you want here?" He said, "I have proclaimed your praise in the ears of mortals, but they were deaf to me. So I come to you that you yourself may hear me and reply." "Turn back," came the cry from within. "Here is no ear for you. I have sunk my hearing in the deafness of mortals."[75]

In this, as in other portions of Buber's writings, we have a parallel to Erikson's emphasis upon the importance of mutuality. For Erikson, it is experienced first by the infant in relation to the mother, a hallowed presence. At the close of life, looking for the face through the glass darkly, the mutuality of vision seeks revelation in that which transcends the ordinary dimensions of human existence.[76]

If the rituals of healthy religion foster trust in the child, we must recall in this consideration of the adult stages that it is the generative adult who institutionalizes the ritual in religion. If play must be allowed for in childhood, and is itself a signal of transcendence, as Berger has suggested, it is the mature adult who makes the provision for play and in so doing participates in play as its sponsor, if not its model.

Actually, for Berger, it is not childhood play alone that is specified as a signal of transcendence. Adults who suspend the rules of the serious game of life in order to experience the limitless boundaries of imagination in play also transcend time and self in so doing.

In Berger's words,

> In later life play brings about a beatific reiteration of childhood. When adults play with genuine joy, they momentarily regain the deathlessness of childhood. This becomes most apparent when such play occurs in the actual face of acute suffering and dying. It is this that stirs us about men making music in a city under bombardment or a man doing mathematics on his deathbed.[77]

If it is the adolescent who searches for an ideology in which theology may be an integral part, as it was for Luther, Gandhi, and others, then we must recall who it is that is to provide the ideology. It is the generative adult. Don Browning has thoughtfully developed the significance of Generative Man,[78] as noted earlier. Although we have suggested that no one stage in Erikson's system should be made normative, as Browning does with the seventh stage of generativity, nevertheless his work is worth careful consideration.

To generate rather than stagnate is certainly a dimension of creativity hinting at a Creator who created in his own image. He endowed his creation to be co-workers with himself, as the Judeo-Christian tradition has long taught. Generativity, with care as its virtue, signals a dimension of ultimacy beyond the ordinary, to combine Berger's signals and Gilkey's dimensions of ultimacy.

And what of the religious dimension of the final stage, integrity vs. despair or disgust? According to Langdon Gilkey, any time we stand before mystery, the unexplainable, the joyous, the sad, birth or death, we may experience the dimension of ultimacy.[79]

We have noted previously Erikson's hesitancy to discuss that which transcends life beyond death.[80] He does speak of facing it with integrity rather than despair, with the renewed hope of childlike trust rather than hopelessness.

In one of Peter Berger's later books he introduces a signal of transcendence beyond the five outlined in *A Rumor of Angels*. Here is an appropriate counterpart to Erikson's stage of integrity vs. despair. It is perhaps all the more significant as Berger describes the city of New York as a signal of transcendence. The Statue of Liberty offers hope to all who would become citizens, stepchildren, if you will, in the American family. The magic of the city is a reminder that man is basically playful, and legitimately so, says Berger. Play was one of his earlier signals of transcendence and he alludes to that here:

> A Chicagoan will know what to say to all of this: These people can't be serious. Precisely! The opposite of being serious is being playful; the invincible playfulness of New York City is, I believe, in itself a signal of transcendence. Homo ludens is closer to redemption than homo faber; the clown is more a sacramental figure than the engineer. . . . Anyway, I think it is good theology to expect the Kingdom of God to be a very playful affair—and in that, at the very least, it will resemble New York more than Chicago![81]

Repeating his claim that transcendence may be discovered in and through the particulars, the everyday experiences of life, Berger concludes his book with these words:

> There is a route I drive regularly, between Rutgers University in New Jersey, where I teach, and Brooklyn, where I live. It crosses

from Staten Island over the Verrazano-Narrows Bridge. It has often occurred to me, especially in the evening when the light is soft and the contours of visual reality seem to lack firmness, that the entrance to heaven may well look something like this wonderful bridge, with its majestic arcs and its breathtaking vistas on both sides. I wish for all of us that we will be part of this traffic in the evening of our lives, that we will be forgiven the toll at the gate, and that we will know that, in the city on the other side of (the) bridge, what awaits us is home. I, for one, will not be overly surprised if the gatekeeper addresses me in a Brooklyn accent.[82]

The cycle of life begins in trust and ends there. Integrity, or the old man's reasons, as Erikson interprets Blake, "are at their best, blessed (again) by playful childlikeness."[83] By trust.

In his section on "Shared Visions," in *Toys and Reasons*,[84] Erikson relates the way in which Christian theology is "seen" in the painting *Annunciation*. He reminds his readers that "An Annunciation, of course, is a visitation announcing the Eternal Prospect, the expectation that the child to be born will be the Child who will forever save in man some portion of what childhood promises: The 'Kingdom.' "[85]

His detailed application of the painting to life and ideology need not be repeated here, except to note his conclusion, for it significantly relates to our chapter's theme on the religious dimension of life. "Perspective at its best gives a transcendent order to what is visible from a given position in space, and leads from what is closest to a point revealed in the far distance. . . . We treasure Rembrandt for illuminating so grandly and so simply the transcendence of everyday hereness."[86]

This chapter has been an exploration of the life cycle, an attempt to interpret tacitly what may be known of transcendence in the particulars of the here and now. We shall turn more explicitly in the concluding chapter to make some assertions about Erik H. Erikson as a homo religiosus, and to ask some questions about modernity's readiness to look once more at the religious depths and dimensions of human experience.

NOTES

1. In reading Erikson, one is often reminded of that earlier American psychologist who made an inductive study of religious experience, William James. For his conclusion that there is something More than the physical, observable reality, see *The Varieties of Religious Experience* (New York: Collier Books, 1961) pp. 393–402.
2. Erikson, *Insight*, p. 163.
3. Jerome Bruner, *On Knowing: Essays for the Left Hand* (New York: Atheneum, 1971), p. 102.
4. Erikson, *Toys and Reasons*, p. 17.
5. Ibid., p. 175.
6. Jerry H. Gill, "On Knowing the Dancer from the Dance," *Journal of Aesthetics and Art Criticism* (Winter 1975). Throughout this section I am indebted to Gill, not only for the article on the dance, but for his interaction with me in discussions and for his chapter "Religious Experience" in a book not yet published. In my chapter on "The Religious Dimension," I highlight the relational aspect of religion. For both Gill and Erikson, relational, interactional, responsive, historical, and mediated truths are essential. Gill finds, as I do, these factors especially significant for the Incarnational theology of the Christian tradition in which God became a particular person, yet remained transcendent. Our purpose here is not to develop these aspects of philosophy of religion, but to apply them to Erikson, and the reader is encouraged to explore more deeply the writings of Jerry H. Gill.
7. Ibid., p. 125.
8. The term "signal of transcendence" is used by Peter L. Berger, *A Rumor of Angels: Modern Society and the Rediscovery of the Supernatural* (New York: Doubleday, 1969), pp. 65ff. It will be discussed below.
9. Erikson, *Dimensions of a New Identity*, p. 40.
10. Ibid., p. 47.
11. Erikson, "Reflections on Dr. Borg's Life Cycle," in *Daedalus*, p. 4.
12. Ibid., p. 9.
13. Ibid., p. 11.
14. Ibid.
15. Erikson, *Toys and Reasons*, p. 85.
16. Ibid., pp. 89–90.
17. Erikson, *Young Man Luther*, p. 264.
18. See ibid., p. 277, n. 10.
19. Erikson, *Insight and Responsibility*, p. 140. Also see pp. 136, 139, 152, 175.
20. Peter Berger, *A Rumor of Angels*.
21. Ibid., p. 7.

22. Peter Berger, *The Heretical Imperative* (New York: Anchor Press/ Doubleday, 1979).

23. Ibid., p. 61.

> The deductive option is to reassert the authority of a religious tradition in the face of modern secularity. . . . The reductive option is to reinterpret the traditions in terms of modern secularity, which in turn is taken to be a compelling necessity of participating in modern consciousness. . . . The major disadvantage is that the tradition, with all its religious contents, tends to disappear or dissolve in the process of secularizing translation. (p. 62.)

> The inductive option is to turn to experience as the ground of all religious affirmations—one's own experience to whatever extent that is possible, and the experience embodied in a particular range of traditions. (pp. 62–63.)

24. Berger, *A Rumor of Angels*, p. 66–86.

25. Ibid., pp. 65–66.

26. Ibid., p. 68.

27. Langdon Gilkey, *Naming the Whirlwind: The Renewal of God Language* (Indianapolis and New York: Bobbs-Merrill, 1969), pp. 305ff.

28. Ibid., p. 364.

29. Abraham H. Maslow, *Toward a Psychology of Being*, 2d ed., an Insight Book (Princeton, N.J.: D. Van Nostrand, 1962).

30. Erikson, *Identity: Youth and Crisis*, p. 83.

31. Erikson, *Young Man Luther*, p. 264.

32. Ibid.

33. Ibid.

34. In the past, religious man put himself in total opposition to political and technological man and strove for inner peace through noninvolvement, sacrifice, and faith. He often cultivated masochistic propensities; his ideal was saintliness. . . . Now, I think that Gandhi quite consciously established a new trend in combining politics and religion, and this at least temporarily with great psychological acumen.

> Evans, Dialogue, p. 77. Also see Erikson, *Gandhi's Truth*, p. 22.

35. Erikson, *Gandhi's Truth*, p. 399. Also see pp. 435–36.

36. Erikson, *Insight and Responsibility*, p. 153. We shall discuss Erikson's allowance for a possible exception to faith later.

37. "Hope is the enduring belief in the attainability of fervent wishes, in spite of the dark urges and rages which mark the beginning of existence." Erikson, *Insight and Responsibility*, p. 118.

38. Erikson, *Identity: Youth and Crisis*, pp. 106–107.

39. I Corinthians 13, New Testament.

40. For example, Jurgen Moltmann, *The Theology of Hope* (New York: Harper & Row, 1967).

41. Erikson, *Insight and Responsibility*, p. 118.

42. Donald Capps, *Pastoral Care: A Thematic Approach* (Philadelphia: Westminster Press, 1979), p. 114. The theological themes Capps uses are developed by Paul W. Pruyser, *The Minister as Diagnostician* (Philadelphia: Westminster Press, 1976).

43. Romans 7:15, New Testament (RSV). This one sentence does not communicate the depth of the struggle as much as the context.

44. Erikson, "Dr. Borg's Life Cycle," p. 23.

45. However, there are times when Erikson substitutes the word "wishes" for hopes as in note 37 above. What he there calls "fervent wishes," he identifies with "Primal Trust," and that gives the *depth* of the sense in which he may substitute wish for hope.

46. Erikson, *Toys and Reasons*, p. 92. He refers to the Last Judgment here as a ritual.

47. John H. Gleason, Jr., *Growing Up to God: Eight Steps in Religious Development* (Nashville: Abingdon Press, 1975), pp. 38–48.

48. Rollo May, *Love and Will* (New York: W. W. Norton, 1969), p. 184.

49. Erikson, *Young Man Luther*, pp. 162–63.

50. Ibid., p. 195.

51. Peter Berger, *A Rumor of Angels*, p. 73.

52. Erikson, *Dimensions of a New Identity*, p. 41.

53. Ibid., pp. 42–43.

54. Ibid., p. 42.

55. Ibid., p. 43. Italics his.

56. Ibid., p. 44.

57. Ibid., p. 106.

58. Ibid., p. 95.

59. Erikson, *Young Man Luther*, p. 22. Erikson is obviously leaving open the possibility of an ideology based upon scientific or political thought as well as religious. For our discussion, the significant point is that he does not exclude religion as being antithetic to science or politics.

60. Ibid., p. 206.

61. Ibid., p. 208. In using the word passive for Luther as I have, I do not mean the same kind of passivity Erikson finds in the mysticism of Tauler. See *Young Man Luther*, p. 189.

62. Ibid., pp. 208–209.

63. Peter Homans, ed., *Childhood and Selfhood*, pp. 231–63.

64. Ibid., p. 257.

65. J. F. T. Bugental, *The Search for Authenticity* (New York: Holt, Rinehart and Winston, 1965), p. 355.

66. Ibid., p. 356.

67. Victor E. Frankl, *Man's Search for Meaning* (New York: Washington Square Press, 1963).

68. Elizabeth O'Connor, *Eighth Day of Creation* (Waco, Tex.: Word Books, 1971), pp. 43–44.
69. Gabriel Marcel, *Creative Fidelity* (New York: Noonday Press [div. Farrar, Straus & Giroux], 1964).
70. J. H. Oldham, *Life is Commitment* (New York: Association Press, 1959).
71. H. Richard Niebuhr, *Radical Monotheism and Western Culture* (New York: Harper, 1943), pp. 16–23.
72. Erikson, *Life History*, p. 209.
73. Bill Brinkman, Eastern College, February 24, 1974. Printed by permission.
74. The whole New Testament and the thrust of Christian theology support this claim. Specific references which directly state that God is love and the source of our love are these: I John 4:8, 19.
75. Martin Buber, *Between Man and Man* (New York: Macmillan, 1967), p. 15.
76. Erikson, "Reflections on Dr. Borg's Life Cycle," p. 24; *Young Man Luther*, pp. 263–64.
77. Peter Berger, *A Rumor of Angels*, p. 73.
78. Don Browning, *Generative Man*. See especially his three chapters on Erikson, pp. 145–228.
79. Langdon Gilkey, *Naming the Whirlwind*, pp. 305–413.
80. See n. 38, Chapter VI.
81. Peter Berger, *Facing Up to Modernity* (New York: Basic Books, 1977), p. 217.
82. Ibid., pp. 219–20.
83. Erikson, *Toys and Reasons*, p. 112.
84. Ibid., pp. 121–75.
85. Ibid., p. 123.
86. Ibid., p. 126.

CHAPTER X

Erik H. Erikson:
Homo Religiosus?

One might ask, "Why the Latin? Why not just say, religious man or, in less sexist language, person?" Of course, my use is actually Erikson's designation for Luther, Gandhi, and others. Nevertheless the question is appropriate and may be answered in a number of ways.

First, if one reads *Young Man Luther* it becomes apparent that Erikson became immersed in the Latin through his Luther research. In Chapter 6, "The Meaning of 'Meaning It,'" Erikson traces the history of Christianity since Augustine, and Latin terms appear *en masse! Homo naturalis, Homo spiritualis, concupiscentia,* are just a few of the Latinisms appearing on one page and are perhaps second nature to one who has studied Reformation history and its roots in classical Christianity.[1]

Or perhaps Erikson's reason is no different from any contemporary who chooses to identify a concept by using what may be thought of as a more generic language. Berger speaks of *homo ludens* for man the player. H. Richard Niebuhr, whose ethics we have related to Erikson's position, saw responsibility as being symbolized in the Latin term, *homo dialogicus.* This symbol, for Niebuhr, was a development beyond *homo faber,* man the craftsman, or man the maker, and *homo politicus,* man the citizen, the one who obeys laws. *Homo dialogicus* was a new symbol of man the responder, responsible man.[2]

This second reason for reverting to Latin seems to point more directly to Erikson's use of *homo religiosus*. The term has very special meaning. To speak of religious man is rather common. To speak of *homo religiosus* is not so familiar and therefore may be more purposeful. In other words, Erikson may intend to communicate another dimension or depth to the concept of men and women having a religious nature.

"Homo religiosus" is, in a sense, a term transcending common speech and the reality the words point to is that of persons who experience transcendence in a special way in their lives. Referring to the eighth stage of life, Erikson writes at one point: "This integrity crisis, last in the lives of *ordinary men*, is a lifelong and chronic crisis in a *homo religiosus.*"[3]

Erikson goes on to say that a *homo religiosus* is so different from "ordinary men" that there is almost no place for him in the social order. His interests and understanding are far advanced, far beyond the norm. "We know little of Jesus of Nazareth as a young man, but we certainly cannot even begin to imagine him as middle-aged."[4]

For Erikson, *homo religiosus* is symbolic of a special kind of person, beyond the "ordinary," and the question we face is this: does it apply to Erikson himself? Is his appreciation for the religious dimension more than ordinary? This chapter will deal with that question. The words of Erikson just quoted are a reminder of the symbol we have used for Erikson, stepchild, never quite feeling at home in the family.

First, very briefly, we shall review what we have seen. Secondly, a less precise question will be addressed, "What have we sensed?" Third, we'll take some soundings. What have we heard, or what do we hear, from others who study Erikson's views on religion? This issue is especially significant in its context of modernity, or what some have called postmodernity. Still others describe our age as that of being totally secular or post-Christian. Is it? How does Erikson's position with regard to the religious dimension fit with the spirit of the age, the closing decades of the twentieth century? Finally, how does Erikson's concern for wholeness relate to religion?

What We Have Seen

In Chapter II we referred to the fact that when Erikson disclaimed an ability to be at home in so intellectual a discipline as psychoanalysis, it was Anna Freud who told the young skeptic, whose vocation was primarily that of an artist, "You might help to make them see."[5] Through Erikson's eyes we have "seen" the development of the life cycle through eight stages. He clearly perceives an order in this process, though not one to be rigidly prescribed or circumscribed. There is an order, however.

The order Erikson sees in human development may not be simply dismissed as evolutionary, for beyond physical, natural development there are ethical dimensions that are essential to human development.[6] These are the virtues that emerge with each healthy resolution of the eight crises of the life cycle. It is therefore essential that each generation give to the next an ethical sense and reliable institutional counterparts to the virtues. Chief among these institutions is that of religion for the preservation of the strength of the earliest stage, if trust, hope, and faith are to emerge. We have seen Erikson describe the reality of this order, its need for the ritual and institution of religion, and can therefore conclude that, in his view, religion is essential in the development of the life cycle and the race. We have also seen him postulate that there may be substitutes for religion, and this, too, must be seen clearly. This appears to be only a possibility, however, and never developed in actuality. We shall deal more with his disclaimer regarding the essential nature of religion in the section to follow, regarding what we have sensed.

Secondly, we have seen his development of the identity concept as being crucial to our age. Identity is not privatistic in Erikson's scheme but psychosocial. One finds one's identity in relation to others and ultimately to the Other. What does it mean to say "I"? It is to encounter the deity as the ultimate Other, along with others who attribute to him this eternal quality of numinousness. In Erikson's words, "That is why God, when Moses asked Him who should he say had called him, answered: 'I AM THAT I AM.' "[7]

Erikson's use of the word "God," above, raises the question of meaning. Does he ever really say that there is ontological reality to God? Responses to this question vary. We may note, however, a number of interesting references in Erikson's writings without belaboring the point.

In his dialogue with Huey Newton the question of God arises. Newton had implied that people create their own God, or dispose of him when they assume control themselves. Erikson responded with the observation that he could not understand Newton's concept of God. Could there exist a common brotherhood without a single fatherhood? And if we want the brotherhood to survive, can we dismiss the reality of that fatherhood? Then Erikson concludes with the words, "There is something very simple to be said here which is that both a father and a god are irreversible."[8]

Because these comments about God occur in the context of the question of fatherhood and brotherhood, we must not exaggerate their implications. Erikson and Newton were speaking on more than one level. The question of earthly fathers being needed for earthly brothers may signal a transcendent notion of a Father God for some. That appears to be Erikson's point, or, if not Erikson's, it is mine.

A second example of Erikson's use of the concept of God occurs in an extension of his earlier autobiographical comments, a section entitled "Postscript and Outlook" in *Life History and the Historical Moment*. Erikson acknowledges that psychoanalysis has explained our need for a deity. (I shall return to this passage to compare it with an earlier formulation in our section on "Sense.") Erikson sounds generally within his Freudian tradition as he acknowledges man's need for a god, adding that for both existential and evolutionary reasons humanity may need such a god. "For a community of I's may well be able to believe in a common fund of grace or destiny only to the extent that all acknowledge a Super-I that each I partakes in: a Being that Is."[9]

We must be clear here. He is not necessarily saying that the Being Is. He is saying that there may be good reasons for such a belief. For that reason, many have interpreted Erikson as one who fits within the traditional Freudian interpretation of religion, that our concept of God is a projection of our need for a God.

But just when we think we have "seen" what Erikson means, we have another picture. It is not clear, but it does admit to a different interpretation. When Erikson attended a conference at the Divinity School of the University of Chicago in 1975, Peter Homans read a paper on "Erikson's Understanding of Religion."[10] Don Browning wrote a review of that conference in *Criterion* (Spring 1976). He told of Homans's paper and of his conclusion that Erikson is more positive than Freud in his concept of religion as projection, and then Browning adds these words:

> Erikson surprised the conference by taking some exception to the idea that he held the view that the origin of religion was projection. . . . He cautioned the audience against seeing projection in religion in analogy to paranoid projection. "In religion, man does not just project something onto nothing. He is probably projecting something onto some reality which is actually there. There may even be an interaction between man's projection and this reality."[11]

Here the issue is before us very clearly as an enigma. What we see and what we sense may be antithetical. However, Erikson sounds as though he finds it plausible to believe in the reality of the Being, God. Yet his use of the word "probably" keeps him from being unequivocal about the issue. Theology is not his field. Psychology is. We see his reason for avoiding dogmatism by returning to his earlier essay. We hear him say, "At any rate, what religion calls grace and sin transcend the goals of therapy—that is, the relative comfort of adaptation and the reasonable management of guilt."[12] It is not just the goals of therapy but its province which religion transcends, and Erikson chooses not to speak authoritatively in disciplines outside of psychoanalysis. That there are strong hints as to his position we may infer and interpret as we choose and as we have. So much for his references to God, at this point.

Erikson is, then, aware of the aid religion can provide in the establishment of basic trust and identity. In the integrity stage, also, religion has a role to play: helping us to face the reality of death, without fear, at the end of our one and only life cycle.

In a tribute to theologian Paul Tillich, who apparently was his friend during his years at Harvard, Erikson had this to say:

> When he was among us, Paul Tillich combined his opposites— and his occasional extremes—in what he called his *glaeubiger Realismus*, his blend of realism and faith, his utter sensual and spiritual Hereness. He has now gone beyond the borderline—unspeakable and inexorable—of all borderlines. From our side of it, we who

> knew him can say with assurance that as long as we are here, Paulus
> Tillich will be here.[13]

"Unspeakable and inexorable" is Erikson's way of describing that which lies beyond the life cycle. That it is a mystery beyond our understanding is what we see clearly in all his writings.

Still another aspect of Erikson's thought which is explicitly developed is the importance of ritual in life. Religious ritual rekindles basic trust and is essential for infancy, identity, and integrity. Every stage, of course, draws up into it the strengths of the previous stages. These three, however,—the trust, identity, and integrity stages—seem to be key in Erikson's development of the need and usefulness of ritual.

Finally, there is his growing interest in the ethical. This has been treated previously and needs only to be commented upon here. The Golden Rule is Erikson's baseline for ethics. But we must consider that he does reformulate the Rule as we have come to know it in the Christian tradition. Admitting the variations in its use among religions and cultures, Erikson simply states, "My base line is the Golden Rule, which advocates that one should do (or not do) to another what one wishes to be (or not to be) done by."[14]

The change that Erikson makes in the Golden Rule is a certain implication of self-interest in the pursuit of helping another. This may or may not be considered by some to be in keeping with the Christian tradition which has at its center the love that loves because that is its nature rather than because of the worthiness of the one loved or other possible consequences. Erikson clearly believes that the exercise of the Golden Rule will strengthen both the doer and the recipient of the action.[15]

The point of greater significance for us is that he selects a religious concept for his baseline in ethics. And in defense of his position, while self-interest may be included in his reformulation, so is self-love in the Christian tradition when we are told to love our neighbors *as ourselves.* Erikson's reformulation may not be as foreign to the Judeo-Christian tradition as it is to some interpreters of that tradition.

The place of religion for Erikson is clearly seen in the areas we have identified as well as others. We move on now to another hemisphere, that of left-handed knowing—what does one intuitively sense when reading Erikson regarding the religious dimension? Of course sense often emerges from sight and there is a reciprocal relationship by which they cannot be clearly separated. After all, have we not made the point that integration of left and right, not bipolar orientation, is our goal?

What Do We Sense?

To speak of sensing Erikson's relation to religion is quite in keeping with how he also defines that phenomenon. In his book *Young Man Luther* he squarely faces the traditional "dichotomy of psychoanalysis and religion," saying, "I will not approach it like a man with a chip on each shoulder. Psychology endeavors to establish what is demonstrably true in human behavior, including such behavior as expresses what to human beings seems true and feels true."[16] Here, both the rational and intuitive are included in Erikson's description of psychology. He sees a difference, however, in the way in which psychology and religion are to be approached.

In contrast to psychology, "religion, on the other hand, elaborates on what *feels* profoundly true even though it is not demonstrable. . . ."[17] He goes on to state that it is not his purpose to criticize religious dogma as it relates to Luther. His purpose is to investigate how the isms of the Reformation era offered Luther in one form or another ideologies that would or would not be useful in his quest for identity.

The previous section of this chapter highlighted Erikson's equivocation with regard to the possibility of deity, and that is the first thing I would note about what we sense in Erikson's treatment of religion in general. There is ambiguity. On the one hand he sometimes speaks of mankind's creating its own gods.[18] Then there is the statement made in Chicago, referred to above, that we may project our concept of deity but that we probably project "something onto some reality which is actually there."[19]

Inasmuch as this latter statement was made more recently than many of Erikson's other comments regarding projection, and inasmuch as it is his latest book, *Toys and Reasons*, which gives so much credence to the validity of ritual, especially religion, as that which restores trust, it may be that Erikson's position is not so much one of ambiguity as it is that of development.

That Erikson may have changed his mind regarding the validity of the religious dimension can in no way be argued conclusively. There is this interesting change in wording, however, in one of his revisions of earlier remarks. In Erikson's 1970 *Daedalus* article on "Autobiographic Notes on the Identity Crisis," he wrote:

> Behind all this may well be another and wider identity crisis. Psychoanalysis in line with the Enlightenment, has *debunked* the belief (and the need to believe) in a deity. It has suggested that the god image "really" reflects the infantile image of the father, as, indeed, it does in transparent cultural variations.[20]

In revising that article for his book *Life History and the Historical Moment*, the gist of what psychoanalysis has done was not changed, but the sense of Erikson's own attitude is felt in his change of wording. The book was published five years later than the *Daedalus* article. The same passage reads as follows: "Behind all this may well be another, an existential identity crisis. Psychoanalysis, in line with the Enlightenment, has offered a *rational explanation* for the belief (and the need to believe) in a deity."[21] (The third sentence quoted from the journal source remains unchanged.) The words that strike me as implying a more sympathetic attitude toward religion are *debunk*, which is stricken from the earlier version, and its substitute, *rational explanation*. Rationally explaining something is an entirely different undertaking from setting out to debunk it. In light of Erikson's statement in Chicago regarding our projection of a deity as being projection onto something which is probably there, the change in wording takes on new significance.

Other ways in which one senses a tendency toward a more sympathetic view of religion in Erikson's writings are in his attention to religious figures, use of religious terms, and statements about religion that leave one sensing the kind of nostalgia he often describes in others.

The two outstanding religious figures to whom Erikson has given a great deal of attention are Martin Luther and Mohandas Gandhi. It is noteworthy that in referring to both of these persons Erikson admits a sense of identification. In a chapter of *Life History* entitled "On 'Psycho-Historical' Evidence," Erikson refers to a "pervasive aspect of a reviewer's identification with his subject."[22]

Just prior to that statement he has said that "my transference to Gandhi no doubt harbored an adolescent search for a spiritual fatherhood, augmented by the fact that my own father, whom I had never seen, had taken on a mythical quality in my early years." Then he goes on to relate his interest in Gandhi and Luther. Erikson states that in the experience of writing his book on Luther, he vicariously lived out some of his " 'protestant' impulses." Moving along in his interest in the adult stages, Gandhi was an appropriate subject. His students suggested that this work might well be called, " 'Middle-Aged Mahatma.' "[23]

What were the "protestant" impulses Erikson lived out vicariously in his writing of *Young Man Luther?* From a psychological vantage point one could easily make a case for Erikson as a reformer of Freudianism. After all, we have noted how he has worked to free psychoanalysis from its inwardness, downwardness, and its looking back to origins. His protests on the psychoanalytic level have been symbolically nailed to the doctor's door. Erikson wants to free psychological man from enslavement to the id or superego. Man is a responsible being. It is not our drives from within or our commands from without, but our choices made in a balanced ego-oriented identity that count for Erikson. His protests are obviously not exhausted by this brief summary.

But we must return to the question. What "protestant" impulses was Erikson referring to in his autobiographic comment above? We have reflected upon the question from a psychological perspective. What about the religious? Our clue here comes from an interview Robert Coles once had with Erikson. There he stated, "What some genuinely Lutheran elements in Christianity have come to mean to me is indicated in my book on young Luther."[24]

The reader is forced to return to *Young Man Luther* and ask just what he senses of Erikson's own identification with "some genuinely Lutheran elements in Christianity." A key chapter in that book, for me, is one to which I have often referred, Chapter VI, "The Meaning of

'Meaning It.' "[25] It is in that chapter that Erikson takes us, with Luther, to Rome. The whole of the Christian tradition is summarized from the Pauline era to Luther's day. Then the reader is given insight into the struggle of Luther's crisis of identity and faith, along with its resolution, his liberation from past bondage. Not that Luther ever became free from all of the negative polarities of the eight stages of life. He did not, and Erikson, as always, includes both poles. Luther's way of expressing the polar tension is described by Erikson with understanding. "The whole person includes certain total states in his balances: we are, Luther proclaimed, totally sinners (*totus homo peccator*) and totally just (*totus homo justus*), always both damned and blessed, both alive and dead."[26]

Our best clue to Erikson's identification comes with this explanation: "Meaning it, then, is not a matter of credal protestation; verbal explicitness is not a sign of faith. Meaning it, means to be at one with an ideology in the process of rejuvenation. . . ."[27]

One can only sense that in tracing Luther's identity crisis and resolution which (as for all life crises) was never fully resolved, Erikson identifies with the liberator. Just how much of the Lutheran ideology is a part of that liberation is open to speculation. Erikson does not tell us. We sense closeness, however, in several ways.

In his Preface to *Young Man Luther*, Erikson tells of spending a night with a friend in a little village in Germany. He was a wandering artist at the time. His friend's father, a Protestant pastor, said table grace at breakfast, repeating the Lord's Prayer. Erikson recalls that it was the first time he remembers really having heard that prayer. More significantly, he remembers that on that morning he "had the experience, as seldom before or after, of *a wholeness* captured in a few simple words, of poetry fusing the aesthetic and the moral. . . ."[28]

Erikson goes on to indicate the importance of that event in the "corner of Europe from which Schweitzer came."[29] He suggests that perhaps the whole book on Luther is kind of a tribute to that spring morning. Here the aesthetic, political, and religious dimensions fuse in imagery, but the sense is one of nostalgic identification with Erikson's subject matter.[30]

We have dealt at length with what we may sense of Erikson's

identification as a homo religiosus in his work on Luther. Similar feelings are aroused in reading and rereading *Gandhi's Truth*. He makes the claim there that "Gandhi, I think, would make his own those pronouncements of Luther which I once singled out as the essence of religious actualism . . . ."[31]

From Luther and Gandhi as a base there are a great many other religious persons who have become the focus of Erikson's observing eyes. An exhaustive list is not necessary here, but the following names occur enough within Erikson's writings to deserve inclusion in any attention given to the religious figures he has studied: William James, St. Francis, Thomas Jefferson as an editor of the New Testament, Søren Kierkegaard, Paul Tillich, and Jesus.

As well as religious figures we would mention the religious terms Erikson uses, such as sin, grace, and contrition, or the images and configurations that surface so often, such as the smiling face of God in mutuality, or his use of the cross in therapy. There is a sense of the homo religiosus that is *felt* in reading Erikson as well as what we see more directly in his formulations.

Soundings

In any attempt to review a person's life, works, and orientation, attention must obviously be given to how others see and hear and interpret. This section on soundings, therefore, will sample how a few others have responded to Erikson.[32]

We shall begin with Robert Coles, one of Erikson's earliest interpreters and students. In the section of his book on Erikson's writing *Gandhi's Truth*, Coles quotes Erikson's reference to Gandhi who said he wrote as the Spirit moved him. Gandhi went on to say that the great steps he had taken in his life were directed, he believed, by the Spirit.[33]

Erikson's own response is this: "If I did not believe something of this kind, I would not be writing this book."[34]

Coles concludes, "In a way, that is that—except for one thing: *Gandhi's Truth* is also meant to show the truth a psychoanalyst (*and* a historian *and* a writer *and*, in his own way, a religious man) comes upon when inspired by one like the Mahatma."[35] Coles rightly describes Erikson's multiple interests. Note that he calls Erikson, "in his own way, a religious man." Knowing the identity theory of Erikson, we might ask, "Could we expect Erikson to be a religious man in any other way?" Coles dedicated his book on Erikson "To Cesar Chavez, who like Erik Erikson ... struggled to make things clear...."[36]

From Coles, one of the earliest interpreters of Erikson, we jump to the contemporary scene to mention a number of scholars who have found in Erikson a homo religiosus for modernity, people such as Don Browning and Peter Homans.

For Browning, generative man is normative. After carefully examining the options offered by Philip Rieff in Psychological Man, Norman Brown in Dionysian Man, Erich Fromm in Productive Man, Browning concludes that Erikson's Generative Man is normative for our time:

> Generative man is a religious man. His religion provides him with a commanding world image and a vigorous ritual enactment which sums up, yet somehow renews and enriches, the rituals of everyday life, both those of his children and of himself, and those of his own childhood. His religion sanctions him to indulge in a "generalized generativity of institutions."[37]

Browning is concerned that our understanding of Erikson as a homo religiosus be seen in these terms of generativity and not just in identity. As Erikson shifted his interest in later years to ethical concerns, so Browning interprets his importance in terms of the larger milieu and Erikson's vision of the wider identity that may be generated.

Peter Homans edited the book *Childhood and Selfhood: Essays on Tradition, Religion, and Modernity in the Psychology of Erik H. Erikson.* One of the fundamental problems which Homans sees in Erikson's interpretation of religion is between "the *sui generis* nature of religious reality," and "the view of religion as the projection of some infrastructure."[38] Homans interprets Erikson as trying to have both positions and is critical of him at this point.

When Erikson speaks of religion as transcendence, he is identifying with the theologians who consider religion to be in a category of its own, as having a *sui generis* origin. Homans believes, however, that Erikson's theory rests primarily upon a notion of religion as projection. We have pointed out Erikson's ambiguity in this matter and can only affirm that Homans raises an issue that needs clarification.

My view is that Erikson would not agree to the need for an either/or position. Religion may be projection on man's part, but if it is projection onto something that is real, a Being who is God, then transcendence is a reality that is beyond the scope of our rational or objective sciences to explore. Yet it is a reality.

Paul Roazen, a Freudian scholar to whose book we have referred earlier,[39] is not nearly as hesitant to take a position. He writes that "Erikson is now a believing Christian. . . ."[40] Later he refers to Erikson as having undergone a religious conversion.[41] His basis for such conclusions are not very clear and only Erikson himself could verify their accuracy.[42]

In our soundings of how others have responded to Erikson's interest in religion, we must note a collection of essays discussed briefly in an earlier chapter on Erikson's concept of psycho-history, *Encounter with Erikson: Historical Interpretation and Religious Biography.*[43] Of the many contributions this collection of essays makes to our study, perhaps one of the most interesting is that of Donald Capps.

It is Capps's conclusion that the argument about Erikson's psycho-history is misplaced. When the historians quarrel about the accuracy of Erikson's data, and the psychologists question using their methodology to analyze historical personages, the problem is a matter of misunderstanding what Erikson is about.

The genius of Erikson, according to Donald Capps, is that he has given us a new genre of biography. More in line with the old hagiography (lives of religious persons) but a vast improvement upon it, Erikson has devised a new genre "which we may call religious biography."[44]

For this reason, that Erikson has created a new genre of religious biography, as well as for many others outlined in the book, Capps and his co-editors have concluded that Erikson has made an important contribution to the field of religious studies. They see him as having had a

> catalytic effect upon religious studies. He has been responsible for shaping religious understanding and imagination, and has made aspects of religious consciousness accessible. In its present and future shape, religious studies is something other than it would have been had there been no Erik Erikson, and had he not worked long,

persistently, and creatively in the fields of psychoanalysis and psychohistory.[45]

Several other interesting observations are made in this volume. Walter Capps writes the concluding essay, "Erikson's Orientation as Process Philosopher."[46] In defending Erikson from his critics, who sometimes accuse Erikson of reducing what is essentially theocentric to the egocentric, especially in his *Young Man Luther*, Capps has this to say:

> What Erikson's critics sometimes fail to realize, however, is that *Young Man Luther* offers description and interpretation rather than explanation. Erikson was not concerned to account for religion or to explain it away. Rather, he was simply opening up such areas of inquiry to new lines of interpretation, and more as a lesson to psychologists than to theologicans [*sic*] and church historians.[47]

While making this defense, Capps also concedes that Erikson did introduce a new approach. "Yes, in doing this, Erikson did indeed come to arrange hallowed materials, theologically speaking, around an 'alien' point of orientation."[48]

With Capps, however, I would question Erikson's critics. Was he really all that reductionistic in his treatment of *Young Man Luther*? Or is it time for theologians to be more open to the light that other disciplines may shed upon their subject matter? Must faith forego psychological understanding? It has historically interrelated and interacted with philosophy; why not with psychology? To understand the psychological dynamics of religious experience is not to explain away the sacred. Erikson is quite careful to avoid just that in his refusal to deal with dogma. My personal conviction, somewhat in defense of Erikson, is that we need more, not less, bridge-building between religion and life if meaning is to be found in the midst of our secular society, meaning which for religion has transcendent dimensions.

Walter Capps also has a section in his conclusion dealing with "Current Religious Change."[49] He discusses the crisis of belief and the unrest in religious circles, the transition of many religious persons, nuns and priests, changing both outwardly and inwardly. There has been a sense in which religious persons have felt their transitions in faith to have affected their self concept, especially when they have tried to hold "to the tenets of the faith without being in touch with their 'true selves.' "[50] Capps develops the need in these persons to integrate their formerly authoritarian position (superego) with the new found feeling level (libidinal forces), into "a perceptively functioning ego."[51]

An example of Capps's point, for me, is an article appearing in the *Christian Century* a few years ago entitled "Returning to the Fold: Disbelief Within the Community of Faith." Its author, Donald E. Miller, traces his own life pilgrimage from an early orthodoxy through the normal changes of postadolescent rebellion. Aware of his need, however, he continued to search for a meaningful ideology and orientation to life. He traces his pilgrimage, his decision to continue in the ritual, especially that of "the sacrament of holy communion and the liturgical forms that surround it. I suppose that this 'beliefless obedience' sprang from the realization that though I could not control my feelings of belief, I could at least exercise some control over my behavior."[52]

What is of special interest is Miller's own analysis of what was going on within him. His search was not so much for beliefs, or experience of a narcissistic variety. What he wanted was "an identity—or more broadly stated, a tradition in which I could locate myself. . . . I wanted (almost desperately) a transcendent identity—not 'transcendent' so much in a metaphysical sense as in a psychosocial sense, with metaphysical overtones."[53]

He goes on to say that he was searching for a community with stability and permanence. "The whole movement back to a commitment to the church started to make more sense when I reread Erik Erikson's discussion of identity as being tied to the discovery of an ideology, a belief system, which gives one a transcendent fix on the meaning and purpose for existence."[54] Miller also feels that Erikson's understanding of the need for a moratorium during which time alternatives may be explored makes sense.

There are others, as well, who have found in Erikson a homo religiosus for our time.[55] And what of our time? Is modernity, or postmodernity, a time when Erikson with his left- and right-handedness will be heard? We must briefly consider why Erikson may be a prophet, as a homo religiosus, in a scientific age that many envisioned would answer all questions including the mystery of transcendence.

Modernity

Does religion make sense in the modern world? That is the question being asked by technology's children. However, technology's children may not be all that ready to accept their parentage. In quest of identity, they are rebelling quite naturally against their computerized heritage. Has the Enlightenment been all that enlightening if it has locked us into a rigid objectivism, scientism, and rationalism?

Throughout this book we have used as a referent the thesis of another developmental psychologist, Jerome Bruner. Knowing is not confined to the right-handed method of the verbal, rational, and scientifically verifiable approach to reality. Knowing is also a left-handed experience of discerning subjectively, intuitively, and interpreting metaphorically.

We have seen how Erik Erikson appropriately fits into this framework with his disciplined subjectivity and refusal to accept the Cartesian straight jacket. Do modern men and women make sense of this interpretation?

Definitions of modernity and postmodernity are endless. We have referred to Peter Berger, a contemporary sociologist, a number of times; he is one of many who wrestle with the issue explicitly stated in the title of one of his books, *Facing Up to Modernity*.[56] We noted earlier his signal of transcendence in the conclusion of that work, the bridge from New Jersey into New York, symbolic of the bridge from the city of man to the city of God.[57]

Peter Homans and his colleagues have also struggled with the issue of the relationship of the religious dimension to modernity.[58] In Homans's chapter "The Significance of Erikson's Psychology for Modern Understandings of Religion," he makes this claim: "Erikson's psychology is above all else a theory of modernity—that is, a theory of how the modern person can live in the modern world."[59]

H. Paul Santmire, in his Epilogue to *Critical Issues in Modern Religion*, entitled "The Birthing of Post-Modern Religion,"[60] claims that we are now living in a postmodern age. The Cartesian formula of a rational base for everything, including religion, is no longer acceptable. Rational control has proven to be an impossible dream. Erikson's concept of trust makes more sense for contemporary persons.

Erikson himself does not specifically analyze modernity or postmodernity. He does describe the alternatives to identity in our rootless, alienated, lonely world. He concludes his book *Life History* with these words: "Beyond anxiety and fear we may face that existential dread which awakens universal resources of faith and fellowship."[61]

The context of Erikson's work, our historical era, has been and is one of existential dread. In developing his theory and vision of a new identity that will not ignore the malignancies of the past, he does direct us to new "resources of faith and fellowship."

What are those resources? Some would feel that faith in psychoanalysis itself is enough. It is true that Erikson often speaks of outworn ideologies, of religions that have lost their vitality, or which have become exploitive.[62] Where those religious institutions are revitalized, however, and ideologies rethought, new resources of faith will be forthcoming.

Peter Homans expressed it well in a footnote in the introduction to the book he edited. Referring to Erikson's own conclusion to *Childhood and Society*, "Beyond Anxiety," Homans states:

> In this chapter . . . Erikson discusses the anxieties of contemporary Americans and offers his clinical knowledge as a solution. In doing so, Erikson assumes that a properly reformulated interpretation of psychoanalytic theory can meet the need of a modern world for meaning—a need created by the decline of the power of traditional religion to bind the individual into a meaningful social structure. What modernity lacks is stability, the key to stability is tradition, and the key to tradition is religion.[63]

Modernity's need is clear. It is religion. In 1950 and again in his 1963 edition of *Childhood and Society*, Erikson may have assumed that "a properly reformulated interpretation of psychoanalytic theory can meet the need of a modern world for meaning." He may still believe that. However, he has definitely added the religious dimension to psychoanalytic theory, and his later writings have at least opened up a new option in how one interprets his understanding of religion.

In Pursuit of Wholeness

Throughout this book the concept of wholeness has been emphasized as one of Erikson's concerns. We have noted his use of wholeness over against totalism and the limits of pseudospecies. These will be briefly reviewed below. In the religious context, what does wholeness mean for Erikson, however? And why is it a concern? For reasons that will become apparent, we conclude our study with this discussion of his pursuit of wholeness.

In an earlier chapter we noted Erikson's interest in Jefferson's version of the Gospels. He appears intrigued by the fact that this political innovator would take the time and have the enthusiasm for such a project. He also finds Jefferson's inclusions and exclusions to be provocative.

Erikson chides Jefferson for completely overlooking Jesus' healing ministry. To Erikson it is significant that Jesus was a healer. In his first book, *Childhood and Society*, he discussed the fact that the clinician of today has his heritage in religion. " 'Clinical' once designated the function of a priest at the sickbed when the somatic struggle seemed to be coming to an end, and when the soul needed guidance for a lonely meeting with its Maker."[64]

While there has been a change in our thinking concerning the use of the term "clinician," Erikson suggests that "it is regaining some of its old connotation, for we learn that a neurotic person, no matter where and how and why he feels sick, is crippled at the core, no matter what you call that ordered or ordering core."[65]

When Erikson reviews Jefferson's edition of the Gospels, therefore, he is critical of the omission of Jesus' healing ministry. In fact he states that he cannot forgive Jefferson for such an oversight even if it was quite intentional to support Jefferson's own view that Jesus was not a miracle worker. In words that reveal deep conviction, Erikson writes, "To me, the decisive therapeutic event in the Gospels appears in Luke 8:48, and Mark 5:25–35. It is the story of a woman who had lost not only blood for twelve years, but also all her money on physicians who had not helped her at all."[66]

Erikson proceeds to quote the event from the Gospel record. The woman, who had heard of Jesus' healing power, joined the crowd pressing in upon him. She felt that just to touch the hem of his garment would be sufficient. When she did touch him, Jesus was aware that virtue had gone out of him and asked who it was that had touched him. His disciples found it hard to believe that he could even ask who had touched him when so many were pressing against him, but he clarified the situation by looking directly at the woman, who in fear fell at his feet, telling her story of seeking health from many doctors, spending all her money, and not being healed. Jesus' response to her was that her faith had made her *whole* and that she should go in *peace*. These italicized words are of greater significance than they may appear, a fact we shall develop later.

As Erikson ends his quotation of the Gospel story he writes, "This story conveys themes which renew their urging presence in each age: There is the assumption of certain quantities lost and regained and with them a quality of wholeness."[67]

After continuing to relate this theme to Jefferson, Erikson states that "Transformations in the over-all sense of identity . . . bring with them new approaches to sickness and madness."[68] The ellipsis just above represents a parenthetical statement in which Erikson reminds his readers that the Greco-Roman world and the new Christian kingdom were at polar opposites and that a transformation ensued that had its effect upon the American identity as well as the ancient. This idea of Christianity's transforming identity, or culture, and helping to produce a new identity is a familiar one to the current religious scene in which one of H. Richard Niebuhr's books develops a fivefold typology regarding the relationship of Christ and culture.[69]

While it is beyond the scope of our interests to fully discuss Niebuhr's typology, it is significant that Erikson here appears to fit more into Niebuhr's fifth category, in which Christ and the Christian kingdom are transforming the ancient and American world, or, at least for Erikson, its identity. This, in contrast to Jefferson, whose concern to keep Jesus free from traditional miracle-working concepts would fit more readily into a Christ-of-culture type, an accommodating kind of relationship.

In concluding his treatment of this part of Jefferson's identity, Erikson comments on the fact that the transformation referred to represents "an internalization of the cause as well as the cure of sickness ('your faith will make you whole') and thus by a greater ethical awareness on the parts of both healer and to be healed."[70]

Erikson's final comment is also informative to us in our quest to understand his religious orientation. It shows once again that religion and psychology are not polarized in his thought, but synthesized. "How, in our time, insight thus joined faith as the therapeutic agent of wholeness, even as the theorizing about mysterious quantities continued—that, too, we will return to in the second lecture."[71]

The two themes that we wish to develop at this point are, first, that there is a pursuit on Erikson's part, and second, that the goal is wholeness.

In discussing Erikson's vision of wholeness as it relates to religion we must again be clear that Erikson is not always pleased with the religious perspective. He highlights both the positive and negative elements of religion as they relate to wholeness. Positively, religion provides the means whereby wholeness may be regained through its rituals and their appropriate relation to the stages of the life cycle. Negatively, religion has often been totalistic, cold, and cruel.[72]

The introduction of the theme of totalism appropriately opens the discussion to what wholeness is not. In Chapter V, in our discussion of the "Dangers of Confusion," we quoted at length a passage in which Erikson contrasts wholeness and totalism. The Gestalt of totalism is one of excluding other persons and other ideas. It is directly counter to efforts to integrate and attempt a sense of coherence of diversified parts.

In totalism, absolute boundaries are delineated admitting no form of divergence from the norm. In totalism that which is included must remain within; that which is excluded is barred from entrance with an uncompromising rigidity. Such totalism is often a transitional stage, especially in the identity crisis, and, therefore, it is important for more mature wholism to be tolerant of others' totalism.

The first polarity to wholeness, therefore, is totalism. The second is that of the pseudospecies. This concept has also been discussed previously, both in developing the concept of identity and in the wider application to ethics. In his encyclopedia article on psychosocial identity Erikson defines pseudospecies in this historical context:

Historical considerations lead back into man's prehistory and evolution. Only gradually emerging as one mankind conscious of itself and responsible to and for itself, man has been divided into pseudospecies (tribes and nations, castes and classes), each with its own over-defined identity and each reinforced by mortal prejudice against its images of other pseudospecies.[73]

Here it would sound as though Erikson is optimistic in assuming that there is a possibility of moving beyond the pseudospecies into the kind of wholeness that would embrace all humanity, a kind of world race, world religion, etc. That optimism does prevail in his writings; one senses, however, a slight accommodation to the reality of species remaining distinct within the whole in his later writings and is perhaps implied by his use of the term pseudo-species for those groups which have unduly isolated themselves from the whole. An example of his positive use of the dialectic between the parts and the whole is noted in *Toys and Reasons*. There he points out that a sense of destiny, or election to a special calling, can in a positive sense "contribute to the highest achievements in citizenship, courage, and workmanship and can, in fact, weld together in new loyalties (*civis Romanus*, Christian love) previously inimical entities."[74]

Here the reference to Christian love has special relevance to our interest in Erikson's religious position. It would appear that for him Christianity need not be classified as one of those religions that must be interpreted in totalistic terms.

Wholeness is polarized in Erikson's thought with totalism, pseudospecies, and, thirdly, with adjustment. I have already stated that Erikson is, to my way of thinking, a transformationist, not a conformist. He tackles this question in the final chapter, "Psychoanalysis: Adjustment or Freedom?", of his book *Life History and The Historical Moment*.[75] Luther did not adjust, he exercised his freedom to adapt to new realities. Erikson, whom I see as a kind of Luther for our age, does not opt for the comfort of adjustment, but challenges us to move beyond our self-imposed boundaries to a new human type; in Christian terms, to a new City.

The issue of adjustment is a significant one. Psychoanalysis has often been accused of simply balancing the frictions of the id, ego, and superego, producing personal acceptance and conformity to the status quo, socially. As a transformationist, an ethical idealist, Erikson challenges society's preconceptions of the therapist's role. We shall mention two other instances in which he displays his move beyond conformity to a new sense of commitment, both from his "Reflections on Dr. Borg's Life Cycle."

In commenting on Bergman's portrait of Dr. Borg, Erikson considers the subject of greatness, making this statement: "And the greatest, more often than not, are those rare persons who have questioned the status quo and have become immortal by creating a new one."[76] And again in commenting on Dr. Borg's somewhat arrested development of those strengths beyond identity, because of his loss of love and overidentification with his occupation, Erikson notes: "In this connection, it must be emphasized that all the psychosocial strengths associated with our scheme postulate an active adaptation rather than a passive adjustment—that is, they change the environment even as they make selective use of its opportunities."[77]

Fourthly, wholeness does not mean freedom from conflict. The polarities and dialectical method of Erikson always admit and embrace the positive and negative, working toward a new synthesis. That applies to the crises of the life cycle, the cycle of generations, and to the movement of history toward wholeness.

From this list of what wholeness is not, it should be more clear as to what wholeness is for Erikson. In human development it is that integration of trust and mistrust moving on through the life cycle towards integrity. "Wholeness emphasizes a sound, organic, progressive mutuality between diversified functions and parts within an entirety, the boundaries of which are open and fluid."[78]

Obviously, wholeness for the individual life cycle involves the cycle of generations: societal, historical, religious, and cultural forces interacting with the developing person.

I quoted earlier that experience of Erikson's in first hearing the Lord's Prayer recited as a table grace and his response of sensing "a wholeness captured in a few simple words, of poetry fusing the esthetic and the moral. . . ."[79] But wholeness for Erikson is also a vision of humanity that can move beyond "my kind to mankind." It is the wider identity to which we have often alluded.

In returning to the individual life development, wholeness for Erikson is a balance between the drives of the libidinal forces, the tyranny of an overactive conscience, or superego, which finds its locus in the ego, the I. Here is the place where wholeness emerges in relation to the Super I, God. Whether one agrees with those interpreters who consider Erikson's view of God to be mere projection, as it was for Freud, or with my discussion above in which I cited Erikson's own words that we probably are projecting something onto reality, onto a Being who is there, it is evident that wholeness has transcendent dimensions for Erikson.

In *Toys and Reasons* Erikson has an extended discussion of a child whose play scene suggested to him the figure of a cross with its horizontal and vertical dimensions.[80] The same symbol is picked up in his discussion of Dr. Borg's life cycle. What are the dimensions of adulthood?

> As a Navajo medicine man recently put it when asked by a friend for a definition of what is human: indicating the figure of a cross, he said that a person was most human where the (vertical) connection between the ground of creation and the Great Spirit met the (horizontal) one between the individual and all other human beings.[81]

That is also a fitting definition of wholeness.

I have clearly stated that identity for Erikson is not a narcissistic, self-centered kind of introspection. Certainly, however, it does involve that core of being called the "I," and how that "I" perceives itself and interprets the perceptions of others. It is therefore fitting to relate Erikson to Dietrich Bonhoeffer, who is the author of the phrase "man come of age." Indeed, a book we have cited previously, *Critical Issues in Modern Religion*, groups Freud, Bonhoeffer, and Erikson in the same section dealing with "Psychoanalysis and Religion."[82]

Bonhoeffer is remembered today for many reasons. He died at the hands of the Nazis just prior to Germany's liberation. He was an ethical man *par excellence* and in many ways opposed to the psychologizing of the faith, or at least an overly indulgent introspection. Among his papers, however, is to be found a verse he wrote which asks the identity question. The title, if taken in isolation from the life

Bonhoeffer lived, would be misleading but the verse brings the religious answer to the neurosis of our age:

Who Am I?

Who am I? They often tell me
I step from my cell's confinement
calmly, cheerfully, firmly,
like a squire from his country-house.
Who am I? They often tell me
I talk to my warders freely and friendly and clearly,
as though it were mine to command.
Who am I? They also tell me
I bear the days of misfortune equably, smilingly, proudly,
like one accustomed to win.

Am I then really all that which other men tell of?
Or am I only what I know of myself,
restless and longing and sick, like a bird in a cage,
struggling for breath, as though hands were compressing
* my throat,*
yearning for colours, for flowers, for the voices of birds,
thirsting for words of kindness, for neighbourliness,
tossing in expectation of great events,
powerlessly trembling for friends at an infinite distance,
weary and empty at praying, at thinking, at making,
faint, and ready to say farewell to it all?
Who am I? This or the other?
Am I one person today, and tomorrow another?
Am I both at once? A hypocrite before others,
and before myself a contemptibly woebegone weakling?
Or is something within me still like a beaten army,
fleeing in disorder from victory already achieved?

Who am I? They mock me, these lonely questions of mine.
Whoever I am, thou knowest, O God, I am thine.[83]

Here is Erikson's "I" facing the "Super I" and, in a sense, finding wholeness. Bonhoeffer died by hanging shortly after having led the ritual of Holy Communion, that reenactment of the Christian's reminder of basic trust. Those who witnessed those last days testify to a sense of integrity and joy in the German martyr's countenance—always, and especially, in the days prior to his death.

Wholeness, finally, must be related to the larger historical context of the Judeo-Christian tradition. It is what life is all about for religious as well as psychological persons.

In the Hebrew "Shalom," which we commonly translate as "peace," there is a basic meaning of wholeness and health. In the Greek root sōs, from which we have our doctrine of salvation called soteriology, the meaning is also that of wholeness or health. To have salvation, peace, health, is to have wholeness. Jesus also called himself a healer who had come to make men whole.

I suggest that another Gospel story of healing be considered as fitting for Erikson's pursuit. Erikson occasionally refers to Proteus in his *Dimensions of a New Identity*. Earlier, we noted that he astutely reminds us that we misunderstand Protean man if we think that there is no real core identity to the manyness of that mythological figure. Therefore, for our identity crisis as Protean persons—many persons within the one—the following story of Jesus' healing ministry instructs us in our pursuit of wholeness. It is one I believe Erikson would favor including in any religious discussion of identity:

> So they came to the other side of the lake, into the country of the Gerasenes. As he stepped ashore, a man possessed by an unclean spirit came up to him from among the tombs where he had his dwelling. He could no longer be controlled; even chains were useless; he had often been fettered and chained up, but he had snapped his chains and broken the fetters. No one was strong enough to master him. And so, unceasingly, night and day, he would cry aloud among the tombs and on the hill-sides and cut himself with stones. When he saw Jesus in the distance, he ran and flung himself down before him, shouting loudly, "What do you want with me, Jesus, son of the Most High God? In God's name do not torment me." (For Jesus was already saying to him, "Out, unclean spirit, come out of this man!") Jesus asked him, "What is

your name?" "My name is Legion," he said, "there are so many of us." And he begged hard that Jesus would not send him out of the country. Now there happened to be a large herd of pigs feeding on the hill-side, and the spirits begged him, "Send us among the pigs and let us go into them." He gave them leave; and the unclean spirits came out and went into the pigs; and the herd, of about two thousand, rushed over the edge into the lake and were drowned.

The men in charge of them took to their heels and carried the news to the town and country-side; and the people came out to see what had happened. They came to Jesus and saw the madman who had been possessed by the legion of devils, sitting there clothed and in his right mind; and they were afraid.[84]

In verse 15 the words "right mind" may also be translated as "whole," or at least it has that connotation, inasmuch as the root Greek word used for "sound mind" is the same as that for "wholeness."

What Erikson pursues, Luther found, the demoniac experienced: wholeness. Psychosocially, it will be pursued from infant trust to the integrity of old age. Here, too, is a signal of transcendence, a dimension of life that on the one hand is pursued, and on the other hand, given: Peace!

NOTES

1. Erikson, *Young Man Luther*, p. 184.
2. Niebuhr, *The Responsible Self*, p. 160.
3. Erikson, *Young Man Luther*, p. 261. Italics for "ordinary men," mine.
4. Ibid.
5. Erikson, *Life History*, p. 30.
6. See his essay "Adjustment or Freedom," *Life History*, p. 261.
7. Erikson, *Identity: Youth and Crisis*, p. 220.
8. Erikson, *In Search of Common Ground*, pp. 142–43.
9. Erikson, *Life History*, p. 108.
10. Homans's paper appears in the book he edited, *Childhood and Selfhood*, and is entitled "The Significance of Erikson's *Psychology for Modern Understanding of Religion*," pp. 231–63.
11. *Criterion*, University of Chicago (Spring 1976), p. 25.
12. Erikson, *Life History*, p. 108.
13. Erikson, "Words for Paul Tillich," *Harvard Divinity School Bulletin*, XXX: 2 (1966), p. 15.

14. Erikson, *Insight and Responsibility*, p. 220.

15. An example of Erikson's use of the rule is found in his "Reflections on Dr. Borg's Life Cycle," *Daedalus*, p. 10. "For if the simplest moral rule is not to do to another what you would not wish to have done to you, the ethical rule of adulthood is to do to others what will help them, even as it helps you, to grow."

16. Erikson, *Young Man Luther*, p. 21.

17. Ibid., italics mine.

18. Erikson, *Insight and Responsibility*, p. 131. Other examples of ambivalence are as follows: In *Childhood and Society,* pp. 277–78, he alludes to the fact that religions may exploit a sense of evil as well as foster trust; on pp. 250–51, he discusses the relativity of all institutions to a particular age and era. In *Identity: Youth and Crisis*, pp. 83–84, he states that "much cruel, cold, and exclusive totalness has dominated some phases of the history of organized religion." He also reminds his readers that contemporary self-made man does not seem to find the wholeness in religion that primitive man found, and this to modern man's detriment.

19. See note 11, above.

20. "Autobiographic Notes," p. 757. Italics mine.

21. Erikson, *Life History*, p. 108. Italics mine.

22. Ibid., p. 149.

23. Ibid., p. 147.

24. Coles, *Erik H. Erikson*, p. 181.

25. Erikson, *Young Man Luther*, pp. 170–222.

26. Ibid., p. 216.

27. Ibid., p. 210.

28. Ibid., p. 10. Italics mine.

29. Ibid.

30. Ibid., pp. 265–66.

31. Erikson, *Gandhi's Truth*, p. 398.

32. My purpose here is to take soundings of how others have responded in light of my question, shall we call Erikson a homo religiosus? Therefore, others who have reviewed his works who do not deal with the religious issue are not here being considered.

33. Coles, *Erik H. Erikson*, pp. 358–59.

34. Erikson, *Gandhi's Truth*, p. 230.

35. Coles, *Erik H. Erikson*, p. 359. Italics his.

36. Ibid., title page.

37. Browning, *Generative Man*, p. 205. The phrase in this quotation, "generalized generativity of institutions," is Brownings's quotation of Erikson in "Ontogeny of Ritualization," in *Psychoanalysis—A General Psychology: Essays in Honor of Heinz Hartmann,* ed. Rudolph M. Loewenstein and others (International Universities Press, 1966) pp. 602–603.

38. Homans, *Childhood and Selfhood*, p. 258.

39. Roazen, *Erik H. Erikson: The Power and Limits of a Vision.*

40. Ibid., p. 95.

41. Ibid., p. 168.

42. In response to my inquiry about his claims, Roazen could only allude to having seen a crucifix on the wall in Erikson's office when he, Roazen, had visited with him in Widener Library, Harvard.

43. A list of those who have found Erikson to be of interest would be informative and significant. The editors of *Encounter with Erikson*, are Donald Capps, Walter H. Capps, and M. Gerald Bradford (Missoula, Mont.: Scholars Press, 1977).

44. Donald Capps, "Theme and Event: Gandhi's Truth as Religious Biography," in *Encounter with Erikson*, p. 147.

45. Capps, Capps, and Bradford, *Encounter*, p. xi.

46. Ibid., pp. 401–19.

47. Ibid., p. 410.

48. Ibid., p. 411.

49. Ibid., pp. 413–17.

50. Ibid., p. 414.

51. Ibid., p. 415.

52. Donald E. Miller, "Returning to the Fold: Disbelief Within the Community of Faith," *Christian Century* (September 21, 1977), p. 810. More recently Miller has again acknowledged the value of Erikson's concepts in a theological context:

> To revitalize liberalism we must admit to the frustration and despair of lacking a metaphysically rooted identity. Commitment and identity, as Erik Erikson has demonstrated, are integrally tied to ideology—and any ideology which we cannot affirm as rooted in "the very nature of things" will not long sustain our attention.

Donald E. Miller, "Spiritual Discipline: Countering Contemporary Culture," *Christian Century*, XCVII: 10 (March 19, 1980).

53. Donald E. Miller, "Returning to the Fold," p. 812.

54. Ibid.

55. Ernest Wallwork, "Erik H. Erikson: Psychosocial Resources for Faith," in Johnson et al., *Critical Issues in Modern Religion*, pp. 354–56.

56. Peter L. Berger, *Facing Up to Modernity: Excursions in Society, Politics and Religion* (New York: Basic Books, 1977).

57. Ibid., pp. 219–20. There is an interesting debate between Berger, the sociologist, and a number of theologians who also attempt to find signals of transcendence within everyday experience. To Berger, however, these theologians are reductionistic, or tend to be, in their approach. His indictments and their responses may be found both in their writings and

in a series of articles appearing as follows: "Secular Theology and the Rejection of the Supernatural: Reflections on Recent Trends," Peter Berger in *Theological Studies*, 38:1 (March 1977). For the responses of those Berger indicted, see "Responses to Peter Berger: Langdon Gilkey, Schubert M. Ogden, and David Tracy," in *Theological Studies*, 39:3 (September 1978). David Tracy is one who interprets our era as one of postmodernity, and his book *Blessed Rage for Order: The New Pluralism in Theology* (New York: Seabury Press, 1978) is one that readers will find of interest. He seeks to develop a theological anthropology.

58. Homans, ed., *Childhood and Selfhood*.

59. Ibid., p. 248. See entire section on "Erikson's Psychology and Contemporary Theories of Religion," pp. 248–58.

60. Johnson et al., *Critical Issues*, pp. 435–55.

61. Erikson, *Life History*, p. 264.

62. See note 18, above.

63. Homans, ed., *Childhood and Selfhood*, p. 54, note 37.

64. Erikson, *Childhood and Society*, p. 24.

65. Ibid.

66. Erikson, *Dimensions of a New Identity*, p. 48.

67. Ibid., p. 49.

68. Ibid.

69. H. Richard Niebuhr, *Christ and Culture*, Harper Torchbooks (New York: Harper, 1951).

70. Erikson, *Dimensions of a New Identity*, pp. 49–50.

71. Ibid.

72. Erikson, *Identity: Youth and Crisis*, pp. 83–84.

73. Erikson, "Psychosocial Identity," *IESS*, p. 62.

74. Erikson, *Toys and Reasons*, pp. 76–77. Also see pp. 168–69 for his discussion of the dialectics of the elements comprising a new human type.

75. Erikson, *Life History*, pp. 248–64.

76. Erikson, "Reflections on Dr. Borg's Life Cycle," p. 18.

77. Ibid., p. 25.

78. Erikson, *Identity: Youth and Crisis*, p. 80–81.

79. Erikson, *Young Man Luther*, p. 10.

80. Erikson, *Toys and Reasons*, pp. 31–39; 99.

81. Erikson, "Reflections on Dr. Borg's Life Cycle," p. 18.

82. Johnson et al., *Critical Issues*, pp. 251–364.

83. Dietrich Bonhoeffer, *Letters and Papers from Prison*, rev. ed., edited Eberhard Bethge (New York: Macmillan, 1967), pp. 188–89.

84. Mark 5:1–15, New English Bible.

Epilogue

As Anna Freud prophetically anticipated, Erikson has helped us to see. On the basis of reality, the actual experiences of life, Erikson has imaginatively formulated his theory. There is a difference between fantasy and imagination. The latter is related to reality.

The real, for Erikson, is always in polar tension: trust vs. mistrust, integrity vs. despair, good vs. evil, wholeness vs. totalism. Therefore, while we find a vision of a wider identity in Erikson, not unlike the Biblical vision of the lion with the lamb, we also find an honest admission of the obstacles to be encountered along the way. These obstacles could as easily lead to the negative identity of pseudospecieshood as to the wider identity of wholeness.

To imagine is to play with images. Erikson does that, and I hope our encounter with Erikson has stirred our imaginations to ask the question of the child at play, "What if?" As a child, our son John asked that question so often that the family called him the "What iffer." It remains the question beyond childhood, on into the identity crisis, and becomes the ultimate question of life.

What if knowledge comes to us through the left as well as the right hand, through intuitive means and the experiential as well as the rational and experimental?

What if Erikson's disciplined subjectivity makes more sense than the rigid limitations of objectivity and verifiability?

What if basic trust is more essential to existence than being in control? And if the universe is to be trusted, and if religion ritualizes trust, then what of religion for our age?

Did we really mature with the Enlightenment, when we limited our respectable family of studies to scientifically verifiable truth alone? What if religion, the stepchild of enlightened persons, really belongs in the family with full recognition and acceptance?

What if the transcendent is clearly signaled in the everyday experiences of life?

What if the question cited in the Introduction, asked by a seemingly despairing rock group, "Is there anybody there?" is answered by the Biblical, "I AM THAT I AM"? Erikson reminds us that this was God's statement to Moses in declaring *His* identity.

Erikson raises these questions, or at least stimulates us to raise them. In the Introduction I said that he really does not go far enough, but perhaps he goes as far as one can go, anthropologically, in playing with configurations and raising questions.

If the idea he suggests, that the "I" of identity needs the transcendent "Super I," God, to really sense completeness, then it is for the theologians to begin to relate their truth to Erikson's stimulating development of the life cycle with all of its complementarities and interactions.

As Erikson found his protestant impulses satisfied in studying the young man Luther, so I have found my Christian heritage reaffirmed in Erikson's affirmations about the nature of life. His social psychology has enriched my theology.

For this I express my gratitude to Erikson, who sees the royal road to truth in play, and who has stimulated me to play with the ideas presented in this book.

Index

Books on Psychology and Counseling from The Seabury Press

ERICH FROMM
On Disobedience and Other Essays

Erich Fromm assembled and revised these essays just before his death in 1980. He assesses the basic requirements for a fully human life — the needs for rootedness, relatedness, transcendence, and identity — and criticizes the social structures which form obstacles to their fulfillment.
144pp

DAVID G. MYERS
The Inflated Self: Human Illusions and the Biblical Call to Hope

"One of the few books to effectively combine general psychology with theology, it provides convincing — even scary — arguments for the necessity of using scientifically based psychology to reduce the personal biases we all carry."

Richard L. Gorsuch

Pbk 208pp   Fuller Theological Seminary

RONALD R. LEE
Clergy and Clients: The Practice of Pastoral Psychotherapy

"Clearly written.... The logic is always evident.... The most creative presentation of structure which I have seen.... A valuable book, to be read and re-read."   *Journal of Pastoral Care*

"A work that can be used to improve the techniques and skills of a pastor.... Well worth reading ... an excellent tool."
192pp   *The Christian Century*

JOHN L.C. MITMAN
Pre-marital Counseling: A Manual for Clergy and Counselors

"This manual is truly what it claims to be: a practical guide — without being a mere 'how-to' book. Part of its practicality is the clarity of its presentation and the common sense of its contents. Though relatively concise, it is remarkably encompassing."

G. Marian Kinget, author of On Being Human
and consultant to the Roman Catholic Diocese of Lansing

"A well-explained digest of the crucial concerns, and practical suggestions for helping counselors explore them. Should make pre-marital counseling more systematic and effective."

Craig Dykstra

144pp   Louisville Presbyterian Seminary